TRANSITION AND DEVELOPMENT
IN ALGERIA:
ECONOMIC, SOCIAL AND CULTURAL
CHALLENGES

Edited by Margaret A. Majumdar and Mohammed Saad

intellect™
Bristol, UK
Portland, OR, USA

First Published in the UK in 2005 by
Intellect Books, PO Box 862, Bristol BS99 1DE, UK.
First Published in the USA in 2005 by
Intellect Books, ISBS, 920 NE 58th Ave. Suite 300, Portland, Oregon 97213-3786, USA.

A catalogue record for this book is available from the British Library

ISBN 1-84150-074-7
Cover Design: Gabriel Solomons
Copy Editor: Julie Strudwick
Production: May Yao

Printed and bound in Great Britain by Antony Rowe Ltd.

Table of Contents

Acknowledgements

The editors would like to record their thanks to all those who have played a part in bringing this volume to fruition. Firstly, we are indebted to the contributors, who have brought their expertise, knowledge and insights to bear on the questions facing Algeria today and also taken part in and enriched the ongoing debates around these issues, from a wide variety of perspectives. We are also grateful to all those who participated in, and helped to organise, the workshops on Algeria, which have prompted this publication, with a particular mention for academic and administrative colleagues, as well as family and friends. Special thanks are due to those institutions and organisations which sponsored and supported these events, including the Society for Algerian Studies, BP, Anadarko, the Bristol Business School, the Faculty of Languages and European Studies of the University of West of England and the School of Humanities and Social Sciences of the University of Glamorgan. Last but not least, we warmly acknowledge the invaluable support of Peter James and Alex Harding for their help in preparing the final text.

Margaret A. Majumdar, Mohammed Saad

Notes on Contributors

Kay Adamson is lecturer in Sociology in the School of Law and Social Sciences at Glasgow Caledonian University. Previously she taught sociology at the University of Sunderland. She has published two books: *Political and Economic Thought and Practice in Nineteenth-Century France and the Colonization of Algeria* (2002) and *Algeria: a Study in Competing Ideologies* (1998). She contributed to *Francophone Studies: The Essential Glossary*, ed. M. A. Majumdar (2002) and has published in the *Journal of Algerian Studies*. She also teaches on contemporary issues of nationalism, migration, racism and Islam in Europe and in the field of social justice.

Mahfoud Amara is a Research Fellow at the School of Sports & Exercise Sciences, Loughborough University. He is researching the study of globalisation, sport and local cultures. His research interests include sport and politics; the relation between sport, nationalism and nation state building; sport in colonial and post-colonial history; sport modernity and postmodernity; Olympism; pan-Arabism and pan-Islamism; postmodern sociology and discourse analysis.

Zine M. Barka is Professor of Public Finance at the University of Tlemcen and a Visiting Professor at the University of Le Mans. He was a Research Fellow in the Department of Economics of the University of Illinois at Urbana - Champaign. His teaching and research interests include public finance, growth and budget procedures in MENA Countries with reference to Algeria, tax and fiscal policy.

Mahfoud Benosman is Dean of the Faculty of Economics and Management at Annaba University. He was a member of the Privatisation Council from 1996 to 1999. He focuses on economic reforms, industrial restructuring and privatisation.

Dai Jones is Vice President, New Business Development and Gas Marketing, of BP and Director Algeria - BP Exploration (in Salah) Ltd and BP Exploration (in Amenas) Ltd. He has wide experience of international business and in-depth knowledge of the business culture and current reforms taking place in Algeria. He has negotiated major contracts with the Algerian authorities and led investment projects in Algeria and other countries.

Jeremy Keenan is Research Associate in the Department of Social Anthropology, Cambridge University. He has extensive knowledge of Algeria's Saharan regions, being the author of *The Tuareg: People of Ahaggar* (1977, reprint 2001) and *Sahara Man: Travelling with the Tuareg* (2001). As Director of Saharatec, he also has extensive experience of tourism in the Algerian Sahara.

Naaman Kessous is lecturer in French Studies at the University of Lancaster. His main research interests include: French Politics since 1945, Frantz Fanon and the African Diaspora; Politics, Culture and Society in pre- and post-colonial Algeria.

He is the author of *Rousseau and Fourier: Two French Precursors of Marxism* (1996) and a contributor to *Francophone Studies: The Essential Glossary*, ed. M. A. Majumdar (2002). He is currently working on an edited book on forty years of Algerian independence.

Cathie Lloyd is a Senior Research Officer at the International Development Centre (QEH), Oxford. Her work has focused on gender, antiracism, social movements and civil society with particular reference to the women's movement in North Africa and the Maghrebian diaspora. Recent publications include *Rethinking Antiracisms: From Theory to Practice* (2001).

Margaret A. Majumdar is Visiting Professor of Francophone Studies at the University of Portsmouth. She was a founding editor of the *Bulletin of Francophone Africa* and has published widely on Francophone colonial/ postcolonial political theory and discourse, Algerian national identity and Maghrebian and Caribbean literature. Books include *Althusser and the End of Leninism?* (1995) and *Francophone Studies: The Essential Glossary* (2002).

Hakim Meliani is a Senior Lecturer in the Faculty of Economics and Management at the University of Setif (Algeria). He gained a Master in Accounting from Glasgow University in 1988 and is currently completing a doctorate on the emerging markets. His work focused essentially on emerging economies, foreign direct investment, privatisation and financial economic reforms.

Cherif Merrouche is a Senior Lecturer in Accounting and Finance at Caledonian Business School. His teaching, research and consultancy focus on international accounting, management accounting, financial management, adult education and training in the financial sector, and the issue of international governmental and non-profit accounting. Cherif Merrouche has undertaken research and/or consultancy in the UK, Armenia, Albania, North Africa, Kenya, Tanzania and Taiwan.

Mohammed Miliani is Professor and Director of Research at the University of Oran. His main teaching and research interests include higher education, culture and communication; didactics of languages; learning strategies; educational psychology; didactics; research methodology. He is a very active member of many committees which include the National University Committee; the intersector-based Committee for the programming, co-ordination, promotion & evaluation of Scientific & Technological Development in 'Education, Culture & Communication'; the National Committee for Degree Equivalencies; the National Committee for the Reform of the Languages Curricula; the Scientific Council of the Research Centre in Social and Cultural Anthropology; the National Pedagogical Committee on *Berber language and culture*. Mohammed Miliani is leading several research projects on language, culture and education and has published widely.

Mohammed Saad is a Reader in Innovation and Operations Management and Head of the School of Operations and Information Management at the Bristol Business

School, University of the West of England. His academic activities focus on innovation, learning, supply chain management and technology transfer. He also undertakes consultancy work, including advising a number of organisations and governmental institutions on innovation, more collaborative inter-organisational relationships and procurement approaches. He is co-founder and co-editor of a new journal, *The International Journal of Technology Management and Sustainable Development*. His most recent publications include *Development Through Technology Transfer - Creating New Organisational and Cultural Understanding* (2000) and *Managing Innovation in Construction* (2003).

Introduction

Algeria, with its 2.4 million square kilometres, is the second largest country in Africa (one-third of the size of the US and five times that of France). More than two million square kilometres are desert or semi-arid steppes extending into the southern Sahara region, but the country also contains a fertile strip of cultivable land concentrated along the coast of the Mediterranean Sea.

A bloody eight-year revolution brought independence to Algeria's population, which, in 1962, was about ten million. By 2002, the number had risen to nearly 30 million. After the departure of the French *colons*, which brought the economy to a halt, there was a clear consensus for instituting a socialist system to run the Algerian society and its economy, in order to provide the population with badly needed jobs, education and health. During the 1960s and 1970s, Algeria was striving to build a strong, independent and sustainable economy. The development of the economy was to be attained through a significant industrial base as rapidly as possible. This required a massive programme of investment from 1967 to 1984, reaching a peak in the period 1967-1979, followed by a downward trend between 1980 and 1989. Algeria's vast oil and gas reserves and external borrowing during the 1970s and 1980s financed heavy investment to develop an industrial sector that relied on capital-intensive production technology. There is now a growing recognition that this strategy, based on the model of industrialising industries, has fallen short of achieving its ambitious objectives. This has led to a multidimensional crisis (political, social, cultural and economic) with a strong demotivation at all levels, a lack of trust towards managers and leaders and hence a lack of sense of direction and belonging.

It was the dramatic revolt of October 1988 that compelled the government to institute a more serious and accelerated programme of reforms. This revolt was attributed to an unacceptably slow pace of political, social, cultural and economic reform, as well as critical shortages caused by the 1986 oil price drop and ensuing decrease in hydrocarbon export earnings, which account for 90 per cent of Algeria's export earnings. The main goals set out in this reform programme were to transform the national economy from a tightly controlled system to a market-oriented one, to introduce democracy and a multiparty system to replace the single-party FLN-state, and to promote a national culture which recognises the existence of different languages and cultures - each with its different beliefs, values, ideas and points of view.

For growth to occur, the society as a whole needs to operate in an environment which consists of sound institutions and laws, law enforcement, accountability, transparency, and genuine and credible governance. Deeper institutional reforms are needed to create this type of environment in which enhanced economic, political, social and cultural initiatives can take place. The absence of such an environment will continue to sustain the emergence of a counter culture with a strong informal sector, black market, corruption and injustice. It will also impede investment in Algeria and the return of growth, desperately needed to address the severe issue of unemployment. The Algerian labour force has been growing at an annual average rate of 4 per cent between 1985 and 2002, but the growth in employment has lagged seriously behind. This has led to an acute level of unemployment (30 per cent).

In addition, this period of transition has been characterised by a significant level of political instability and social unrest, which culminated in a decade of armed conflict and bloody violence, following the cancellation by the army, in the face of the likely victory of the *Front Islamique du Salut* (FIS), of the second round of the national elections, scheduled to take place in January 1992 and the first ones under the multi-party system instituted in 1989. While the country is still struggling to cope with the aftermath of this bloody period and has yet to resolve the power struggles, both open and covert, between individuals, groups, parties, movements and the different institutions of the state itself, in order to establish a state of law and lawful, constitutional governance, it is also still wrestling with the underlying problems and issues in the economic, social and cultural spheres. While these different spheres naturally have their own specific tensions, conflicts and potentialities for progress, there is also evidence that they are all affected by the main characteristics of Algeria's difficult development process and the shifts in focus away from the monoculture of the central planning system and its single ideology, along with the crisis of authority and legitimacy of the major public institutions.

Much of the literature on Algeria and the crisis of recent years has concentrated almost exclusively on the political dimension - the violent armed struggles, the different strategies proposed to bring peace to the country, the tactics of the various players in political parties and movements, as well as in the military, the complex web of international political relations and external pressures which have had an important role to play in further complicating the situation (see Roberts 2003).

The aim of this book, however, is to look more closely at other, often neglected, but equally important processes that make up the reality of Algerian life and society. While in no way arguing that an analysis of these processes can be divorced from an understanding of the political domain, the particular focus of the volume is on those aspects that impinge on the basic infrastructure, as well as the social and cultural fabric of the nation, in its development through a period of economic and social upheavals and transformation. It considers why, during this period, the changes, while often generally considered necessary and desired, have nonetheless been, if not aborted, then frequently stalled and disappointing in their results so far. It attempts to examine the nature of the processes of change and development, as well as the underlying causes for the existence of obstacles preventing the movement forward.

This book is based on a selection of papers presented at the fourth and fifth workshops on Algeria, which were held at the University of the West of England (Bristol) in June 2000 and 2001. The range of perspectives provided by the selected papers is related to our deliberate attempt to adopt a multidisciplinary approach to examine the complex and multidimensional situation of the transition process in Algeria. This multidisciplinary perspective emanates from a synergistic combination of the different disciplines, experiences and perspectives of the authors, who come from a range of backgrounds and three different countries (Algeria, United Kingdom and France).

The book examines the programme of reforms introduced over the past decade and explores some of the problematic issues relating to these developments. It also addresses the impact on society of these developments and assesses the ways in which strategies to deal with the multidimensional crisis currently affecting the country are being implemented and challenged.

Part I (Economic Policy and Change) focuses on the transformation of the national economy from a tightly controlled centralised system to a market-oriented one. The first chapter explores the theoretical background underpinning policy choices relating to the Algerian economy. It suggests that, in part, an understanding of the current problems which face the Algerian economy and, consequently, possible solutions, requires a re-examination of the life and work of the late French economist François Perroux. The Algerian economic model known as 'industrialising industries', which was implemented by President Boumedienne (1967-1979), was an attempt by Perroux and others to put into practice an economic theory of growth and development. Chapter 2 provides an assessment of the relevance of the reforms introduced during the 1990s to support the privatisation programme and the long-term requirements of the Algerian economy as a whole. This investigation includes an evaluation of the Algerian past and present financial systems, as well as the political and social climate that would accommodate future changes. The purpose of chapter 3 is, firstly, to find out whether the accounting system currently in use in Algeria has the necessary characteristics to meet the information needs of its users and, secondly, to establish whether the present accounting system has the ability to generate reliable and relevant information for decision making, particularly in a market economy. This chapter endeavours to determine whether there is a need for accounting reform in Algeria, through government regulation and the development and strengthening of the accounting profession. Chapter 4 examines the origins of the current crisis, assesses the economic and social implications of the reforms and highlights the need for a more appropriate management of people, learning and culture. It argues that Algerian institutions, organisations and businesses can no longer afford to adopt organisational arrangements and learning mechanisms based on the use of mechanistic and bureaucratic structures which impede initiative, motivation, commitment and participation of the workforce at all levels. It highlights the intricate relationships that link culture with human motivation and behaviour, systems of authority and the rule of law, and growth.

The second part of the book, Women and Society, raises the important issues of the effect of social change on women's lives, as well as their role in the development process. Chapter 5 discusses the complexities and ambiguities of the processes of change, as they have affected women. A great emphasis is placed upon the context of the last two decades and the impact of the Family Code, violence and economic liberalisation upon the position of women. Chapter 6 focuses more specifically upon the contribution of rural women to the Algerian society and economy.

In Part III, some of the key difficulties relating to the constitution of the Algerian nation and national culture are explored, along with their implications with regard to the present multifaceted crisis, as well as their impact on future development. The aim of chapter 7 is to provide an in-depth understanding of nation building in Algeria and the transition process, through an assessment of the concepts of alienation and violence in the works of Frantz Fanon. The theme of Algerian nationhood, and the problems associated with it, is pursued in chapter 8, with a specific focus on the notion of the New Man, and its relevance to the Algerian context. Chapter 9 highlights the entangled situation of languages in Algeria, and examines their impact on the economic, social, cultural and political crises. It also reveals the strong collusion between language reforms and political struggle and advocates the need for a balance between the nation and state building process within a framework of greater democracy, transparency and freedom, in which the existence of different cultures and languages is recognised.

The final part of the book (Part IV) sets some of the key development and transitional issues within the wider global economic, social and political framework, with particular regard to the impact on Algeria of its participation in the global economy. Chapter 10 highlights the impact of globalisation upon Algerian football, as, with professionalism taking over the sport, it marks its transition from a cultural and political vehicle, to a profitable economic activity. It examines the historical role of sport (particularly football) in Algeria, during the colonial and postcolonial periods and its implications for the discourse of political and national identity. The objective of chapter 11 is to propose a comprehensive discussion, through the specific case of tourism in the South of Algeria (Sahara), of the development orientation of this industry. It reviews the key political, economic, social, cultural and environmental factors that need to be taken into consideration in such an analysis. Finally, chapter 12 provides a practical analysis of the management of the transition in Algeria, from the perspective of a major foreign investor.

1 ESTABLISHING UTOPIA: EXPLORING THE POLITICAL ORIGINS OF ECONOMIC POLICY IN ALGERIA[1]

Kay Adamson

Introduction

The aim of this paper is to suggest that a part of understanding the current problems which face the Algerian economy and, consequently, possible solutions, requires a re-examination of the life and work of the late French economist François Perroux. Perroux, who was a significant figure in both post-World War II French and post-independence Algerian economic policy-making, also left behind an immense body of economic writings. The Algerian 'economic model' which took shape in the late 1960s and 1970s and was then implemented by President Boumedienne, was an attempt by Perroux and others to put into practice an economic theory of growth and development. Whilst there is a substantial body of criticism of the outcomes of this experiment, that critique has attributed its failings to the political sphere; thus the model itself has been subject to rather less scrutiny. Yet authors such as De Soto (2000) and Frank (1998), on the one hand, and Castells (1998), on the other, have not only offered very different visions of the way in which economies of the developing countries work but also of the way in which economic activity at the global level works. It is not simply a matter of technical adjustment of the Algerian economy that is necessary, but of a deeper rethink of some of the starting points from which the current structures have developed.

This chapter revisits a number of issues concerned with the relationship between ideology and systemic economic and political change. Part of the reason for doing so stems from the distance, highlighted by three recent studies, that lies between the different solutions to what has previously seemed to be an intractable problem - how to account for the gap between the industrialised economies of the West and the poorest of the rest of the world. The disparity in the nature of the agenda for change which they each offer, is an indication of the absence of consensus, not about the existence of the problem of economic inequality between states, but about the reasons why it has persisted irrespective of whether or not the countries concerned have followed a 'Left' or 'Right' economic and political agenda. Three of the authors referred to - Hernando De Soto, Andre Gunder Frank and Manual Castells have all, over many years, made contributions to the discussion; indeed it was Frank whose evocative 'development of underdevelopment' thesis[2] inspired a generation of commentators on political and economic problems in the Third World. Since then, Frank has taken up the challenge posed by the world systems' theory associated with Immanuel Wallerstein.[3] *ReOrient* (1998) is Frank's response to the arguments raised by Wallerstein. In contrast, Castells who has been examining the impact of the technology shift encapsulated by the phrase the 'information age' explores the capacity of different types of societies to benefit from the rapid technological changes of the last ten years (Castells 1998). De Soto who was intimately involved in economic reform policies under the Peruvian president, Alberto Fujimori, offers, in *The Mystery of Capital* (De Soto 2000), a deceptively simple argument for why poor countries have remained poor. His argument has two principal strands. The first is that the poor of the developing countries are only poor because they are unable to realise the capital resources, which are in their possession. De Soto then identifies property as the most significant of these capital resources. His argument is that it is the non-realisation as a capital resource of property that imposes limits on the capacity of poor people to escape their poverty. The second part of his argument is that the difficulties in registering title are the consequence of the existence in poor countries of large bureaucracies, which depend upon the operation of long and complex procedures to register title. The result is that most individuals are deterred from the attempt to register title by the nature of the processes involved and as a result are prevented from making maximum use of their capital resources.

Castells, Frank and de Soto however, can be seen as reflecting a concern which was originally posed when the Spanish and Portuguese colonies in South America won their political emancipation in the nineteenth century, and which has preoccupied economists and others ever since. It was a concern that took on a new meaning in the 1960s and 1970s when the political emancipation of European colonial empires in Africa and Asia took place. It was this central question of what political emancipation meant for the economy, which inspired Perroux, Hirschman (1981) and others in the 1950s and 1960s, and led to a focus on the nature of economic growth and the links between growth and economic development. Frank can be seen in many ways as representative of a critical perspective on the work of these authors; and yet it may also be argued that they all actually shared a fundamental assumption, which lies at the heart of not only the programmes for growth and development but also the critique. This fundamental assumption, apparent also in De Soto, was that articulated by Brenner (1977). Brenner's argument was that work on development, irrespective of its Left/Right credentials, was reliant upon Adam Smith's thesis on capitalist development in Book I of *The Wealth of Nations* (1776). As a result, both Left and Right had a tendency to perceive the question of development as a problem primarily of markets. Certainly, by perceiving the issue in this way, what is offered is the possibility that issues of economic development can be resolved by appropriate processes of adjustment, that is, it can be imagined in terms of the adoption of the right policies. However, if the core problem is not one of markets but is instead an outcome, as Brenner argues and as Castells also argues, of production relations or technology, then the economic development issues are very different and, equally importantly, much more difficult to overcome.

It is Brenner's contention that to understand capitalist economic development, the first thing that needs to be understood is how the social productive relations, which underpinned the accumulation of capital on an extended scale, originated (Brenner 1977: 27). The key to the problem, he argues, is not therefore the organisation of exchange relations and markets but the social/class relations which pertained. This same question can be posed in a slightly different way, as Mohammad Saad[4] did in a thought-provoking presentation which explored the role played by 'culture' in determining the nature of a country's economic development style. In doing so, he also pointed to the failure of models of economic development, which focus on development exclusively as an issue of markets, financial institutions and the quantitative aspects of the infrastructure of production processes. Thus, from its point of conceptualisation, the economy is viewed through the restrictive prism of exchange relations, and, as a result, it becomes divorced from its own system or systems of cultural signification. One consequence of this narrowing of perspective is that such questions as the manner in which society views ideas of the 'good' are not considered to be of the same importance as the nominal presence of banks, firms and markets. However, what constitutes the idea of the 'good', i.e. 'good' development, 'good' employment, 'good' conduct, have a fundamental impact on the processes of economic development itself. In other words, just as there is a sense in which there are considered to be, on the one hand, 'good' jobs and, on the other, 'bad' jobs and that deciding which are which involves cultural and/or moral views and decision-making as much as an economic process.[5] In this sense, it seems useful to reflect upon some of the ideological underpinning of the choices which were made about the direction of Algerian economic policy in the first ten years after independence. Central to the decisions which were taken about economic policy in the 1960s was the premise that the Algerian economy would be able to catch up and more quickly if it made certain specific choices about the types of industries that would underpin her economy and be promoted by the state. Even if those decisions were, as was argued above, premised on the availability and accessibility of markets, it was still the case that not all of the decisions which were taken reflected the economic aims of either the state or its advisers. Some of the choices were also concerned with how it was felt things ought to be, hence the importance, at the political and the ideological level, of the place given to the relationship between industry and agriculture. This relationship was and is essentially problematic, not least because the precise nature of the articulation between it and other areas of economic activity is obscured by the concern of social thinkers, dating back to the nineteenth century, with the consequences for society of the social dislocations which are perceived to accompany processes of industrialisation. As a result, there has been a tendency towards an idealisation of the place of agriculture in post-colonial economies and the accompanying tendency to solve political and social problems arising from the uncertainties of industrialisation by means of the manipulation of the agricultural sector.

One way to begin to explore these questions is to revisit the ideas of two French economists who both directly and indirectly, played significant roles in establishing the actual framework of post-independence Algerian economic and industrial policy, i.e. François Perroux and Gérard Destanne de Bernis. There are a number of reasons for focusing on both Perroux and de Bernis, in that whilst it is de Bernis's perhaps somewhat technicist interpretation by which the model has come to be known in practice, yet much of the theoretical basis of the model is contained in the work of Perroux himself. Furthermore, although the attractiveness of the Perroux model was due to certain innovative arguments about the role, in particular, of 'power' in economic relations, there are clear links between the ideas of Perroux and other contemporary economists, such as Albert Hirschman, and between Perroux and nineteenth-century economic and political ideas including those of Saint-Simon and Karl Marx. In a sense, what needs to be subject to scrutiny are some of the fundamental ideas which have underpinned both centre left and radical economic thinking. At the same time, whilst it might seem that such models have been left well behind as a result of the economic reforms of the 1990s, nevertheless there is still a critique of the changes which have taken place in which fundamental elements of the critique reflect the original ideas of the Perroux model, for example, Said Bouamama's *Les Racines de l'Intégrisme* (2000). In this sense too, it is necessary to consider the two presumed social negatives of economic growth, namely the inability of agriculture to grow at the same pace as the industrial sector, and the incapacity of the reforms to deliver employment. However, neither the policies proposed by Perroux and de Bernis, nor the critique to which these policies have been subjected, took place in a vacuum; they had deep roots in French and European social and economic thinking of the nineteenth as well as the twentieth centuries. This means that it is necessary to look beyond the policies themselves in order that a better understanding of their meaning can be achieved.

1. Locating Algeria in French Economic and Political Ideas

It is important to understand the role of Algeria as an interface in the articulation of economic and political ideas because it helps to explain aspects of both post-independence economic policy-making and its critique. At the same time, the idea of Algeria as such an interface should not be restricted to the twentieth century and the post-independence period. This is because her economic base and the foundations of economic ideas about the nature and character of the economic development that would be possible were laid in the nineteenth century. They were also constructed using the same basic understandings of the capitalist economic development process.

Algeria played a role in the articulation of French visions of a just society from a very early stage in France's colonisation, as is evident from the range and number of reports which appeared on the nature and future of the colonisation project. These were sometimes the result of investigatory visits to Algeria - Prosper Enfantin (1842), Adolphe Blanqui (1840), or they represented a mix of general political reflection supported later by an investigatory visit - Alexis de Tocqueville, or it was simply impossible to exclude a consideration of the place of Algeria in a wider French vision of her political and economic role in the Mediterranean region - Michel Chevalier, or Algeria was viewed as a new land of opportunity where it would be possible to realise the republican dream of equality - Pierre Leroux.[6] In this way Algeria was not only incorporated within the wider vision of the world that revolution and counter-revolution had bequeathed to Frenchmen, but she also provided the empirical evidence for the social and economic processes of capitalist development. If this seems to be a large claim, it has to be remembered that one of the major influences on political and economic ideas of the period was Claude Henri Saint-Simon, and that many of those who found their way to Algeria were directly or indirectly influenced by his ideas. These include Enfantin, Blanqui, Chevalier and Leroux, and, as will be seen later, Perroux himself would draw upon Saint-Simonian ideas. Other figures in the development of socialist ideas in France, such as Jules Ferry and Jean Jaurès would also visit Algeria and report back to a French public their findings. This special place of Algeria as being part of, but not quite, France would be manifested again in the immediate aftermath of independence when a range of commentators expressing a variety of different socialist visions would attempt to influence post-independence Algerian economic policy-making just as they had attempted to do over a century earlier.

The influence of Saint-Simon on French nineteenth-century thinking and beyond, however, represents only one side of the equation. On the other side is the influence on French economic thinking of Adam Smith in particular but also other eighteenth- and nineteenth-century Anglo-Scottish economic ideas and the effect of both of these strands on the way in which economic development in Algeria was seen. To illustrate different aspects of these influences, the contributions to contemporary nineteenth-century debate by Enfantin, Blanqui and Chevalier are particularly useful. Of these three, it is only Enfantin who sought by his visit as a member of the 'Algerian Scientific Commission of 1840-42' to apply Saint-Simonian ideas directly to Algeria. Blanqui, who was sent by the Academy of Moral and Political Sciences in 1839 to examine the economic situation in Algeria and prospects for a French colonial project, was sympathetic to some Saint-Simonian ideas but also to Anglo-Scottish economic ideas and, in particular, those of Adam Smith - he wrote the Introduction to the 1843 translation by Garnier of *The Wealth of Nations*.[7] Chevalier's association with the Saint-Simonians may have been brief but it left a visible legacy in his thinking, whilst he was politically the most influential of the three through his advocacy, negotiation and finally successful signing of the 1860 Anglo-French free trade treaty.[8]

What then was the essence of their ideas and what do these ideas reveal about the ways in which the building of what were undoubtedly perceived to be 'modern' economic relations in Algeria was seen? Perhaps the first observation to be made is that following from Saint-Simon, there was an underlying assumption that it was the European who was possessed of the necessary creative dynamic to breathe life into the economy that France had found in Algeria. However, each chose to take a different focus on what they perceived to be the way forward. Although Enfantin has a lengthy discussion of 'property relations' and the advantages and disadvantages of French and Algerian/Muslim systems of the latter, he nevertheless takes the view that Muslim society in Algeria had become immobile. This leads him to advocate the principle of 'industrial association' in the form of the *société anonyme*.[9] Blanqui also comments on the nature of property relations but takes the view that they are caught between two negative forces - religious and military - but that these can be transformed by free movement of people and goods. Even so, for Blanqui, the real key to the effective use of the opportunities that Algeria provided, was to institute an economic policy centred on the development of Algiers as a major Mediterranean commercial 'entrepôt'. There are clear links between this vision and that constructed by Chevalier in his elaboration of the idea of a 'Mediterranean system' in which Algeria becomes an integral part in the creation of a Mediterranean economic power house and plays the same catalytic role as the American West was doing for the economy of the United States.[10] Finally, Leroux was also close to Saint-Simonian ideas and thought that if only French men and women could be persuaded to emigrate to Algeria, it would be possible to build there the utopian socialist world which it appeared to him would be almost impossible to build within France itself. He therefore proposed to the Assembly of the short-lived Second Republic that emigration to Algeria should be encouraged so that the establishment of such communities in Algeria could occur. However, in a more general sense, Saint-Simonians and Saint-Simonian ideas also influenced the evolution of the colonial project in Algeria. Saint-Simonians such as Ismail Urbain sought to articulate a different vision of the relationship between Europeans and Muslims in Algeria whilst other Saint-Simonians such as Warnier sought to impose a draconian colonial state upon Muslim Algeria (Emerit 1941).

If these were the ideas that were circulating and influencing economic thinking in France when she began her colonial project in Algeria, what is it that they embody which links them to Perroux, de Bernis and Brenner's argument that underpinning the majority of ideas on post-independence economic development in the 1960s and 1970s were Smithian notions? In the first place, Perroux himself was familiar with the ideas of Saint-Simon and in his introduction to a collection of articles on the subject of the usefulness of the ideas of Saint-Simon and the Saint-Simonians in the twentieth century, he argued that the neglect of these ideas had been due to their subversive character on the one hand, and on the other, that Marxism had been better able to express 'the sense of the "revolt of the disinherited classes"' but that Saint-Simonian ideas also provided certain valuable lessons. Indeed Bocage in his study of Perroux's economic theory (Bocage 1985: 38) argues that Perroux's opposition of dominant and dominated units 'is reminiscent of the contrast between the industrialist and the idlers' (*oisifs*) of Saint-Simon.

Brenner's argument is that, from Paul Sweezy to Immanuel Wallerstein and Andre Gunder Frank, what you have is an updated reading of Book I of *The Wealth of Nations*, but one which puts to one side Smith's initial argument that the development of a society's wealth should be seen as the result of the productivity of its labour, and that productivity of labour was itself the consequence of the specialisation of productive tasks. That means the separation of agriculture and manufacturing, and their assignment respectively to country and town. However, rather than following through the implications that this poses, Brenner argued that it was Smith's subsequent discussion of specialisation and how specialisation was intimately linked to the development of trade, resulting in a situation where 'the division of labour is limited by the extent of the market' (Brenner 1977: 34) that is the idea that one finds percolating through economic development literature of whatever colour during the 1960s and 1970s. Taking this argument and adding to the frame the Saint-Simonian current that had also influenced the first ideas about economic development in Algeria, then there are some important implications for the understanding of the particular difficulties encountered by the post-independence Algerian economic policy-makers, including the idealistic role which was given to agriculture. In particular, the attempts that were made during the Agrarian Revolution to reverse the flow of labour from countryside to the towns, when the political requirement to compensate the urban dispossessed by investment in the countryside led to a series of policies which sought to reframe the economic agenda by land redistribution policies and agrarian programmes, alongside the industrial investment, resulting in the switching of resources from productive to unproductive production.

The purpose of the above discussion has been to illustrate that contradictory discourses concerning the economic development of Algeria are not only not new but have deep roots and that these influenced both the policy proposals which were put forward and the radical critique that they received. Thus the European radical left's agenda for the post-independence Algeria economy and its choice of terrain - *autogestion* or self-management - was as much about their own search for alternatives to the dominant non-capitalist economic model of the day - soviet state planning - as it was a self-reflective analysis of Algerian economic potential at the time. In other words, it was very similar to Enfantin's search for communal forms of property ownership in Algeria, and Leroux's view that it was in Algeria that it would be possible to establish the socialist communities of which he dreamed.

Given the volume of Perroux's published economic writings - far more extensive than that of de Bernis himself, even if it was de Bernis's articulation of the model that is the form with which we are most familiar, and the influence which Perroux had on post World War II French economic thinking (partly through his establishment of the Institute of Applied Economic Sciences in 1944 and his editorship of the journal *Economie appliquée*), it is surprising that there is not greater familiarity with his economic writing in the Anglo-Saxon world. This is not to ignore the study of his 'general economic theory' by Ducarmel Bocage in 1985. The aim here is to revisit some of the main strands of his economic thinking in conjunction with their articulation by de Bernis, and also to consider how these ideas were used and reinterpreted by the Algerian economic theorist, Hamid Temmar. The contemporary critique by radical French critics such as Raffinot & Jacquemot (1977) has already been referred to, but it is still useful to remember that they considered the Algerian model to be inspired by Perroux and that it was a depiction of industrialisation which saw it as 'a cumulative process structuring the social whole by the intensive use of machine systems and permitting the growth at a decreasing cost of its benefits to human beings' (Raffinot & Jacquemot 1977: 141).[11]

2. The Perroux/de Bernis Model of 'Industrialising Industries'

The framework of the 'industrialising industries' model can be found in Perroux's *L'Economie du XXième siècle* (1991 [1961]: 51) in the long introductory essay entitled 'General equilibrium and harmonised growth' and in de Bernis's 1966 and 1968 articles in *Economie appliquée*, 'Industrialising industries and the base of a policy of regional integration' and 'Industrialising industries and regional economic integration'. The presentation of the 'industrialising industries' model by Perroux in *L'Economie du XXième siècle* forms an integral part of his discussion of the history of the theory of general equilibrium in economics from the eighteenth century onwards and it is useful to give an outline of the argument that Perroux follows in order to reach his 'industrialising industries' model.

Perroux's version identifies, as key elements in this history, Jean-Baptiste Say's 1831 distinction between the entrepreneur and the capitalist that had arisen from the question of the role of the service sector in the economy, and secondly, the distinction drawn more generally in eighteenth-century economic writing between the idea of the saver and the entrepreneur-capitalist as active, and the worker as passive. A distinction which, he argued, modern economic writing had transformed into one where investment and manufacture of the means of production were perceived as active, savings plus consumption as the consequences of product changes, and waged work as in the process of becoming active. As a result of all these new groups of activities - in which organisation, social mediation had become more important, Perroux argued that classes also changed in terms of both their form and their content which had the effect of creating a new Third Estate (Perroux 1991: 25). Perroux's other main reference is the notion of 'interdependence' contained in the Walras-Pareto model of general equilibrium, even if he did not consider that he could subscribe to their general model. Whilst finding useful their nominal elements of consumer-worker and entrepreneur, in which what had to be achieved was an equilibrium between the consumer and the entrepreneur, he concluded that it was insufficiently supple to deal with what he called 'dynamic situations'. These 'dynamic situations' included both relations that occurred outside of those concerning exchange and trade, and those that involved 'macro-units'. This led him to incorporate into his model the concept of 'power relation' which he derived from his rejection of the American economist Edward Hastings Chamberlin's view that the economic power asserted by any given economic unit was not directly or even solely related to price and quantity variables (Perroux 1991: 42)[12] but was, as Bocage describes it, 'an expression of the asymmetrical relationships of human agency and groups of human agents in the social universe' (Bocage 1985: 15) in which, firstly, knowledge/information, and, secondly, *contrainte* (or coercion/ pressure) with leadership and domination whether partial or total, are important (Perroux 1991: 42-5).

In Perroux's model, the market was seen as a particular kind of macro-unit, the structure of which reflected the trade-off between the power relation and group relations. By adopting this view of the market as one particular type of macro-unity, he could identify it as 'a coherent institution' which operated within the context of a range of other institutions such as the state which itself had to be seen as the result of a cumulative number of 'social armistices' that had been arrived at by historical '*rapport des forces*' between groups (Perroux 1991: 48-9). Consequently, for Perroux, economic reality was a 'set of obvious or hidden power relationships, a network of interactions between unequal forces, that is, between dominant and dominated partners' (Bocage 1985: 30). He was therefore able to assign to government 'a constructive role in transforming the classical version of capitalism into a form of welfare or regulated market economy' and partly also because, in his eyes, it was the 'power phenomenon' that was responsible for perverting what he called 'the utopian competitive ideal' (Bocage 1985: 21). However, from this brief discussion, it is possible to see why Perroux's view of the relationships between production, the market and the state had obvious attractions for policy-makers dealing with the aftermath of the anticolonial struggle. It is also interesting to reflect that in this discussion, Perroux is less concerned about questions of market than either de Bernis or, as Brenner (1977) pointed out, much of the radical left critique.

The relationships which he has been describing are then set up diagrammatically as two alternative sets of relations of interdependence (Perroux 1991) where Model A is primarily about relations between industries and Model B is about the interaction between industry and agriculture. However, central to both models was the idea that within any economy there are, for the sake of convenience, 'motor industries' (Perroux 1991: 17) which for good or bad, impact on the actions of others, to change organisational structures. These changes result in economic progress - individually, collectively, sectorially - hence also the role of 'development poles' which are, in effect, the particular application of the general analysis. In the context of Algeria in 1962, clearly the key to the change promotion idea of the 'motor industries' is that of 'energy'. However, it was actually the version B of the model which is the one which was closest to the strategy which was adopted in Algeria after independence, in which agriculture acts as the lynchpin between categories: on the one hand, raising productivity sufficiently to absorb production from the new industrial sectors and, on the other, that increased agricultural productivity feeding into food and food processing industries.

The differing positioning of agriculture in the two models is of considerable significance because, as will be seen from de Bernis, the question of the relationship between agriculture and industry was a key political issue. Furthermore, the positioning of agriculture as an integral part of the model is particularly interesting, as in much of the current writing on globalisation, agriculture is conspicuous by its absence from the analytical framework. If agriculture is barely considered in these contemporary writings, the treatment of the agricultural sector in the 'industrialising industries' model was also central to the radical critique of it. The significance of the role and place of agriculture within any model of economic development may have lost its centrality, but its real importance may lie in its capacity to raise major issues about the imagining of the political and social order. In this context, it is useful to refer to the huge divergence in perceptions in the United Kingdom about appropriate strategies to deal with the foot and mouth outbreak, which began in March 2001. At issue has been the importance or non-importance of agriculture itself to the UK economy, and it seems clear, certainly in the reading of both de Bernis (1966) and Temmar (1973) that there was an uncritical assumption that agriculture and those who worked in it, ought to be seen to be as much at the centre of the development model as were the industrial sectors themselves. Again, there are parallels with the political and economic history of Algeria in the nineteenth century, when, in spite of the fact that the majority of European settlers lived in the cities, much of the political debate focused on and was dictated by an image of the countryside and its needs, which did not reflect economic realities but which gave rise to a view of agriculture as a site of struggle.

De Bernis's contribution to the utilisation of Perroux's economic theory was to stress the idea that there were some industrial sectors and industries which were better able to promote the cause of industrialisation. In his 1966 article, he used the example of Renault to illustrate how it became the source of origin for the growth of a machine tool industry in France, thus stressing not only the motor industry idea but also the growth pole notion. However, he also makes an observation to the effect that the modern industries of the time presupposed an industrial base created during the first phase of industrialisation. The implication of this observation seems to be equally pertinent today, and is at the heart of the dilemma that Castells (1998) has raised. Essentially, Castells argues that the speed of technological innovation makes the idea of catching up, as in the case of the former Soviet Union, largely a utopian dream. However, at the time that de Bernis was advocating his version of the 'motor industries'/'development poles' thesis, it seemed at least theoretically possible that the conditions of industrialisation could be artificially constructed by choosing to focus on particular industries and, most importantly, iron and steel, with the energy industry as an alternative substitute. Similarly, in the Franks (1998) version of the 'world system', using the energy industry as the means of buying into this system ought at least to be theoretically possible, as it appears to be able to offer the means to overcome those asymmetrical power relations, which Perroux had identified. However, in the same way that the iron and steel industry can no longer be considered to be an essential element of economic power, the problem for the oil producers is that while they may be able to influence the terms of trade (markets), they are less able to manage the technological innovations on the production side. In many ways, de Bernis acknowledged this problem in his 1968 article; however his response is an argument based on a view of the national state as, in most cases, too small to sustain the growth needs of the majority of industrial sectors. Thus, his solution for what he identified as 'semi-industrialised regions' was a three-pronged policy involving rationalisation, regional specialisation and harmonisation. Once these had been achieved, he envisaged that there ought to be co-ordination of planning between countries.

De Bernis had also categorically rejected, in his 1966 article, the role of consumer/consumption industries as a route to development, arguing that they acted as a break on broader development processes, because they did not possess, in his view, the required 'snowball' effect that had been attributed to them. However, de Bernis's own choice of iron and steel as one of the principal motor industries, rather than offering the solution to the problems which Perroux had earlier highlighted, seems to be reflecting what had been the European historical experience. Thus, when these industries began to contract and 'rationalise' during the 1980s, de Bernis's 'semi-industrialised regions' were ill-prepared to respond. Moreover, the route that he advocated in 1968, that is regional specialisation as a means to move towards regional economic integration, also seems to be a reflection of the experience of Europe and, this time, that of the European Union rather than the political and economic realities of the 'semi-industrialised regions' themselves.

Conclusion

In conclusion, the importance of the Perroux/de Bernis ideas in the establishment of economic thinking by the post-independence Algerian state cannot be underestimated. Their appeal can be gauged from the Preface which Perroux wrote to *Problèmes de l'Algérie indépendante* (1963). Here Perroux writes that Algeria has to achieve in a short period all those tasks, both political and economic, which states like France achieved over a long period of time, if she is to overcome 'the perils of a disarticulated economy, an exterior balance which is impossible to equilibrate without aid ...' but very much in the sense of Algeria as an autonomous unit. Thus one of the primary critiques that one would make today of this model and of the contemporary critique of it, is the view that economic strategy was an internal matter.

Notes

1   This paper was substantially revised as a result of the debates which took place during the 2001, Fifth Workshop on Algeria, University of the West of England - Bristol Business School.

2   Frank has shifted the focus of his argument from the 'development of underdevelopment thesis' of his early work (1967), to one that extends the idea of a global economy or 'world system' beyond the 1600 date used by Wallerstein. This argument is explored in Frank & Gills (1993), Frank (1998) takes the argument an additional step by suggesting that the economic dominance of the West has to be seen as predicated on the economic decline of the East.

3   Immanuel Wallerstein argues that one has to see the world as a single economic system with its different parts dependent upon one another. However, central to this dependence has been its skewing towards the dominant powers within western capitalism. For a summary version of his general thesis, see Frank & Gills (1993: 292-6).

4   Mohammed Saad, 'Matching culture and reforms - Issues and challenges', presentation on 30 June 2001, Fifth Workshop on Algeria, University of the West of England - Bristol Business School.

5   Illustration of this can be found in an article by Roula Khalaf '"Saudi jobs" desert that feeds terror', *Financial Times*, 19 October 2001, where she describes a situation in which a young man seeking a job, nevertheless expects the job to meet his conditions 'a single shift, usual in government but not in the private sector. He wants his office to be next to his house. And he will not accept a monthly salary under SR2,500 ($667).'

6   I deal with the detail of these ideas in Adamson (1999/2000 & 2002).

7   Germain Garnier had a first translation of Adam Smith's *The Wealth of Nations* in 1802, a second edition appeared in 1821, with a new edition revised by Adolphe Blanqui and including biographical notes published in 1843.

8   For a detailed study of the Free Trade Treaty of 1860 between England and France, see Dunham (1930).

9   *Société anonyme* is the equivalent of a limited company.

10 A detailed discussion of Chevalier's visit to the United States and his account of his visit *Le Tableau de l'Amérique* is to be found in Walch (1975).

11 'Un processus cumulatif structurant l'ensemble social par l'emploi intensif de systèmes de machines et permettant l'augmentation à un taux décroissant des objets bénéfiques au groupe humain'. In Raffinot & Jacquemot's text, this appears in quotation marks but they do not cite the source.

12 Edward Hastings Chamberlin is known for his work on the theory of the firm and his ideas were a considerable influence on Perroux (see Béraud & Faccarello 2000). Although he is not being discussed here, Hirschman, with his concept of growth disequilibrium, also argued that if development was to take place, it would be necessary to establish 'motor industries' which he identified as iron and steel, and mechanical engineering.

2 The Tortuous and Uncompleted Privatisation Process in Algeria

Mohammed Saad, Hakim Meliani and Mahfoud Benosman

Introduction

This chapter investigates the relevance of the current reforms by assessing their effectiveness in meeting and supporting the objectives of the privatisation programme and the long-term requirements of the Algerian economy as a whole. This investigation includes an evaluation of the Algerian past and present financial systems as well as the political and social climate that would accommodate future changes. It will also include a review of the two main financial systems used in the developed economies, which are essentially described as either bank-based or market-based financial systems. This chapter highlights the incomplete structural reforms and the weaknesses of the Algerian financial institutions. It concludes with policy recommendations focusing on the need for a better structured, managed and regulated financial system.

1. The Collapse of the Centralised Economic System

Following Algeria's independence in 1962, economic development policies and programmes were oriented towards the expansion of the industrial base with the aim of providing substitutes for imported products. This was to be achieved through a centrally planned economy, which is described in more detail in chapter four. Economic policy choices emphasising planning and heavy industries have prompted the state to create and rely on state-owned companies to implement its development strategy (Saad 2000). The state has thus become a major economic actor owning most companies and being the largest employer. It has been providing 70 per cent of industrial production, 80 per cent of value added and 76.9 per cent of total employment. As shown in Table 1, the size and the role of the public sector in the economy remains large and continues to expand. Through the government's 'return of growth' programme, the size of the public sector, as measured by total government expenditures over GDP, increased from 25.6 per cent, in 1990 to 31.3 per cent in 2001 and 35 per cent in 2002 (Callier & Koranchelian 2002). However, those state-owned companies, which form the basis of the Algerian economy, are often characterised by inefficiency, under-utilisation of capacity, mismanagement, heavy debt and corruption.

Table 1. Importance of the Public Enterprise Sector (1989-2000)

	Value added to productive sector in %	Wages in %
1989	54.2	73.6
1990	57.1	73.4
1991	58.3	67.9
1992	56.5	66.3
1993	52.3	63.7
1994	53.4	66.8
1995	54.6	65.4
1996	54.3	62.5
1997	54.3	57.1
1998	46.4	55.0
1999	48.2	51.7
2000	57.8	51.5

Source: Algerian Authorities and World Bank

Over the past four decades, Algeria has not been able to achieve high and sustainable growth rates. Productivity growth has also been negative during most of these decades. After an initial phase of rapid growth in the 1960s and 1970s with 6.4 per cent on average between 1966 and 1980, Algeria's growth performance was at best modest (2.3 per cent) from 1981 to 2001 and even negative in the early 1990s (Callier & Koranchelian 2002).

However, during most of the 40 years since its independence in 1962, Algeria's investment rate has been one of the highest in the world. It averaged 32 per cent of GDP annually from 1971 to 2000. Human capital, proxied by the average number of years of schooling for the population aged 25, also grew rapidly, as illustrated in Table 2 (Callier & Koranchelian 2002). As the stock of factors of production grew faster than output, total factor productivity growth has been negative.

Table 2. Algerian Growth

	Productivity	Physical capital	Human capital	GDP
1965–70	3.9	2.2	5.0	6.4
1970–75	-1.3	7.1	9.1	5.2
1975–80	-4.6	10.3	14.8	6.2
1980–85	-2.3	5.3	9.0	5.2
1985–90	-4.2	3.0	8.5	0.1
1990–95	-4.3	1.0	9.0	0.3
1995–2000	-1.8	1.3	8.7	3.1
1965–2000	-2.1	4.5	9.5	3.8

Sources: Bosworth, Collins & Chen (1995), Barro & Lee (2000) and Callier & Koranchelian (2002).

The Algerian strategy for economic development has fallen short of achieving its ambitious objectives. This failure is often perceived as one of the main origins of the political, social and economic crisis faced by the country for more than a decade. The Algerian economy and society are essentially characterised by a very poor performance of the agriculture and manufacturing sectors, a strong dependency on hydrocarbons, a high level of debts, unemployment (30 per cent), shortage of housing and corruption. In 1994, the debts were equal to 70 per cent of GDP and the service of the debts was equal to 96 per cent of total income from exports.

The collapse of this economic and political system has pressurised the Algerian authorities into introducing a sweeping programme of political and economic reforms. Macroeconomic stabilisation and structural reforms were initiated by the end of the 1980s. They were aimed at establishing the conditions for sustainable long-term growth and for attracting foreign direct investment. They included correcting macroeconomic imbalances and price distortions, containing inflation, promoting private sector development, reforming and re-structuring public enterprises and integrating the economy into world markets. Developing a successful economy was therefore driven by the need, for the first time, to create a favourable macroeconomic environment which should create the conditions for a real price and inflation stability and would promote investment and production and hence job creation. One of the main goals of these reforms was aimed at transforming the national economy from a tightly controlled centralised system (command and control system of the 1970s and 1980s) to a market-oriented one and hence reducing the role of the state.

2. The Introduction of the Reforms

The collapse of the strategy of development has made the shift towards market economy and privatisation major features of the reforms. In 1989, after more than three decades of central planning, Algeria introduced a comprehensive set of reforms aimed at achieving macroeconomic stabilisation setting the foundations to achieve economic growth, liberalisation and privatisation.

In 1990, new money and credit laws were launched. Budget deficits were eliminated and inflation significantly reduced. The local currency (Dinar) became fully convertible but was drastically devalued. Subsidies were phased out and controls on retail prices and margins were lifted for most goods and services. However, the cost and implications of these reforms and transition are increasingly affecting the social cohesion and political stability of the country. An effective social safety-net system needed to accompany these radical reforms, and privatisation and the re-structuring of the large Algerian public sector are still missing.

The transition process towards a market economy rests on an economic transformation programme in which structural reforms aim at laying the basis of a truly competitive economy. This process started in 1988 with the law on the autonomy of enterprises, which became effective only in 1994 with the implementation of the Structural Adjustment Programme (SAP). This SAP, which ended in 1998 on the eve of the presidential elections won by Lamine Zeroual, delineated the framework from which originated most of the stabilisation and re-structuring policies, essentially aimed at creating the conditions for the return of growth. This programme included:

• A drastic devaluation of the local currency (Dinar);

• A removal of state subsidies;

• A reduction in the budget deficit; and

• The initiation of a gradual privatisation programme.

The SAP had several objectives aimed at improving the macro-economy, which would generate conditions for economic growth in Algeria. As part of the deal, the Algerian government was also required by the IMF to address acute social problems such as housing shortage and unemployment. The Algerian government was, for instance, asked to invest in labour intensive activities and to reduce its dependency on oil and gas.

A noteworthy emphasis was placed upon re-structuring state-owned enterprises as a result of their significant influence on the economy. The transition to a market economy requires, for instance, removing or modifying controls and regulations that distort price mechanisms and competition. The re-structuring of the public economic sector in Algeria is driven by the following two main objectives:

• To transform the public enterprise into a 'firm': i.e. an economic structure subject to the sole challenge of efficiency and profitability; and

• To increase the share of the private sector in the formation of the national product.

This is appearing to be a complex and challenging task, given the state's profound dominance in all sectors of the economy. State-owned enterprises account for 75 per cent of total formal sector industrial employment. They have always been highly subsidised and used as a means to achieve social objectives such as job creation. As a consequence, these state-owned enterprises are being helped by a compliant public banking sector. These firms became bloated and unproductive but remained intact despite poor performance. Industrial production fell by half during the decade from 1986 to 1996, while industrial employment experienced no net change, indicating an increase in the number of effectively redundant workers. Most industrial public enterprises currently operate at a mere 35 per cent capacity.

Reforms have not had all the expected consequences. A good number of state-owned companies have preserved their monopoly despite the legal reforms and are deeply in debt. The transition is far from completed. It is painfully going through difficult stages, in the face of social, cultural, bureaucratic and ideological barriers. Internal adjustment reforms began as early as 1988; the bill on money and credit, promoting the liberalisation of economic structures, dates back to 1990, but the agreements with the IMF, which have speeded up liberalisation, were signed only in 1994-95.

At the macroeconomic level, the assessment of the results remains mitigated. The incidence of the deepening of external shocks on internal equilibrium conveys the risk of further increasing a vulnerability that the domestic economy has already displayed, three years into the implementation of a brutal adjustment process. The weakness of the national economy with too great a dependence *vis-à-vis* oil exports (a key adjustment variable), increases the legitimate fear of the worsening of the overall economic situation if the extreme constraints are to prevail any further.

At the economic policy level, the concern is about the management of a transition from a macroeconomic level to a microeconomic level, in order to break the duality that still characterises the real and monetary spheres, so as to introduce coherence between the two levels of regulation.

3. The Privatisation Programme

As already mentioned, the structural adjustments were aimed at liberalising the capital market to enable the private sectors to invest and acquire state assets. Privatisations are perceived as a tool to help the Algerian economy reorganise and modernise itself and hence develop its efficiency and competitiveness. It is also seen as a means to attract foreign investment. Privatisations have been taking place in a context of transition, fundamental re-structuring, transformation of the economy, as well as political instability.

Privatisations are an essential component of economic reforms and are justified by the recent microeconomic literature, based on the idea that the private firm has an intrinsic ability of being more efficient than its public counterpart (Leibenstein 1989). In 1995, the privatisation of around 500 companies was announced. In spite of internal social troubles, 140 companies were privatised. The privatisation process is slow and is still in its infancy even if the commitment to it is clear: 'everything can be privatised, including the hydrocarbons'.[1] The lack of clarity about its pace can be explained by two main reasons. First, the Algerian state-owned companies are not attracting the interest of investors. Second, the Algerian privatisation strategy has not yet generated a clear consensus, as it is still strongly rejected by the main trade unions and other strong and often unknown political forces.

3.1. Objectives of the Privatisation

Through its privatisation programme, Algeria is striving hard to improve a series of key economic, social and technological factors vital to the return of growth. The main objectives of this programme are:

- To increase the size of the private sector in the economy and reduce state intervention;

- To strengthen the process of industrial re-structuring;

- To promote partnerships and technology transfer;

- To alleviate the technological, financial and market constraints;

- To mobilise additional resources through attractive measures in order to ease the burden of foreign debt; and

- To preserve employment via workers' concessions contracts.

In addition, privatisation is also seen as a means to enhance technological and management capability, develop a real culture of business and management leading to efficiency and competitiveness, and promote exports. The objectives of the privatisation programme can be considered as challenging as well as ambitious given the significant delays, setbacks and resistance, the low level of foreign investment and the poor technical and financial state of most Algerian firms and industries to be privatised.

3.2. The Changing Structures in Charge of Governing Privatisation
From 1988 to early 2003, the structures in charge of governing privatisation have been constantly modified and sometimes radically changed. State-owned companies continue to be used for the introduction of new experiments and change driven by unclear and sometimes contradictory political and economic motives ('La Zone industrielle paralysée', *Liberté*, 28 July 1997, p. 3).

The state National Council Participation Fund (NCPF), as defined by the Decree N° 95.404, led to the regrouping of the state-owned companies into eleven national Public Holdings. Public Holdings were created to replace the previous prevailing form of organisation known as Participation Funds, which were dissolved in December 1996. The implementation of such Holdings became effective in mid 1996. Their status is basically that of modern firms. Their main mission is to re-structure the state-owned companies and actively prepare their transition to the mechanisms of the market economy.

The formation of these Holdings was essentially based upon the idea of clusters of state companies belonging to the same branch or sector activity, such as mechanics, steel, mining, and electronics and computing. In June 2000, the NCPF reviewed this configuration and reduced the number of Holdings to create six large Holdings. The fundamental principle underlying the structure of Holdings was not always easy to respect. The new Holding known as 'Services' was formed from scattered companies operating in a wide range of different activities, which include transport, distribution, publishing and tourism. Regional Holdings were also created to re-structure local public enterprises.

With the view to reducing and completely removing dependency on the state, Public Holdings, unlike the previous Participation Funds, control 100 per cent of the social capital of state-owned companies and are provided with complete authority and power. Participation Funds were merely acting as state fiduciary agents without real power and effective decision-making authority.

The overabundance of texts without clarification as to their scope of intervention has led to the problem of multiplication of intervening parties in the definition and the setting up of privatisation programmes. The insufficient delimitation of the commission of control prerogatives also remains another serious drawback of these reforms. The confusion and lack of clear boundaries engendered by these texts has led to an overlapping of prerogatives between the Council of Privatisation and the Public Holdings. In addition, the effectiveness of the privatisation process is significantly impeded by the heavy bureaucratic system of the evaluation procedures and the lack of experience of the members of the council. There is also a confusion prevailing in the conception and management of the policy of privatisation. The exclusion of so-called 'strategic' sectors from the scope of privatisation is the most significant indication of a serious failing in the conception of Algeria's policy of liberalisation.

4. Financial Reforms

The ongoing reforms and privatisation in Algeria require fundamental financial reforms, which would help promote and sustain the economic and social development. The re-alignment and re-structuring of the financial sector requires a better structured, managed, and regulated financial system (Kaser & Allsopp 1992; Rybczynski 1991; Corbett & Mayer 1991).

4.1. Main Financial Institutions in Algeria

As already mentioned, following its independence in 1962, Algeria undertook the construction of a socialist economy supported by heavy industrialisation and substantial investment in human capital. The political ideology has been a major influence in the establishment of a centralised financial system resulting in the creation of strong state financial institutions to support and finance the ambitious programme of development. The tasks and responsibilities of these state-owned banks increased, while, at the same time, their level of independence was significantly reduced and their role became very passive. The Central Bank, which was set up in December 1962, has always been very dependent upon the government. The 'Caisse Algérienne de Développement' (CAD) was created in May 1963 to finance state investment projects. This bank played a major role in launching the first major Algerian state-owned companies such as SONATRACH (oil company), SNS (steel company), CNAN (shipment company). The 'Caisse Algérienne de Développement' (CAD) was replaced by the Algerian Bank of

Development in May 1973 in order to finance the economic development and improve the financial position of most state-owned companies. The 'Caisse Nationale d'Epargne et de Prévoyance' was formed in August 1964 as a Savings Fund to promote and boost housing policies. The 'Banque Nationale d'Algérie (BNA) and the 'Crédit Populaire d'Algérie' (CPA) were both created in 1966 to fund the increasingly ambitious programme of industrial development. In 1967, the 'Banque Extérieure d'Algérie' (BAE) was created to support and promote development and transactions with foreign companies.

It is clear that the process of 'Algerianisation' and thus the nationalisation of the main financial institutions enabled the state to own and control the main flow of credit. A similar and parallel development of state control and ownership also occurred from 1965 to 1975 in the other sectors of the Algerian economy. This led to a significant collusion between the economic and political spheres, resulting from a high level of state intervention and domination in all sectors of the economy, including the financial institutions. For political reasons, banks had to keep offering loans to state-owned companies, in spite of their very poor performance and financial situation (Soliman 1991). The role of Algerian financial institutions was passive and merely restricted to providing the financial backing to the state's plans by automatically issuing credit and loans for approved expenditures. Their activities became almost purely accounting in nature. The role of credit evaluation was hardly performed.

4.2. Recent Liberalisation Policies

With the introduction of the economic reforms and the re-structuring of the economy, there has been, since the early 1990s, a gradual liberalisation of the financial institutions that has resulted in an increased involvement of private and foreign banks. The Baraka Bank, a joint venture between Saudi Arabia and Algeria, was created in December 1990. June of the same year also saw the creation of the Joint Offshore Bank (BAMIC), between Libya and Algeria. In addition to national private banks, several foreign banks, such as Arab International Bank (ABC), Arab Investment Bank (AIB), City Bank, Société Générale, Natexis, Ryan Bank, started operating in Algeria.

The main objectives of the reforms of the financial institutions are:

• To introduce competition and modernisation,

• To move the banks from directed credit to market-determined allocation of credit;

• To reduce state domination;

• To strengthen banking supervision; and

• To complete portfolio re-structuring.

However, on the whole, the Algerian financial system remains broadly underdeveloped and heavily controlled by the government (95 per cent of assets and 90 per cent of lending). It essentially consists of the central bank and six state-owned banks, plus a marginal participation of foreign financial institutions with small operations mainly focused on high profit, low risk transactions. It is strongly argued that the process of the economic reforms and the programme of privatisation are seriously impeded by this heavy bureaucratic and state-owned financial system, which is far from changing its past behaviour and mind-set. In addition, the market for credit is still far from being adequately developed (Callier & Koranchelian 2003).

4.3. Financial Structures in Developed Economies

The main role of financial systems is to mobilise the funds of a large number of individual savers towards the funding of larger-scale enterprises. The way such funds are mobilised and allocated varies from one economy to the other. Furthermore, the process of mobilisation may heavily influence the activities, directions, growth and even success of individual firms or even industries at large. It was shown theoretically by Modigliani & Miller (1958), applying competitive equilibrium analysis to corporate finance, that there is no relation between corporate finance and the performance of the firm, in the absence of taxation and capital market imperfections. However, as early as 1962, it was recognised that the varying approaches towards financing significantly affect economic development and industrial enterprise. Gerschenkron (1962) argued that there was a significant discrepancy between the English bank, essentially designed to serve as a source of short-term capital, and the German bank, designed to finance the long-term needs of the economy. The German banks advise and maintain interest in corporate activities and provide technical support and market know-how accumulated by their staff (Pollard 1989).

In terms of financial activities, there are significant differences existing between the various economies of the developed countries. Systems may be characterised as either bank-based or market-based financial systems. Germany and Japan are clear illustrations of economies, which have developed banked-based systems. On the other hand, the United States and the United Kingdom are typical of market-based financial systems.

Bank-based systems not only provide long-term capital, but also play an active role in the financing and general directions of corporate strategy. They also provide advisory and brokerage services for both individuals and firms; about half of all shares are deposited with banks, thus they not only minimise transaction costs, but also act as custodians of these shares by, for example, utilising their voting rights. In addition to the credit evaluation of prospective borrowers at the initial stage and the setting of terms on which finance is provided, bank-based systems provide subsequent monitoring (Corbett 1987). Unlike the usual practice of monitoring accounting performance and management, it is quite usual for Japanese loans officers to visit firms on a regular basis, often more than once a week. Another distinguishing factor of Japanese banks is that when firms encounter financial hardship, direct managerial control by banks can occur, in which the firm's main bank can organise the response of creditors, re-schedule loans and even provide specialised and trained staff. They may intervene and assist businesses in times of poor performance.

In market-based systems, capital markets exert control over the management activities of the firm. Control is generally associated with takeovers - a process that acts as a discipline on firms, allowing control to be transferred from inefficient to efficient ones. Competition for control by other firms, through takeovers, suggests that corporate efficiency must increase, since inefficient companies would always be under pressure. However, in practice, it has been proven to be deficient in several respects, especially since it often results in hostile takeovers. In addition to being an extremely provocative and aggressive process of publicly demonstrating the incompetence of the rival management, it is very costly in terms of resources, time and distraction from other management duties.

4.4. Financial Reforms Needed For Privatisation And Industrial Development

The current changes aiming at the privatisation of state-owned firms require a coherent policy that embarks on a strategic re-alignment and re-structuring of industry (Soliman 1991). There needs to be a simultaneous re-structuring of the financial structures in order to accommodate such changes. The financial system will, furthermore, determine the consequent development of the industrial sector as a whole.

The present financial system in Algeria is inadequate to accommodate the break-up of the industrial public sector. There needs to be a more appropriately structured, managed and regulated financial system. The alternative financial systems operating in the developed countries, namely the bank-based system typical in Germany and Japan, or the market-based system that is prevalent in the United States and the United Kingdom, have to be assessed in order to evaluate the reforms in the financial system that would be most suitable, yet realistically obtainable, for the needs, demands and development of the Algerian industrial sector. Would therefore a market-based system be viable in Algeria?

The stock exchange in Algeria has been very passive in the development of the industrial sector. The January 1998 bond issue of SONATRACH was the first operation on the Algerian capital market. Its success opened the way for other operations such as ERIAD/SETIF (capital increase through an IPO in November 1998), SAIDAL group and EL AURASSI Hotel (launched on the stock exchange successively in February and June 1999). The first trading session was held on 13 September 1999 with the successive listing of the companies. Without doubt, the revival of a vibrant stock exchange would be a contributory factor in the overall development of the financial system. However, there are some concerns as to the relevance of this strategy to the successful implementation of the privatisation programme aimed at promoting and sustaining development. This strategy may obstruct the long-term growth of firms quoted on the stock exchange. In addition, it has often been difficult to induce people to participate in such activities. Recent experience has shown little interest and willingness to contribute to the transaction operations in the stock market. Hence, the possibility of selling a large quantity of shares to a large number of small investors is extremely remote. Relying on large investments may lead to a transfer of a state monopoly to a private monopoly. Furthermore, without strict regulatory bodies, there may be a tendency to drastically alter the firm's activities, which may not only be detrimental to the government policies of industrial development but also to other non-participating stakeholders, such as the employees, as often happens in the hostile takeover transactions in the United States (Corbett & Mayer 1991).

Conclusion

The current policy in Algeria has essentially been focused on the market-system, as the main instrument for the implementation of the privatisation programme. However, the relevance, feasibility and impact of such a choice have not been sufficiently investigated.

An alternative approach, based on a bank-based system, may be more appropriate to re-structure the Algerian economy and provide a sustainable and long-term development. Germany and Japan, which have adopted such a system, have experienced long-term success, stability and development in the main sectors of their economy. Such a strategy, involving a new, active role for the Algerian banking institutions, requires them to be modernised, made independent and empowered in terms of the autonomy, skills and expertise needed to take on new and additional responsibilities. The success of the Algerian privatisation programme is dependent upon a coherent and strategic re-alignment and re-structuring of the whole economy. This re-alignment may also need to take into consideration the religious practices and the issue of the interest rate.

Finally, there is also a need to change the culture[2] and the focus of regulatory institutions from central planning and bureaucracy to a system based on greater coordination between the different institutions, transparency, openness, efficiency and accountability.

Notes

1   As declared by the Minister in charge of privatisation, Hamid Temmar.

2   The need for a change of the culture is discussed in chapter five.

3 The Role of Accounting in Economies in Transition: The Case of Algeria

Cherif Merrouche

Introduction

Does accounting play a vital role in the achievement of economic growth? Specialists in the field believe that in developing countries, accounting should be considered as an important pillar, contributing to the implementation of the development process. Needles (1976: 45) stresses that 'despite the difficulty of proving the causality between the two highly correlated variables of economic development and accounting technology, there is little doubt that accounting is an important factor in achieving the goal of economic growth by a developing country'. Yet, why should we expect accounting to be of help in the economic development process? Solomons (1980: 7) argues that:

> *Accounting itself cannot feed the hungry or cure the sick or bring enlightenment to the illiterate. Yet, it has a part to play in all these advances. Whenever scarce resources need to be economized, there is work for the accountant to do; and the scarcer the resources are, the more important it is that they should not be misdirected or misappropriated.*

Enthoven (1973, 1979) also points out that a sound accounting system is an essential element in the economic development of developing countries. It is generally accepted that economic development can be analysed and planned by various forms of 'models'. In addition, while quantitative economic (econometric) model building helps us to know more about the working of an economy and to project systematically its structure, accounting information systems play an important part in these economic models. Similar arguments are made by Chandler & Holzer (1981); Jensen & Arrington (1983); Lin & Deng (1992); Belkaoui (1994); Radebaugh & Gray (1997); Abdul-Rahaman (1998); Ndzinge & Briston (1999). Hence, in broad terms, it is widely accepted that accounting information has the potential to play a very important role in many of the debates on the issues affecting economic development. In fact, some have gone so far as to suggest that it would be impossible for developing countries to join the global economy without a strong accounting profession. In fact, it may be possible to point out that a country's economic development is similar to a jigsaw. While the contribution of any one piece of the jigsaw may not be of equal proportion to the individual and collective contribution of the other pieces, it still remains the case, that the absence of any piece would unquestionably have a detrimental impact on the overall appearance of the jigsaw. Ndzinge & Briston (1999: 32) suggest that:

> There are many factors which have a role to play in the economic development. This development depends on such factors as a country's natural and human resources, the political climate and the fiscal policies. Although accounting is only one component in the entire system of economic development, it should not be regarded as dispensable, for removal of just one element of any system could easily lead to the system malfunctioning. Accounting can play the vital role of catalyst in the economic development process and this deserves serious attention from developing countries.

Accounting in developing countries has received little attention in the international accounting literature. Until 1977, little was published on African and Asian countries. With few exceptions (Enthoven 1979, Wallace 1999), there seems to be little interest in the study of accounting in Africa. If we consider the development and practice of accounting in former French colonies (Francophone Africa), the picture is even bleaker. Unlike in the former British colonies, accounting in Francophone Africa has been neglected in the works of Anglo-Saxon researchers.

The purpose of this chapter is, firstly, to find out the state of accounting in Algeria from independence to the present, by tracing the different factors that individually and collectively contributed to determining its (accounting) trajectory. Secondly, it seeks to establish whether the current accounting system has the ability to generate reliable and relevant information for decision-making in the transition from a command to a market economy. Thirdly, it attempts to fill part of the aforementioned gap in the literature by contributing to the conceptual body of knowledge in international accounting and the developmental theory of accounting practices in different environments.

It provides a brief review of the preferred Algerian mechanism for implementing economic development policies following independence in 1962 and addresses the issue of how the perceived weaknesses experienced by the newly independent country with the inherited 1957 French accountancy plan (PCG: *Plan Comptable Général*) led Algeria in 1972 to the necessity of creating a new accountancy plan (PCN: *Plan Comptable National*). It then focuses on the gradual Algerian economic transition from a command economy toward a market economy and the impact of this change on accounting in transition. In the final section, some suggestions are made as to the accounting changes necessary in the transition from a planned to a market economy.

1. Economic Development Path

During the colonial period, the Algerian economy was managed for the sole interest of the coloniser. From an economic point of view, Algeria was considered as a market, a source of both agricultural products and cheap labour. Fertile lands the length of the Mediterranean coast were confiscated and given to French settlers and related agricultural entities. As a result, the majority of the Algerian population was pushed towards the mountains where the land is naturally harsh and most unproductive. France's other main priority was to exploit intensively its colony's mineral resources.

Following independence in 1962, the Algerian economy experienced severe difficulties as a result of the massive exodus of French landowners, industrialists and administrators. The lack of a contingency plan for such an eventuality made matters even worse. The absence of suitably qualified Algerians to take over after the French human exodus drastically complicated an already complex situation. The agricultural sector had been in decline since 1959 and the industrial sector was rather weak to have had any noticeable impact on the needs of the country.

In the wake of the colonial exodus, the Algerian authorities had little short-term alternative but to take over substantial responsibilities in virtually all the sectors of the economy. Furthermore, postcolonial amnesia is symptomatic of the urge for historical self-invention or the need to make a new start. It is then not surprising to find that, not long after independence the 'state exercised all powers: executive, legislative and judicial. It became the principal agent of industrialisation and development, hence reinforcing its political, social and cultural omnipresence within society' (Bennoune 1988: 122). The Algerian-preferred mechanism for implementing economic development rested largely on a series of State-Owned Enterprises (SOEs) the main characteristics and functions of which were highly influenced by state policy.

Table 1. Algerian State Owned Enterprises

Economic Activity	Name of SOE
• Petroleum	SONATRACH
• Electricity and Gas	SONELGAZ
• Mining	SONAREM
• Steel	S.N.S
• Metal Equipment	S.N. METAL
• Mechanical Equipment	SONACOME
• Electrical and Electronic Equipment	SONELEC
• Building Materials	S.N.M.C
• Textile	SONITEX
• Leather and Skins	SONIPEC
• Tobacco	S.N.T.A
• Foodstuffs	S.N. SEMPAC
• Paper	SONIC
• Wood and Furniture	S.N.L.B
• Chemicals and Para chemicals	S.N.I.C
• Traditional Crafts	S.N.A.T
• Transport (Land, Sea, Air)	SNTF, SNTV, SNTR, CNAN, AIR ALGERIE
• Livestock and Fisheries	ONAB, ONALAIT

Source: Algerian Ministry of Industry 1974.

These enterprises grew out of necessity and were created for political, economic, social and historic reasons. There was a need to promote self-reliance in strategic sectors of the economy, provide infrastructural facilities for promoting a balanced and diversified economic structure in development and increase employment. The overall objective of each of these enterprises was 'profitability' taken not solely in its strict financial sense but intended to embrace also the social aspects; the aim here being not to achieve profits for the benefit of a few, but to maximise productivity for the purpose of satisfying the needs of the country as a whole.

The various SOEs appear to have been conceived as the main instruments for state intervention in the overall planned effort for economic development. By the beginning of the 1980s, these enterprises were the main engine of the economic development of the country, responsible for the production and distribution of a variety of products and services ranging from mining, steel, household appliances, construction of houses, transport, livestock and fisheries to manufacturing clothes and shoes (see Table 1). The only part of the economy that remained under private control was, for some practical purposes, a fraction of the traditional sector, some small manufactures and small-scale retail trade.

2. Organisational Structure

One important peculiarity of the formal structure of these enterprises (or at least some of them) was characterised by the progressive enforcement and implementation of a system of participative management. Both historic developments and the need for greater state control have contributed towards preserving and even enhancing structural patterns of a 'conventional type' comparable to the structural forms and mechanisms found in enterprises of non-socialist oriented countries. As a result, a bi-polar system of authority structure may be discerned in these enterprises.

On the one hand stands the authority structure born from both the colonial inheritance and state policies, while, on the other, emerges a form of structure centred upon promoting a system of participative management. These characteristics are reflective of 'a priori' and 'a posteriori' traits, pointing to pluri-dimensional features inherent in the complexities of the Algerian socio-political and economic context. These two somewhat contradictory structures are clearly reflected in the way the SOE operates. On the one hand, the SOE has more in common with a privately owned entity in that:

• It is subject to commercial law;

• It is financially autonomous;

• It is subject to the same fiscal policy as that applying to privately owned entities;

• It aims to make a profit or at least break even.

On the other, the SOE is different from a privately owned enterprise and has more in common with socialist enterprises found elsewhere in the world in that:

• Its capital belongs to the state;

• It is owned by the state;

• Its managing director (chief executive) is appointed by the relevant guardianship ministry (*tutelle*);

• Part of its profit is paid to the state's treasury;

• Another part of the profit is paid to the employees;

• Self-financing including investments is not allowed;

• Seeking and/or granting loans is not allowed.

It appears then that the Algerian SOE is a hybrid organisation. As an enterprise and in common with a privately owned entity, it sells its output to its customers on the market place. It therefore performs similar functions such as production, finance and marketing to those undertaken by firms found in the private sector. On the other, as an entity owned and controlled by the state, it is expected to respond and account not only for its activities on the market, but to direct and indirect pressures from bureaucrats, politicians and the public at large.

Having so many 'masters' to account to naturally results in a plethora of objectives. This may be equivalent to having no objectives at all and, obviously, conflict over objectives at the enterprise level is very possible. This is because it is possible that two types of managers would emerge from such a set-up, each with their own goals and interests. The first type is mainly concerned with running the entity like a private concern and is motivated by economic considerations, profits and growth. The second type perceives its role as a link between the enterprise and other state bodies, including central government, and is anxious to favour those non-commercial and politically motivated objectives. The enterprise in this context is considered as a means to climbing further the political ladder.

The above is best illustrated in the way the SOEs were structured before and after the Charter for the Socialist Organisation of Enterprises, known in Algeria as GSE (*Gestion Socialiste des Entreprises* 1971). Until the beginning of the 1970s, the structural organisation of all SOEs was based on the same model. At the head of the SOE was the managing director (*directeur général*), in principle assisted by the 'Guidance and Control Committee'. The Committee was made up of representatives from the guardianship Ministry and the Ministry of Finance and representatives from the ruling party FLN (*Front de Libération Nationale*) and the National Union of Algerian Workers (UGTA, *Union Générale des Travailleurs Algériens*).

The Committee was to meet three times a year to give its 'opinion' on a range of matters such as the management of the enterprise, the long-term strategy and all other decisions related to the assets of the enterprise and the investments to be made. In reality, the only effective control that took place was that undertaken by the Ministry of Finance's auditors who were based in the SOE's headquarters. The 'Guidance and Control Committee' was replaced in 1971 by the 'Management Council' and the '"Workers" Assembly'. The 'Management Council' is an amalgamation of government designated officials and workers' representatives designated by the Workers' Assembly from amongst its members. The Council is presided over by the government executive director (managing director). The Council deals with the overall functioning of the enterprise and meets at least once a week. The Workers' Assembly is given important prerogatives in terms of control over the management of the enterprise through its rights to control and make proposals and recommendations concerning the overall functioning of the enterprise.

The GSE, together with *Ordonnance* no. 71-74 (16 November 1971), set out the regulations governing the socialist management of SOEs, the essence of which is that the worker is not an ordinary wage earner but a producer-manager. Workers' participation in the management of SOEs was not only at the organisational level; it also played a pivotal role in the production workshops. Through the GSE, the primary aim was to emphasise the socialist character of the economy, as well as having a mechanism in place to win the battle of production.

3. Accountability and Control

The emergence of the state as the major force in the economy resulted in most sectors of the economy being controlled and operated by the state. The central authorities, by means of the national planning mechanism, were in a position to determine the activities of each national enterprise. In fact, it may be argued that the national enterprise is not an autonomous entity, as its corporate plan is highly influenced by, and is a fundamental part of, the national economic plan. The statutory position, rights and obligations of the national enterprise are defined in Article 2, *Ordonnance* no. 75-23 (April 1975), where it is stated that the national enterprise should undertake the task of fulfilling its objectives in the context of the national socio-economic development plan (CNGSE: *Commission Nationale pour la Gestion Socialiste des Entreprises* 1975).

The relationship between the national enterprise and the State administrative bodies is defined in *Ordonnance* no. 75-76 (November 1975) which stipulates that:

> *The socialist enterprise is the principal agent in the attainment of the planned developmental objectives. It is concerned with one or several branches of economic activities and constitutes the basic organisational echelon in the planning process, and within the legal limits of its mission contributes to the economic and socio-cultural development.*

This close relationship between the national enterprise and the strategic aims of the state is further illustrated in the 1976 National Charter (*Charte Nationale*):

> *The socialist enterprise belongs to the state and is the most appropriate tool to concretise the objectives of the revolution through the socialisation of the means of production... The socialist enterprise constitutes the most appropriate structure for the state to build socialism. (86)*

It follows that the SOE plays a critical role in the implementation of the strategic aims of the state and was not therefore regarded as a mere commercial organisation in the sense that its objective was to maximise profit. In pursuit of this aim, it was also expected to have in place short and medium term plans clearly indicating the ways by which the state's objectives would be achieved. On the other hand, apart from its inclusion in the national economic plan, the SOE's managerial decisions would be subjected to further scrutiny by other government agencies (Ministry of Finance, Energy, Transport etc...). In fact, the GSE (1971: 10) clearly states that the SOE 'is directly accountable to the relevant legal authority and should implement all the instructions issued by this authority' and 'should operate on the basis of the central directives of the economy'.

It follows that:

• The SOE is guided by the expansion of production.

• Economic decision-making is centrally determined and the role of market forces is relegated.

• Prices are centrally determined and market prices are suspended.

• Allocation of resources and investment decisions are centrally determined using non-commercial criteria as a basis.

• The private sector is only responsible for a small proportion of the investment decisions.

• The SOE's managers have little incentive and managerial authority to enhance efficiency.

• Production of unprofitable products is tolerated.

• Providing employment is consistent with the aim of the state being the economic and social development agent.

• Political considerations tend on the whole to outweigh economic considerations.

Corresponding to the position illustrated above, it follows that the objectives of national enterprises are different from those of their private counterparts. Economic development will depend upon natural, human and financial resources. Non-economic factors such as education and government policy also play a significant role. Given the role allocated to the various SOEs in the economic development of the country, as discussed above, it follows that the information gathered at the enterprise level will play a significant role in the national economic plan. It has been argued that the accounting needs of the government sector are no less urgent than those for the business enterprise sector, nor is sound government likely to exist without sound governmental accounting.

4. Economic System and Accounting Development

What would then be the role of accounting in the environment discussed above? In the more developed countries, accounting is theoretically perceived to be essentially utilitarian, being conditioned by the requirements of the society in which it is conducted. This theory has often been suggested in the literature. In other words, the framework of political and economic institutions of a given society ought and is expected to impact on the practice of accounting. This theoretical point of view however does not hold when the attention is turned to developing countries. It is widely accepted that developing countries in their attempt to become 'developed' have either inherited wholesale the accounting systems left behind by the colonial administration or imported accounting systems voluntarily from the countries from which they obtained their political independence, or from their new allies through international aid or through development and training programmes (Godfrey et al. 1996, Annisette 1999, Wallace 1999).

As to the adoption of these 'foreign' accounting systems in the African context, Wallace (1999) points out that some countries are better than others in their assimilation of these systems but not better in transforming imported systems to suit their cultures (p. 7). However, as far back as 1972, Algeria had not only rejected the inherited accounting system, but created a new accountancy plan, perceived to be more suitable to its socio-economic and cultural conditions. It is therefore safe to mention here that Algeria's decision to reject the French 1957 PCG was very bold and had even emerged well before its time. This is also bearing in mind that it was argued as late as 1995 that:

> the PCG has inspired the accounting systems put in place by countries such as Cambodia, Spain, Lebanon, Morocco and Russia. The PCG has had also an indirect influence on the development of the accounting systems of Chile, Greece, Iraq, Laos, Madagascar, Portugal, Ukraine and Vietnam. (Burlaud 1995: 100)

It would definitely have been to Algeria's advantage to keep the inherited accounting system already tried and tested in France and Algeria, hence avoiding the need to both re-invent the wheel of accounting development and incur the costs of such re-invention. Or was the desire to create a new accounting system rather a statement of national determinism and a change away from all inherited systems (including accounting) that were based on an enforced colonial system?

At this stage, it is essential to ask why was it necessary for Algeria to reject the inherited PCG? Before answering this question, it is important to describe briefly the French 1957 PCG. The PCG (revised in 1979 and 1984) is essentially a chart of accounts with a system of ledger codes; recommendations on the valuation of assets and determination of costs, expenses, and results; model financial statements and statistical reports; and a discussion of the cost of accounting procedures. The origins of the plan 'lie firmly rooted within the unique features of the French system where the government was in a very powerful position to plan and control all sectors of the economy' (Samuels et al. 1975: 14).

These planning arrangements arose as a response to the realities of the post- World War II situation, when a series of five year economic plans was developed to create an *économie concertée*, with public and private investment working together to rebuild the economy (Godfrey et al. 1999: 228). It was designed to help the French make the transition from an essentially agrarian economy to a modern, internationally focused country. Finally, the PCG is characterised by its macroeconomic orientation, which is different from the microeconomic focus in countries such as the US and the UK, where the emphasis is on the private sector.

5. The Conception and Design of the Algerian Accountancy Plan

In response to Algeria's changing new economic needs, the French PCG was considered an inadequate information system, incapable of responding sufficiently to the country's realities and providing a useful tool for contributing to a better management of the economic development. The French PCG was also criticised for having been designed in a free market economy where state intervention and internal control of the economic activities is limited. It was also argued at the time that, the PCG was much more finance and statistic oriented. Its uniformity was limited to the operations expressed in monetary terms. Therefore, this made it impossible to know the details that would give a real insight into the structure of the production, the costs and prices composition and the nature of the management methods, as would be the case in planned economies such as that of Algeria.

Another criticism of the PCG was that it provided less management information than would be necessary in a planned economy. The planning process expects accounting information to show material and physical elements that are the main ingredients for the management needs and the planning necessities of the new economy. The PCG was useful in an economy based on competition and in markets where supply and demand is the major rule. With that in mind, it was of paramount importance to design and implement a new accountancy plan based on the needs of the emerging new economic environment.

In his address to the Higher Council of Accountancy (CSC: *Conseil Supérieur de la Comptabilité*) the body whose task was to design and implement the PCN, the Minister of Finance (1972) stated:

> *You are to elaborate a new accountancy plan that will become a tool particularly suited to the management necessities of the Algerian planning, as well as the needs of the socialist enterprises. In other words, this is to endow ourselves with an instrument that will ease both forecasting and decision making... we must ensure that the national accounting has at its disposal, for its statistical and forecasting aims, information that is easy to aggregate, clear and significant...*

The CSC was a consultative body under the control of the Ministry of Finance. Its remit was to promote and facilitate the application of accounting at the enterprise level which in turn would result in providing a basis for more complete economic and informational systems necessary for the planning of the economy. Through the PCN, the aim was to achieve the following objectives:

• Provide the necessary information for easing forecasting and decision-making of enterprises at different levels for better economic and management control.

• Show values that are economically and socially significant to the nation as a whole in terms of national accounting statistics needed for central planning.

• Enable the users of accounting information to know the costs and the level of stocks at any time.

• Give comprehensive, clear and precise information to all users of accounting information.

After four years of preparation and consultation, the new system of accounting and reporting came into operation on 1 January 1976. The design stage of the PCN drew on the experience of four French *'Experts Comptables'* from the French National Council of Accountancy, two of whom had taken part in the drafting of the accountancy plan for African French-Speaking Countries (OCAM: *Organisation Commune Africaine et Malgache*) some two years earlier. The PCN requires a meaningful uniform classification of accounts under a clear terminology and standardised methods of recording. It allows for the compilation of statistics by economic activity, thereby facilitating inter-sectoral and inter-enterprise comparisons.

The PCN presented two unique characteristics. Firstly, it was conceived, prepared and implemented because of the needs of the Algerian economy at the time, certainly unlike many developing countries which adopted either the British, the Franco-Spanish-Portuguese, Germanic/Dutch, United States or former Soviet Union and Eastern European accounting systems. Secondly, the PCN not only defined the users of accounting information but, more importantly, ranked them, guided by the principle that the state should own the means of production and that private capital would be acceptable only where it did not exploit the workers. The most important users in the Algerian context were identified as follows:

- The enterprise;

- The tax administration;

- The guardianship ministries;

- The national accounting body.

However, despite the innovations, and, in some instances, the radical departures from the PCG 1957, the orientation of the PCN is towards providing statistical information useful for the economic planning process. It is largely devoid of any management accounting and cost accounting. This could result in managers lacking the necessary tools to plan and control their activities efficiently. In addition, it is conceivable that this lack of guidance in such a critical area, would leave managers with no alternative but to improvise whenever necessary. If we add to this the lack of highly skilled accountants, it would not be surprising to conclude that cost accounting records would either not be kept, kept poorly or even maintained on the basis of the colonial system. Therefore, the value of management accounting as a tool for planning, controlling, communicating, organising and motivating, including budgeting, pricing, revenue and performance measurement, is highly compromised. Consequently, the quality of the financial information reported would not have any particular impact on the outcome of the decision-making process.

Therefore, it is not surprising that despite the fact that the PCN has been in place now for more than 25 years, recent studies (Ouibrahim & Scapens 1989, Jones & Sefiane 1992) have shown that accounting does not appear to feature highly in the day-to-day running of national enterprises and that, in general, Algeria makes rather limited use of accounting data in decision-making. This is consistent with what has already been mentioned, in that the SOE operates with a view to satisfy the objectives assigned to it in the national economic plan. The managing director and the management council are not confronted with the problems of commercial viability, competition and the threat of liquidation or takeover, which characterise companies operating in a market economy.

Consequently, senior managers have a somewhat reduced need for accounting information. They do not operate under uncertainty, as they have no discretion in the choice of strategy, product lines, organisational forms and policies to manage risk. They are not guided by an internalised need to achieve a prescribed goal but by other motivations, which may not form the basis of their performance evaluation. While privately owned entities are owned by shareholders to whom senior managers must legally account (annual report) at least once a year, a national enterprise is owned by the state and the latter is neither a person nor a single organisation. The state acts through a variety of agents (ministers, civil servants, legislators etc.) and these agents invariably see their mission as different from one another. Thus, the balance between autonomy and accountability is rather ambiguous and, unlike private entities, the accounting contribution to enhancing this relationship is rather limited if not non-existent.

6. Gradual State Withdrawal: Privatisations

There are many reasons for the introduction and spread of privatisation. These include, among others, improvement of the government's financial position and subsequently a reduction of the burden on the state's treasury; a strengthening of market forces and competition; improvement of national enterprise performance and encouragement of wider business ownership. In Algeria, the process of privatisation may be argued to have started in 1986 following the massive decline in the oil revenue and the resulting austerity plan put in place by the government. Given the role played by the SOEs since independence, it was not a matter of if, but when their overall performance would come under the spotlight. While the SOEs have registered a huge increase in size over the years and have definitely contributed to the economic development of the country, the way in which resources have been used and most of all, the outcome of the use of these resources translated into financial terms made grim reading (Abdeladim 1998).

The first major reform of the Algerian SOE came in 1988 (*Loi* no. 88-01). The main objective of this reform was to redefine the relationship between the state and the SOE and the role to be played by each party. The aim was clearly to allow the national enterprise to be more autonomous in its activities and decision-making, while the state remained the sole owner of these enterprises.

However, seven years later, the conclusion was that the 'autonomous national enterprise', as perceived by Law no. 88-01, did not really materialise on the ground. The reasons for this 'setback' are many. Amongst them are the continuous presence of the state as the sole owner; the suspicion of the enterprises' senior managers of a system of autonomy conceived and imposed from the top, and the tolerance by the state including the financial bailing out of many national enterprises that kept showing huge losses. The lack of impact made on the management of SOEs following the 1988 reform compelled the Algerian authorities to repeal Law no. 88-01 by Ordinance no. 95-25 (*Ordonnance* no. 95-25, 25 September 1995).

In parallel with similar developments elsewhere, the reform programme put in place in Algeria aims to allow more and more autonomy in making economic decisions and providing financial incentives to managers and employees of these enterprises. The reform programme is characterised by the following features:

• Although the government may still retain ownership of an SOE or may have majority shares, there would be a clear degree of separation of management and ownership.

- There would no longer be direct control over the NCSOE (newly converted SOE) by the state and/or its agencies. Most NCSOEs would become either profit centres and/or investment centres.

- The decision-making process would be in the hands of the NCSOEs' managers or board of directors.

- The activities of NCSOEs would no longer be part of the state's economic planning, but rather integrated through the market mechanism acting on the totality of the separate decisions of numerous independent entrepreneurs.

- Profit would be the primary goal and would increasingly become the sole criterion in the performance measurement of the NCSOEs and their managers.

- NCSOEs would now be operating in relatively freer markets and would be subject to market forces. The state and/or its agencies would no longer guarantee a market for a NCSOE's products or services and would stop subsidising loss-making NCSOEs.

- Only a small number of NCSOEs would have their shares traded on the Algiers Stock Exchange. For other NCSOEs, the value of the firm cannot be determined in a free market and access to finance to fund expansions and or investments would be harder.

- The role of accounting information would be of very critical importance.

7. Conclusion and Recommendations

In its current state, the PCN would not be in a position to meet the challenges that result from the transition from a command to a market economy. In a market economy, accounting is considered as part of the total information system of an entity. In this context, accounting is defined as the process of identifying, measuring and communicating information to permit informed judgements and decisions by users of the information. Therefore, accounting exists for one major purpose. That purpose is to help users of accounting information make informed decisions. In the absence of such a purpose, the preparation of accounting reports may be an unnecessary use of time and resources. As a result, it is clearly the case that the work of the accountants is not only about preparing accounting reports but to participate positively through the information prepared beforehand in influencing the decisions of users.

If accounting is about providing information to allow informed decision-making, its ultimate usefulness would certainly depend on its 'qualitative' characteristics. These are widely accepted to be (a) relevance, (b) reliability, (c) comparability, (d) understandability and (e) timeliness. A major re-structuring of the accounting system currently in place in Algeria is an evident and necessary condition to enhance the country's ability to attract both foreign investments and local capital.

If such investments are progressively to occur, a more up-to-date accounting system taking the new economic realities of the country into account, with an independent audit, has to be set in place.

In addition, the accounting 'profession', to the extent that one exists, has had a low status in Algeria. Accountants are still viewed as bookkeepers or, at best, technicians not decision-makers. The number of qualified accountants is low (by comparison to both Morocco and Tunisia) resulting in a shortage of local accountants at the professional level. The accounting education and training is rather insufficient. Accounting information, to the extent that is produced on time, has not been used in decision-making by investors, creditors, banks and financial institutions. In a market economy, fairly sophisticated investors and creditors are the principal users of financial reports. To be useful, these reports must be prepared and published on time and the information contained in them ought to be accurate, reliable and timely. The need to attract foreign capital investment is a high priority in the transition economies. If such investment is increasingly to materialise, a relevant accounting system with an independent audit has to be set in place.

The Algerian capital market is growing and the Algiers Stock Exchange is currently operating. Capital markets are expected to play a significant part in the economic and social development of the country. The government's economic plans include attracting more foreign capital and boosting capital markets. However, in common with other economies in transition, it is essential to the well-being of the Algerian economy to have an accounting system that takes on board the new economic, political and social realities, by providing users, including management, with good accounting information for decision-making. Such a system would constitute an important step towards economic recovery, while bearing in mind the impact of using the PCN within a planned economy, the continued interaction between fiscal policy and accounting practice, the relatively limited development of auditing and the accounting profession in general and the need for training.

4 Matching Reforms with a New Approach to the Management of People, Learning and Culture

Mohammed Saad

Introduction

Algerian institutions, organisations and businesses are increasingly operating in a complex and uncertain environment, characterised by two crucial challenges. The first includes the transition from the centralised and planned economy to a market economy which involves restructuring all sectors of the economy by removing or modifying controls and regulations that distort price signals and by opening up to international competition. This requires reassessing all administrative, political and managerial rules and procedures in order to create the appropriate climate for the return of growth and address the following severe economic and social problems:

- Poor level of production;

- Strong dependency on hydrocarbons;

- High level of debts;

- High level of unemployment;

- High shortage of housing; and

- Lack of motivation, commitment and trust.

The second challenge concerns the increasing and inevitable opening of the Algerian market to international business, which is essentially driven by the globalisation of competition and an increased pace of change. Experiences from other countries suggest that an effective management of people and their culture is more likely to be successful. It is through empowering people, effective new forms of learning and a supportive and appropriate culture that other societies are developing the capability to face such new and complex situations. This chapter argues that Algerian institutions, organisations and businesses can no longer afford to adopt organisational arrangements and learning mechanisms based on the use of mechanistic and bureaucratic structures which impede initiative, motivation, commitment and participation of the workforce at all levels. It will review the origins of the current crisis, assess the introduction of the reforms and highlight the need for a more appropriate management of people, learning and culture.

1. The Extent of the Algerian Crisis

During the 1960s and 1970s, Algeria was striving hard to build a strong, independent and sustainable economy. The development of the economy was to be attained by establishing a significant industrial sector as rapidly as possible. This has required a massive programme of investment evidenced from 1967 to 1984, reaching a peak in the period 1967-1979, followed by a downwards trend between 1980 and 1989 and a complete decline after 1990. This led to a heavy call for external capital to fund the investment programme introduced in the 1970s under the leadership of President Boumedienne.[1] The level of debt augmented from $3 billion in 1973 to $19 billion in 1980, with a peak in 1977 and 1978 (+74 per cent and 46 per cent).

The economic model of development of the 1970s, which was meant to achieve an introversion of the economy, has in fact led to a strong external dependency (Saad 2000). In addition, and as a result of the collapse of the currency reserve, the fall of oil prices and a critical increase of debt service (80 per cent of external income), imports have reduced and shortages have become part of Algerian daily life, providing ground for increasing social unrest and malaise. This culminated in the dramatic demonstrations and riots of October 1988, which triggered fundamental economic and political changes: multi-partyism and the shift to a market economy.

There is now a growing recognition that the earlier strategy has fallen short of achieving its ambitious objectives. Its outcomes do not reflect at all the very high level of investment. The production system is very poor. The expensive technology acquired from abroad is neither properly operated nor managed - hence, the very low level of use of the installed production capability. Agriculture, which received less attention in terms of investment, is far from meeting the needs of the national market. As a consequence, the level of debt has increased more rapidly than national production and wealth. The increase has been even more intensive for the debt service, which has multiplied 30-fold between 1973 and 1993, while wealth has only been multiplied 5.5-fold. This has led to a multidimensional crisis (political, social, cultural and economic) characterised by the following factors:

• High shortage of housing (1.8 m new houses are needed);

• High unemployment (30 per cent) - there are each year 200,000 young people entering the workforce;

• Poor system of production:

i. Agriculture is neither able to export nor to satisfy the local demand. This has lead to a significant food dependency on foreign markets.

ii. Manufacturing is characterised by three types of constraints (a) high sensitivity towards external constraint as a result of its strong external dependency in terms of inputs, components and machinery; (b) a low level of technological capability and (c) a significant level of under-utilisation of production and manufacturing capacity.

- Economy based on hydrocarbons which are not labour intensive.

- Exports essentially dependent on oil.

This crisis can, to some extent, be associated with a demotivation at all levels, a lack of trust towards managers and leaders, a fragile system of authority and a disrespect for the rule of law, reinforcing corruption. At an organisational level, for example, most employees do not have a sense of pride, commitment and belonging to their organisations, which do not have a clear and appealing corporate image/identity and vision.

2. Evaluation of the Algerian Strategy for Economic and Social Development

After three decades of socialism and a central and planned economy which have failed to achieve the anticipated economic and social objectives, Algeria introduced, by the end of the 1980s, radical reforms aimed at initiating a new society based on the market economy. The Algerian strategy for economic and social development can be described as having gone through four major and distinct phases.

Phase 1: A Cautious and Moderate Start

With Algeria's independence in July 1962, the departure of the French *colons*, who had held a tight stranglehold on the country's administration, nearly brought the economy to a halt, as most Algerians were untrained and hence excluded from managing the economy. The first President of Algeria, Ahmed Ben Bella,[2] reacted by instituting a socialist system aimed at providing jobs and education and improving the poor living conditions of most Algerians. The strategy for economic and social development was essentially based on labour-intensive activities such as light industry and agriculture, which do not require high investments and skills.

Phase 2: A Real and Ambitious Take Off

Houari Boumedienne took over in 1965 through a military coup. His first Three Year Plan (1967-69) marked the beginning of long-term development planning in Algeria. In 1970, a newly created Secretariat of State for Planning took over economic planning from the Ministry of Finance. The new secretariat developed the first Four Year Plan (1970-73) and the second Four Year Plan (1974-77), which emphasised investment in capital-intensive heavy industry at the expense of more labour-intensive small industries. The years from 1977 to 1979 were a transitional period devoted to assessing previous development plans and devising new strategies.

The emphasis placed on manufacturing industries resulted only in an average gross domestic product increase over the decade from the mid1970s to the mid 1980s. But accelerated industrialisation was achieved at the expense of the agricultural sector, whose GDP share declined from 155 in 1965 to 95 in 1985. The decline constrained the government to spend currency on food imports to meet serious food shortages facing a population that was growing at an average annual rate of about 3.2 per cent in the late 1970s. Oil and gas revenues remained Algeria's largest single source of income.

With Boumedienne, the choice shifted towards a development to be achieved through rapid heavy industrialisation from which industries would grow, which in turn would supply other sectors with production equipment, durable consumer goods and other basic needs. It was expected, as illustrated in Figure 1, that this model, known as the industrialising industries model, would integrate and develop the whole economy by creating industrial and sectoral interactions to achieve an introversion of the economy (Bernis 1966 and 1968).

Fig. 1. The Industrialising Industries Model

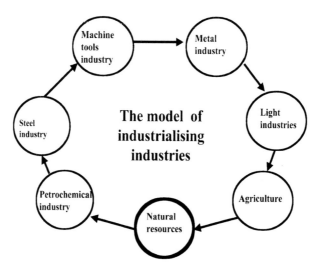

This model was therefore aimed at achieving a certain level of economic growth in a relatively short period of time by acquiring advanced technology which would penetrate into the whole industry and economy through the mechanisms of upstream and downstream integration. This strategy led to heavy investment and to a relatively sustainable economic growth with positive implications on job creation and standard of living. To achieve this objective, Algeria rejected foreign and private investment for ideological motives. However, as we have seen, the policy led Algeria into increasing levels of external debt.

Phase 3: The Undeclared Search for a New Development Option

The early 1980s saw a reversal of the situation and the end of investment in large-scale heavy industry turnkey projects, such as steel mills and oil refineries. Large enterprises were broken into smaller units in order to facilitate effective management and efficiency. Larger amounts of the investment budget were shifted to light industries such as textiles, food processing, and housing construction in order to enhance the economic and social well-being of Algerians. The first Five Year Plan (1980-84) and second Five Year Plan (1985-89) marked a significant policy shift by placing greater emphasis on agriculture and attempting to build a more diversified economy.

This 'U-turn', initiated by President Chadli Bendjedid,[3] was above all motivated by the need to tackle the increasing level of debt, which was reduced from \$19 billion in 1980 to \$15 billion in 1984. However, in spite of the important reduction in investment and the modest debt reduction, the service of the debt had never stopped increasing and had, for instance, reached 35 per cent of exports in 1984.

This phase was also marked by the drastic fall of oil prices (- 46 per cent) in December 1985, which led to a reduction of 35 per cent from export income. Imports were therefore reduced by at least 30 per cent. Supplies of components and machinery to manufacturing suffered a 30 per cent reduction. The rate of utilisation of manufacturing capacity, which was already no higher than 50 per cent (because of lack of know-how and technological capability), was substantially lowered. Growth rates started being negative in 1986 with significant implications for unemployment. This phase was also marked by the devaluation of the dollar and the rise of interest rates making international debts very expensive. In spite of its poor financial capacity between 1985 and 1993, Algeria has never ceased to pay back its debts. This policy was perhaps brave but its impact was very negative, as it did not reduce debt but on the contrary increased it.

As we have already seen, the economic model of development of the 1970s, which was meant to achieve an introversion of the economy, has led to a strong external dependency. In addition, and as a result of the collapse of the currency reserve, the fall of oil prices and a critical increase of debt service (80 per cent of external income), imports were reduced and shortages became part of the Algerian daily life providing ground for increasing social unrest and malaise. This culminated in the dramatic demonstrations and riots of October 1988 that compelled the government to institute a more serious and accelerated economic reform programme.

Phase 4: The Adoption of New Ideological and Economic Options

a) Economic Reforms

It can be argued that the hands of the Algerian authorities, which had been tied for ideological motives, were freed by the dramatic riots of October 1988. After and even before October 1988, the Algerian government cautiously and secretly approached the IMF. Developing a successful economy was therefore driven by the need, for the first time, to create a favourable macro-economic environment, which would create the conditions for a real price and inflation stability and would promote investment and production and hence job creation. The main goals of these new options were to transform the national economy from a tightly controlled centralised system (command and control system of the 1970s and 1980s) to a market-oriented one, create a climate more conducive to foreign investment and increased trade, and encourage domestic savings and investment. Algeria has thus been undergoing a radical programme of macro-economic stabilisation and structural reform, initiated in 1987, aimed at establishing the conditions for sustainable long-term growth and for attracting foreign direct investment. This includes correcting macro-economic imbalances and price distortions, containing inflation, promoting private sector development, reforming and re-structuring public enterprises and integrating the economy into world markets. The government gave management autonomy to two-thirds of the 450 state-owned enterprises, including banks, while instituting a profit accountability system for their managers. The government also eliminated state-controlled monopolies for import and distribution and allowed both Algerian and foreign companies to engage in these activities.

In spite of the political instability, the first Stand-by agreement (31 May 1989) signed with the International Monetary Fund (IMF) was firmly observed and respected, with the adoption of policies based on monetary and financial orthodoxy aimed at paving the way to market mechanisms. The conditions of the second agreement, signed in June 1991, were even harder. The main objectives were to liberalise the economy, allow more business entities to break away from the state and become Public Economic Enterprises (EPE *Entreprises Publiques Économiques*) and attract foreign investment. Algeria was given ten months to introduce reforms, which included:

• End of state monopoly and liberalisation of international trade with greater convertibility of local currency;

• Increase of interest rate;

• Drastic devaluation of the local currency (*Dinar*);

• Phasing out of central control of prices and wages;

• Reform of the fiscal and customs system (introduction of VAT and reduction of customs tariff); and

• Adoption of a social programme aimed at alleviating the negative implications of the programme.

A major area of financial concern is related to Algeria's external debt and debt-service payments. As already discussed, the country's substantial debt dated back to the 1970s (phase 2), when the government borrowed heavily to finance development projects and meet rising consumer needs. When the debt mounted to US$16.9 billion in 1980 (phase 3), the Algerian government decided to limit borrowing to DA50 million a year, which reduced the debt steadily until 1984. However, the debt-service ratio more than doubled between 1985 and 1988, increasing from 35 per cent to 80 per cent. Amortisation payments increased by 38 per cent until they reached US$6.2 billion in 1990. In spite of falling oil production and prices, the government managed to avoid debt rescheduling by cleverly obtaining soft finance and trade credits. To reduce the debt-servicing burden, the government subsequently concentrated on obtaining medium- and long-term loans to repay its financial obligations as soon as they became due.

Algeria has always viewed debt rescheduling as a politically unacceptable step. The government was obliged, however, to make another politically unpopular move in 1991, by reaching a second standby agreement with the IMF. However, this agreement had a positive effect on creditors and potential donors including the World Bank, which decided to grant Algeria a US$300 million structural adjustment loan. The EC also agreed in 1991 to provide a loan worth US$470 million. A year earlier, the BNP had provided a seven-year loan of 1 billion francs to be used in converting short-term borrowing into longer-term loans. Another positive sign was Algeria's apparent determination not to miss debt-service payments despite a debt service exceeding US$7 billion in 1991. However, in 1994, the debts were equal to 70 per cent of GDP and the service of the debts was equal to 96 per cent of total income from exports. Rescheduling, which had hitherto always been rejected by the Algerian authorities, was in 1994 presented as the only alternative available to the country.

With the rescheduling of payments, a programme of stabilisation[4] and a structural adjustment programme (SAP)[5] were negotiated with the IMF to help Algeria introduce economic reforms in order to generate economic growth and produce sufficient surplus to be able to satisfy its financial obligations. This programme, which originally began in 1989, included:

• Devaluation of the local currency (*Dinar*);

• Major cuts in state subsidies;

• A reduction in the budget deficit;

• And the initiation of a gradual privatisation programme.

The structural adjustments were aimed at liberalising the capital market to enable the private sector to invest and acquire state assets. However, in spite of liberalising trade and prices, and devaluing the Dinar, private and foreign investment, apart from the oil and gas industry, is still very low. In October 1991, as part of the fiscal and customs reforms, the Algerian authorities were requested to privatise the large public sector. Privatisation, as discussed in chapter three, is perceived as a way to help the Algerian economy reorganise and modernise itself and attract foreign and private investment. Its main objectives are:

• To increase technological capability;

• To increase management capability;

• To develop a real culture of business and management leading to efficiency and competitiveness; and

• To promote exports.

Essentially, the privatisation programme first started with a large number of SMEs and the privatisation of large companies is still far from happening properly. In 2000, the private sector represented 52 per cent of the added value, 88 per cent of the services, 68 per cent of construction, 65 per cent of the food industry and 38 per cent of manufacturing. There are difficulties that are slowing down this privatisation process. There is a strong resistance from workers and trade unions, who consider these reforms as yet another experiment tried on their companies and are anxious about the short-term (redundancies) and long-term (dissolution of their firms) implications. There is also a strong apprehension regarding the capability of the national private sector to reorganise and modernise the national economy. In addition, Algeria's attractiveness to investors is hampered by the current political crisis, the enormous bureaucratic system and the prevailing anti-business culture.

b) Evaluation of the On-Going Reforms

As shown in Table 1, most macro-economic indicators are very positive with inflation falling to 1.4 per cent in 2002. However, GDP growth remains below the required levels of 6-7 per cent. Reserves have strengthened with $23.1 billion (January 2003), while foreign debts have fallen. For the first time the level of reserves is higher than the level of debts - at $20 billion in January 2003. The debt-service ratio has also improved significantly. In 1994 the debts were equal to 70 per cent of GDP and the service of the debts was equal to 96 per cent of total income from exports. The Central Bank of Algeria data show that the debt burden has been falling very sharply thanks to rescheduling causing the ratio to fall by more than 30 per cent. It went down to 34 per cent in 1995, 27.5 per cent in 1997 and 19.8 per cent in 2002.

Table 1. Main Economic Parameters

	1996	1997	1998	1999	2000	2002
Inflation (%)	21.8	9.0	8.0	8.0	4.0	1.4
Real GDP growth (%)	3.4	2.5	3.8	3.3	3.4	4.2
Reserves ($bn)	5.9	8.0	7.5	11	14	23.1

It is therefore clear that economic parameters may reflect an enhancement of the macro-economic health of the country but this is being achieved through heavy social costs - more unemployment, a lower purchasing power and lower living standards - which may undermine the whole development of the country. On the whole, this programme of reforms was based on macro-economic policies aimed at reducing domestic demand, consumption and public investment, which are still seen as vital for solving the Algerian financial crisis. However, this has resulted in an increase in the level of poverty, even if life expectancy and death rate for children have not been affected. As many as twelve million Algerians live on an income of under $1 per day. These social implications are essentially related to the significant increase of unemployment (30 per cent), freezing of wages and phasing out of subsidies. As a consequence of the adjustment of prices and hence their liberalisation, the cost of living has significantly increased. Food subsidies were phased out by the end of 1996, while increases in gas, electricity, water and telephone prices were gradually implemented. The price of milk has, for instance, multiplied 10-fold. GDP per head has fallen from $2,475 in 1990 to an estimated $1,546 in 1996. The chances of this situation improving for a majority of Algerians seem slim.

Re-structuring of large state companies is also very slow. Complete autonomy, as discussed in chapter three, does not yet exist. The authorities have always been aware that accelerated re-structuring could trigger further unrest, which is one reason why the government remains reluctant to administer anything approaching shock therapy. It is also clear that the Algerian economy is a hostage to political events. Unlike the 1970s and 1980s, the current Algerian economy is operating within a very hostile and uncertain environment. It is extremely dependent upon political, cultural and social constraints over which the government has limited control.

The strong interaction between the economic and political systems in Algeria could explain the reason why the Algerian government has often appeared to opt for half measures rather than dare to adopt clear and unambiguous strategies (interview with Mourad Benachenhou, Minister in charge of the restructuring of the economy, *El Watan*, 22 May 1995). The lack of accountability and the state's interference in allocating tasks and resources to firms, which cause them to deviate from the search for efficiency and profitability, constitute other factors explaining the incoherence of the Algerian system. Business in Algeria is therefore still characterised by:

- Ideological resistance;

- Strong counter culture;

- Poor style of management;

- Complex decision-making process;

- Strong interaction between political and economic systems;

- Lack of trust;

- Lack of strong leadership; and

- A poor system of incentives and motivation.

3. Managing People and Culture: a Pre-Requisite for Successful Reforms in Algeria

The Algerian crisis can be explained by its poor choice of economic policies, their bad implementation and the lack of control and accountability. It can also be associated with the lack of an effective and clear management strategy of people and culture that could bring meaning and purpose to life and work both at the national and organisational level.

This chapter argues that a good cultural model based on fundamental values which address human needs and aspirations on all levels is an invaluable aid to management that can help to get the best from people. Culture is not the most important influence on management but it is the most neglected, as it deals with people and soft issues such as norms, values, beliefs, attitudes, behaviour, motivation and commitment. There is strong relationship between human motivation and culture, as motivation is simply a response to the underlying culture of a society or an organisation that determines the way people think and behave. The purpose of a new and more appropriate management strategy of people and culture is, as shown in Figure 2, to harmonise Algerian people with the new systems and options in a way that enables them to share in their success rather than feel oppressed by their efficiency.

Fig. 2. Culture as a Harmonisation of People and Systems

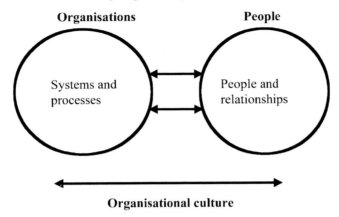

3.1. The Need for an Effective Strategy for the Management of People

Management is the process of achieving organisational objectives effectively, with and through others. This process entails planning, organising, leading, directing, staffing and controlling. For Johnson (2001) managing people/human resources is linked with the following key assumptions regarding:

• People as social capital capable of development;

• The potential for developing coincidence of interest between stakeholders;

• The search for power equalisation for trust and collaboration; and

• Open channels of communication to build trust and commitment.

The main objective of such an effective management strategy is to develop and empower people in order that organisational or indeed national goals can be achieved. This clearly highlights the importance of 'mutuality' in the definition of an effective management of people which needs to be strongly based upon mutual goals, mutual influence, mutual respect, mutual rewards and mutual responsibility (Johnson 2001, Walton 1985). This mutuality is more likely to elicit positive attitudes and behaviour that will generate motivation, which in turn will yield greater commitment and better performance. This strategy based on the commitment and empowerment of people is perceived as a means to provide organisations and nations with a sustained competitive advantage (Kamoche 2000, Harrison 1993). This is echoed by a great body of literature, which considers the extent to which human resources (motivation, commitment, enthusiasm, knowledge, skills, abilities) contribute to firms (Kamoche 2000, and others).

However, human resources management in Algeria is primarily concerned with procedural, administrative tasks like record keeping, manpower planning, salary, wage and benefits administration, employee relations and so forth (Saad 2000). The preoccupation with an administrative agenda is, in part, a reflection of the low priority accorded to strategic, long-term planning and soft issues. It appears that the concern with administrative activities has prevented organisations from taking a more proactive approach in employee development. In addition, most organisations in Algeria are still operating under 'command-and-control' principles. Their structural arrangements are very pyramidal with rigid boundaries, corresponding to the traditional model of organisation known as Fordism. This model is characterised by bureaucratic and mechanistic lines of control. It is a highly departmentalised model of organisation with a heavy reliance on a centralised system and formal procedures for planning and control. This system is also characterised by a rigid separation of 'mental work' from 'manual work', which often leads to alienating and monotonous jobs. Such a system can only be compatible with a society concerned with increasing productivity and industrial output, via the use of techniques operated by an uneducated and unskilled workforce, such as those which led to the successful development of mass-production methods. However, this organisational system fails to involve and empower people and hence their commitment and creativity.

The challenge for Algerian managers thus begins with an improvement in the underlying rationale for managing people particularly through training and career development. The principles of organisational dynamics and motivation, for example, may have to be re-examined and revised to accommodate the new changes and challenges associated with the on-going reforms.

3.2. A More Effective Learning Strategy for the New Organisational and National Challenges

Success in dealing with such significant changes and challenges calls for a new approach to learning. Learning refers to the various processes by which skill and knowledge are acquired by individuals or perhaps organisations. The ability to deal with unpredictable tasks and to respond as quickly as possible to changes from the internal and external environment requires a continuous acquisition of knowledge. To remain viable in a global environment and manage effectively the transition to the market economy, Algerian institutions, organisations and individuals must be able to adapt by continuously learning. In an economy where the only certainty is uncertainty, the one sure source of competitive advantage is knowledge (Nonaka 1996).

Many ideas and models for learning have been put forward in the literature. Some are essentially behavioural; others focus on a supportive learning climate for individuals, and are loosely linked to cultures of empowerment and individual ownership. In this context, Vince (1996) suggests that the starting point is to acknowledge the relationship between learning and change. Plant (1987) claims that the factor most likely to influence our capacity to change is our capacity to learn. Argyris & Schon (1996) and others have highlighted the distinction between single, double and triple loop learning. As illustrated in Figure 3, these new forms of learning have become necessary with a high level of complexity characterised by greater uncertainty and less predictability.

Fig. 3. Learning Versus Complexity

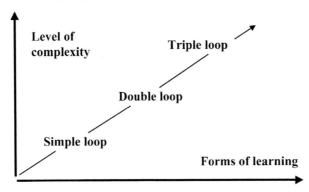

Single-loop learning corresponds to a situation of relative certainty and predictability. As shown in Figure 4, it involves the detection of error within a set of controllable conditions and within the existing and defined norms and values, which constitute the culture of the organisation or institution. With greater complexity, double-loop learning becomes more appropriate. It involves a questioning of norms and values and a re-examination of the fundamentals, which may lead to unlearning a previously held view of the internal and external culture and environment. Triple-loop learning, also known as 'learning how to learn' acknowledges and encourages more interactions with changing environments and places greater emphasis on the learning process rather than the outcome. It implies a more active role in learning by unfolding and understanding the learning process.

Fig. 4. Forms of Learning

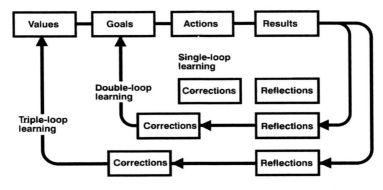

Source: Derived from Argyris & Schon 1996

Thus, effective and new forms of learning involve a lot of unlearning and discomfort. Courage and perseverance are therefore needed. This can be effectively promoted and developed through the 'triple helix' model (Figure 5) involving the government, industry and universities and based on a greater establishment of networks and collaboration.

Fig. 5. Triple Helix Model

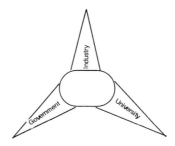

3.3. A New Culture for the On-Going Changes and Reforms

The origin of the term culture derives from Latin; it refers to the cultivation of the soil. It literally means to grow, to produce and, most significantly, to cultivate or improve the mind through learning. In essence, culture is the way people grow and develop through learning and mutual association (Cartwright 1999). It is a powerful determinant of people's beliefs, attitudes and behaviour. It is a complex ensemble which includes the knowledge, beliefs, art, law, morals, customs and all of the other capacities and habits acquired by a member of a society (Calori & De Woot 1994). Culture is vast and complex and includes, as Sadler (1991) claims, a whole range of intangible and soft issue factors. The complexity of culture is clearly highlighted by studies undertaken by Hofstede (1984, 1991), Denison (1990) and others, who investigated organisational culture from different angles and reached the same conclusion as to the intricate configuration and difficulty of controlling and manipulating this concept. Hofstede describes it as consisting of a set of visible but also invisible layers, as highlighted in Figure 6.

Fig. 6. The Complexity of Culture

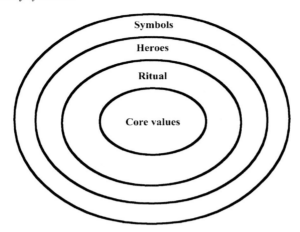

Culture is a group problem-solving tool that enables individuals to survive in a particular environment. It can also be defined as a way of thinking, feeling and reacting that is characteristic of the ways a particular society or a group meets its problems at a particular point in time. It is an organised body or cluster of people who share the same goals, beliefs and values. Culture refers to a system of shared meaning held by members, that distinguishes an organisation from other organisations. The system of shared meaning is a set of key characteristics indicating an organisation's or nation's current customs, traditions and its general way of doing things. It therefore tells people how things are done and what is important. This is why Dressler & Carn (1969) claim that culture is a means to communicate with others through a language that is shared in common. It can also provide its members with standards for distinguishing between what is considered right and wrong, reasonable and unreasonable, and is perceived as a way to bind people together through a sense of belonging and a sense of common purpose.

Cultural change is therefore a process whereby new meaning emerges, leading to the reinterpretation of past experience in order to promote new lines of thinking and actions likely to encourage motivation, learning and commitment. It is indeed a careful re-engineering and even reshaping of the way things are done, aimed at repeating and improving what works and giving up what does not. Cultures can be very stable over time, but they are never static. Indeed, when starting a new project, or when new challenges occur, or when the environment is undergoing rapid change, the nation or organisation's established culture may no longer be appropriate and can be an obstacle to commitment effectiveness. There is therefore a vital need to develop a new set of norms, beliefs and values associated with effective participation, sharing of information and cooperation. Once these new lines of beliefs, norms, conducts and actions are articulated and described, they need to be learnt by the organisation's or nation's members (individual learning) in particular and the organisation in general (organisational or collective learning).

Although the concept of organisational culture is relatively new, the concept and the importance of national and/or societal culture, which is an important part of an organisation's environment, has been taken into account for quite some time. Indeed, differences between national and/or societal cultures often lead to different conceptions and assumptions about organisations and their management (Hofstede 1991). It can also be claimed that, in addition to the national and/or societal culture, organisational culture must be congruent with the technology and industry culture and, above all, with the individual's culture. As illustrated in Figure 7, the different types of culture (national, organisational and individual) are influenced by each other.

Fig. 7. Strong Interaction Between the Different Types of Culture

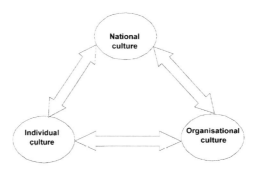

It is vital that Algerian institutions, organisations, leaders and managers strive hard to comprehend the ways to secure the best culture for ensuring a successful introduction of reforms and new options.

3.4. The Key Arguments for Developing a New Strategy for Managing People and Culture

Motivation, growth, authority and change reflect the key critical issues that are currently undermining commitment and the introduction of changes in Algeria.

a) Culture has a Strong Influence on Human Motivation

Change, if it is to work, must involve and alter the perceptions and behaviour of people (Crainer 1996). It also has to carry people along with it. There is now a common belief that competitive advantage may be achieved by organisations through the way their people are managed. Employees have to be regarded as assets. They need to be acquired with care, developed and utilised effectively. Leaders and managers who show respect for their people and value them as human beings are in turn respected and valued. This mutual respect is a powerful relationship bond and helps fulfil the psychological contract between leaders/managers and their subordinates. In so doing, they become a positive source of influence, which implies and promotes positive motivation and personal growth. Negative motivation can only inhibit commitment and growth. A culture is a powerful determinant of human behaviour through the internalisation by its members of its norms, beliefs and values. This leads to adding value to the organisation/group by improving commitment and motivation of people, through such intrinsic values as trust, loyalty, pride, enjoyment and job satisfaction.

Similarly, equality satisfies basic needs for belonging, security and self-esteem, and grants equal rights and opportunities. Inequality reduces self-worth and causes alienation. Thus, when inequality is perceived and felt to be inequitable it becomes a negative motivator with counter-attitudes and behaviours. On the other hand, leaders and managers who show respect for their people and value them as human beings are in turn respected and valued. They fulfil the psychological contract between themselves and their subordinates. In so doing, they become a positive source of influence.

A culture is learned and therefore its values have to be taught. This applies to the cultural values of an organisation, as it does to children at school learning the traditional values of their society and/or community. Values only have power to control and direct (minds and behaviours) when they are deterministic, which is to say when they are internalised. And they will only be internalised when they actually mean something to the persons concerned. When leaders only pay lip service to the values they preach and are found out, then such hypocrisy creates cynicism, scepticism and ridicule. Values determine motivation and motivation delivers outcome. Values are the underlying beliefs and attitudes that help determine conduct. No human beings can exist without values. If values go out of the door, a counter-culture can emerge. A counter-culture is one that has its own system of values and principles and codes of behaviour. A counter-culture within an organisation or a society will have its own economy, that is the 'black economy' or 'trabendo'[6] which is impossible to control.

There is an urgent need for Algerian managers to develop a deep and accurate understanding of motivation. Motivation needs to be understood because it is a simple rule of life that all behaviour is motivated (Lambert 1996). The current Algerian crisis gives clear evidence that if people are not motivated in one direction, they will certainly be motivated in another. Motivation strategy is not, therefore, a matter of manipulation; it is more the planned and conscious development of a positive climate in which the natural process of motivation will be directed at personal and organisational goals which are one and the same. In addition, the emphasis needs to be on rewards rather than sanctions.

It is also worth highlighting the vital role of leadership in designing and creating a motivation strategy at the highest level of the organisation. It is communicated from the highest levels clearly and unambiguously to those who have to make it work. It is not, however, the sole responsibility of the top team. If there is no total involvement, there may well be a change of culture, but it is likely to be a change from confidence and certainty to perplexity and chaos.

b) Relationship Between Culture and Growth

It is increasingly acknowledged that culture and economic performance are so very closely connected as to be inseparable. National cultures have a direct bearing on their national economies and particular kinds of culture are best suited to economic success while others hold nations back. The kind of culture a nation/organisation has, will determine its economic destiny. For instance, a particular kind of culture that grew out of the Eastern cultural philosophies has been phenomenally successful.

The idea of an organisational culture first began to enter management literature in the 1970s as an Americanisation of the Japanese Total Quality production and quality control systems. Its introduction to British management in the 1980s has only recently begun to be more widely adopted (Xenikon & Furnham 1996). Japan's economic achievement is due in large measure to the way the country's traditional culture was able to absorb and improve upon American technology and management methods. From being a relatively backward nation, almost unknown to people in the West, Japan has become the second largest economy in the world in the space of two or three generations. According to Kakuei Tanaka, Prime Minister in the 1970s, their success was due to the mobilisation of an increasingly educated and highly trained working population. Effective management leading to sustained competitive advantage is therefore linked to the establishment of a new and appropriate cultural system with people at its heart. Another example is that of Ireland which emerged from being a relatively poor OECD country to overtake the UK recently in GDP per capita. The explanation for this rise is quite solid: the Irish combined a sound fiscal and strong human development policy, with a commitment to the rule of law.

c) Culture as a System of Authority

The three basic systems of cultural authority are: governance, control and values. The power to control is vested in legitimised (acknowledged) authority. A culture is a system of authority that exercises power through its governance, supported by its people (Cartwright 1999). Authority and rule of law in Algeria need to be notably reinforced by supporting cultural beliefs ('we believe in the rule of law') and values ('we have respect for the law'). Otherwise, people who do not share those cultural beliefs and values will have no respect for authority. They may have respect for the instruments of control (rewards and punishments) but not for its institutions and symbols. The authority of an organisation's or nation's culture is derived from its core nucleus of beliefs and values that are internalised by its people and exercised through leadership and management. A culture is primarily a determinant of human behaviour, which is dependent upon managers and leaders translating and modelling the organisation's or nation's core values as a source of control.

Authority is an essential property of society that is dependent upon people's loyalty. Without authority, leaders and managers are literally powerless. Authority is the instrument by which a culture, a society or an organisation exerts power vested in their leaders, managers, officials and institutions. The psychological power of a culture is what Hofstede described as 'mental programming' and is an essential requirement of leadership. Properly exercised, power can inspire respect, loyalty and trust. Cultural values, when accepted by people, increase power and authority in three ways:

1. People identify with their nation/organisation: they accept its rules when 'it is the right thing to do';

2. People internalise the nation/organisation's values, when they believe they are right;

3. People are motivated to achieve the organisation's objectives.

d) Culture and Change

Today's business is characterised by an increasing level of change and a trend towards greater complexity and uncertainty. Economic activity, business organisations and technology are changing fast, planning horizons are becoming shorter, skills swiftly obsolete, technology and deregulation are generating massive changes leading to new - and sometimes unexpected - alliances of all kinds and changing competitive balances. A new culture is therefore needed to enable Algerian organisations, leaders, managers and employees to deal effectively with these changes.

As cultural values change, so the 'fabric' of society changes - perhaps not in step, but sooner or later new values initiate revised behavioural norms that in turn become institutionalised as the new social order. Culture change is essential if Algerian companies and business are to keep up with the rest of the world, as a culture of continuous improvement is now the aim of all successful organisations. It brings new opportunities for motivation, commitment, creativity and success. Cultural transformation, which is a process of reorganisation in values, attitudes, behavioural norms and management style, is neither an easy nor a short-term project.

Conclusion

A new management strategy of human resources, learning and culture can help Algerian business and organisations harmonise their people with the new systems in a way that enables them to share in their success rather than feel oppressed by their efficiency. A leadership and/or management system without a supportive culture is more likely to have an adverse effect on people's morale and motivation. There is, therefore, an urgent need for leaders and manager to gain a deep and accurate understanding of motivation and to introduce and develop a more appropriate culture. The setting up of a supportive culture should include the development of a learning environment promoting 'pro-activity', whereby people are willing and able to play their role competently.

Cultural change is designed and created at the highest level of the organisation or society, but needs to be communicated clearly and unambiguously to those who have to make it work. In addition, cultural change is a complex and long process and not a one-off thing. Good governance is a key foundation for the successful implementation of changes, which can generate sustainable development and growth. A transformation of the Algerian society and the development of new ways of thinking require credible leaders, a genuine sense of ownership and responsibility on the part of all stakeholders, and a commitment to work together and trust each other.

Education has a vital role to play in this transformation. It can help provide knowledge about social contracts among individuals and between individuals and the state. It can also help to attain the behaviour expected under social contracts and to gain an understanding of the expected consequences of breaking social contracts.

Notes

1   Houari Boumedienne was President of Algeria from June 1965 to December 1978.

2   Ahmed Ben Bella was President from July 1962 to June 1965.

3   After the death of Houari Boumedienne in January 1979, Chadli Bendjedid became President from 1979-1991.

4   From June 1994 to May 1995.

5   From June 1995 to May 1998.

6   The term used in Algeria for the black market.

5 Women in Algeria, Dimensions of a Crisis and of a Resistance

Cathie Lloyd

Introduction

The last two decades of economic liberalism, coupled with violent conflict in Algeria have given rise to a constant pressure on the daily lives of women and men.[1] Periods of multidimensional, intense change have very specific effects on women's lives. Conflict may give rise to new opportunities but also pose greater burdens. For instance, during the War of Independence, women played a variety of roles, which raised the expectation that they might have the freedom to choose different ways of living their lives (Amrane 1991, Amrane-Minne 1999). The hopes of this period were dashed after independence and many of the *moudjahidates* had little choice but to return to quiet domestic lives, or to devote themselves to professional studies. Their activities had a lasting impact also and their example was honoured, but always in a rather distant, mythological way. This experience draws attention to the double-edged nature of women's roles as victims or as heroines. While the nation applauds women's exemplary status as fighters for independence, this also imposes the impossible burden of heroines on a pedestal who are denied personal fulfilment. This process is not unique to Algeria: in many other situations, women have made short-term gains during periods of rapid change, which are clawed back once peace and stability is restored. In the case of Algeria, there are signs of long-term changes in women's position, which suggests a more hopeful future. This chapter will therefore discuss a complex and sometimes ambiguous process of change in women's lives.

The chapter will begin by examining the immediate context of the last two decades and the effects on the position of women, notably of the Family Code, violent conflict and economic liberalisation. These factors, which have tended to the marginalisation and subordination of women, run directly counter to the underlying, long-term trends. I identify steady advances which significantly affect the position of women, including increased levels of education and qualification, rising age at marriage and falling fertility rates. Other long-term trends include more positive attitudes to female children, an outstanding educational achievement and a smaller progress in women taking paid employment outside the home. Finally, I turn to women's role in social and political movements in the last ten years, to suggest that they are becoming increasingly active in the informal public sphere. This is a significant development, likely to leave them with a permanently enhanced position. But it is a prolonged struggle to make the necessary breakthrough to equality partly because of women's legal status, based on the *Code de la Famille*.

1. The Postcolonial Context

At their most blinkered, traditional patriarchal attitudes towards women have reduced their role to that of reproduction: in the 1890s the view was expressed that: 'Woman's function is simply that of procreation, in doing this she is basically the same as a fertile cat',[2] and a century later: 'A woman's function is to reproduce Muslims. If she gives up that role she subverts God's order and pollutes the basis of Islam.'[3] A more enlightened version of this patriarchal view is to put woman on a pedestal; she is expected to be a role model for her children, to act as the repository of family and national honour, but not to determine her own future.

The period of de-colonisation presented many opportunities to women as well as hardships. Education was valued as a way of strengthening the national effort and many activists saw educated women and men as a crucial resource for Algeria's future. There were many different anti-colonial currents. The anti-colonial movement influenced by the early *salafiyas* puritanical movement saw the crisis of Algerian society as due to being distanced from Islam. The most radical position among Muslim 'reformers' was that women had been degraded by misinterpretations of Islam and polluted by colonialism. They wanted women's status to be anchored in the pure origins of Islam. The priority was the re-islamisation of society, which involved the application of the *Shari'a*, the Coranic idea of the 'way', which includes divine prescriptions and the *Figh* (rules which are the result of the interpretation made by Muslim lawyers).

A more liberatory even feminist viewpoint inspired by the Turkish and Egyptian women's movement saw discrimination as linked to feudalism and patriarchy (Amin 1970, 1995). Others were influenced by Western feminism, through their experiences of migration or education abroad, although this often represented men's views of what women should be, rather than a groundswell from women themselves. An Algerian women's movement had to be constructed.

Historically, Algerian women have played an important, if largely unacknowledged, role in public life. Even if we just look back over the past 60 years, their role as freedom fighters or *moudjhidates* in the struggle for independence is widely known. Djamila Amrane argues that their experience shows both the impossibility of excluding women from public life, and the beginning of a new phase of women's presence in Algerian affairs (Amrane-Minne 1999). At the outbreak of the War of Independence in 1954, women were excluded from public life, only 4.5 per cent were literate and they had practically no access to the arena of paid employment. Amrane calculates that there were no more than six women doctors, 25 women teachers at secondary schools and none in Higher Education. The University of

Algiers had only 500 Algerian students including about 50 women (Amrane-Minne 1999: 62). In the nationalist parties, women were restricted to women's only organisations. Despite this marginal position, some 10,949 fighting women, mostly in their twenties, joined the struggle for independence from the outset, accounting for about 3 per cent of all combatants, about the same as for European women's participation in World War II (Amrane 1991). Women provided refuge for resistance fighters, collected money, medicine, clothes and other objects. They shared the deprivation and extremes of violence encountered by their male counterparts. Amrane (1991: 63) emphasises that the key role was played by 'Militant women ... (but that they) were the nucleus around which a whole support network revolved'. In other words, there was an exceptionally broad mobilisation of women who contributed to Algeria's re-found independence.

Louisette Ighilahriz's account of her own capture and torture leaves us in little doubt that they were subject to exceptional ill treatment by the French security forces (Ighilahriz 2001). Amrane (1991) states that about a fifth of all women in the *maquis* were killed in battle. Their ambiguous freedom of movement in the cities was also crucial throughout the campaign, enabling them to use their appearance - either as veiled women or passing as Europeans to move about 'unnoticed' (Fanon 1959).

Even at this stage, women were marginalised by the nationalist elites. Amrane cites the failed candidature to the *Comité National de la Révolution Algérienne* (CNRA) of Nafissa Laliam-Hamoud, as well as the marginalisation of the women's movement in early texts such as the FLN/ALN handbook of August 1956. It reads:

> *It is, therefore, possible, in keeping with the moral values of the Algerian people, to rel-egate [my emphasis - CL] the following duties to women:*
>
> *a. The moral support of fighters and members of the resistance;*
>
> *b. Giving instructions, dealing with provisions and providing refuge;*
>
> *c. Helping the families and children of the maquisards, prisoners and other detainees.*[4]

Most of these duties could be seen as an extension of women's domestic role. During the period of struggle for independence, there had been little support for women's rights as such, as it was thought that women would be emancipated as an indirect consequence of the struggle for national liberation (Bouatta 1997). After independence, they were expected to return to their domestic roles (Balia & Rulleau 1978).

Yet, the majority of those involved in the women's movement saw their struggle as the extension of that for democratic rights. The Tripoli programme of the FLN argued for the equality and the emancipation of women and criticised 'the retrograde mentality about women's role'. In Article 12 of Algeria's first Constitution (1963), the equality of the sexes was affirmed: 'all citizens of both sexes have the same rights and duties'. However, this view was more of an aspiration than a reality, shared only by a minority in society, and, in the mid-1960s, there were several moves by conservative forces to restrict the position of women. This took the form of attempts to draft a code based on the *Shari'a*, which would frame women's status in Algeria. The debate became highly divided between traditional patriarchal views, modern fundamentalist religious positions and secular positions which did not necessarily support women's rights.

Ben Bella's FLN supported the idea of an Arabo-Islamic International emphasising two privileged enemies: the old bourgeoisie, which was compromised because of their dealings with the colonisers, and the commercial petite bourgeoisie (Bouamama 2000: 110). The idea of an Algerian people united in struggle, allowed little space for dissenting voices. It was an environment in which it was all too easy for women to be pushed back into the domestic sphere. The idea of Muslim Socialism, whereby the Muslim egalitarian values of the first *khalifs* would be restored,[5] allowed religious conservatives to take a privileged position.

A committee of *ulémas* proposed in 1963 that polygamy should be extended on the grounds that there were too many war widows and that this would be the best way to deal with the 'extra' women (M'Rabet 1966). In January 1964, the Islamic organisation *Al Qiyam* called for 'a proper Islamic status for women', which would include limiting their activities in the public sphere and banning their participation in sport (Saadi 1991). Just before the overthrow of Ben Bella in 1965, plans were made for legislation to codify family relations, specifically women's position. This designated for a woman the legal status of a minor, with no civil rights, no rights over her children (if there was no father, guardianship of her children would fall to an uncle or cousin), mixed marriages (between Muslim women and non-Muslim men) were prohibited, and polygamy maintained (M'Rabet 1966: 237). Shortly after the coup in 1965, Boumedienne stated:

> There are enemies of women's evolution. There have recently been rumours circulating about the plan for a family code... This propaganda claims that the code will remove all the rights acquired by women. Our reply to this propaganda is simply that women have got to where they are by their own efforts ... and have earned their rights in this society ... the code which is to appear shortly is for the preservation of the rights of women and the Algerian family.[6]

Boumedienne then introduced a new draft, practically identical to the first, which was later also abandoned.

The *moudjahidates'* pressure for women's rights was immobilised by instructions to focus on priority tasks, more important than women's rights - to look after war orphans and help the impoverished. They were urged to wait their 'turn' and to focus on more urgent priorities. In her recently published autobiography, the *moudjahidate* Louisette Ighilahriz writes that once independence had been regained, her parents insisted that she should not delay marriage. But after such a long period in the maquis, in prison, in exile, and then as a financially independent woman, she refused to accept an arranged marriage. She depended on her mother to intercede for her with her father, who had already promised her to several of his comrades while in prison (Ighilahriz 2001: 195). The questioning and self-reliance required in the resistance to colonialism did not always accord easily with the demands of the newly independent state and the new structures of authority.

The *Union Nationale des Femmes Algériennes*, UNFA, was established in 1963 as the official body to address women's concerns. Its objectives were the emancipation of women, to oversee their participation in the political reconstruction of the country and to ensure the social protection of the mother, children and the disabled. Chérifa Bouatta writes:

> *For the majority of women, the most vivid image of the UNFA through the years is that of women's activities, conferences and congresses, chaired by the men of the FLN. (Bouatta 1997: 3)*

It tended to be seen as a transmission belt by which women were informed of the views and decisions of the male leadership of the FLN (M'Rabet 1966) while channelling women's political activities away from the main power-structures which remained male-dominated (Saadi 1991).

Ighilahriz recounts how she became a member of the executive committee of the UNFA in 1974 and remained active in this organisation until 1978 even though frustrated by a very narrow space for manoeuvre. She was full of enthusiasm to realise the promise of women's capacity, which had been proved during the independence struggle. However, she comments that she rapidly realised the enormity of the problem:

> *My task was too much, the weight of tradition was enormous and the number of conservative men extremely high. Wherever I went, I was very well received but in practice, there were dreadful obstacles. (Ighilahriz 2001: 219-20)*

In the 1970s, this conservative viewpoint was expressed by the *police des mœurs* who exhorted 'all fathers who are concerned for their identity and who believe in God ... women (who) walk in the street with naked legs, arms and breasts - the diabolical mixing of men and women on beaches, gardens and leisure centres.'[7] Throughout this period, attempts to draft a Family Code continued, and women's demonstrations and mobilisations responded in protest. This struggle intensified when draft legislation was presented in September 1981. Some of the more outrageous aspects were slightly amended (particularly the clauses limiting women's rights to travel) and the Family Code was finally enacted in July 1984. It established men's dominance over women, providing for the husband to be the head of the family, for men's right to repudiate their wives and institutionalised sexual inequality in inheritance. A woman's consent to her first marriage is mediated by a male guardian who can deny her choice of husband, and the Code legalises polygamy.

This Code has become the most contested legal text in Algeria, underpinning as it does wider repressive practices in society, rooted in a strict interpretation of Islam backed by patriarchal society. Women's associations and political parties have been at the forefront of agitation for its abolition or fundamental reform. Some lawyers claim that the Code is itself unconstitutional because it goes against the provisions for equality between the sexes in the constitution, not to speak of Algeria's international obligations.[8] International bodies frequently question the Code. For instance, the UN Committee on the Elimination of Discrimination Against Women referred, in February 1999, to the Code as one of the factors that permits 'the persistence of cultural stereotypes and patriarchal values as well as polygamy, which violates women's rights'.[9]

When Bouteflika was elected President in 1999, reform of the Code was among the many expectations raised. Bouteflika suggested that the *Haut Conseil Islamique* should study the question according to the spirit of Islam rather than the strict wording of the Coran (*Liberté*, 1 April 1999). The idea was that the Haut *Conseil* would work on the basis of 25 amendments to the Code approved by women at a workshop organised by the Ministry of Solidarity and the Family under Mme Mechernène (*Le Matin*, 14-15 May 1999). These talks reached deadlock in November 1999, and the Code remains unreformed, although recently Ahmed Ouyahia, as Minister of Justice, suggested that a reduced, reformed Family Code would be incorporated in the plans for a new Civil Code (*El Watan*, 9 October 2001). He emphasised that the stability of the country depends on that of the family unit, that the state has a responsibility to prevent children from being thrown out into the street, and to ensure a proper legislation against infanticide. Such assurances have become commonplace and given the tightrope trodden by the authorities between the Islamists and the more secular parties, they tend to be regarded with scepticism in Algeria.

2. Violence Against Women

In the 1990s, women became the privileged targets of terrorist violence. This was directly linked to the role they had been assigned as guardians of the family honour and reputation and the transmission of values to their children. In a period such as the 1980s and 1990s, with rapid social, political and economic change, social norms were fluid, and the resulting vacuum gave scope to the zealots. These people felt that there was a great deal at stake around women's purity, and violence was directed against women who appeared to be transgressing currently acceptable social norms. Mahfoud Bennoune writes of the way in which young women who suggest by the way they dress that they challenge traditional views of their role, are frequently sexually harassed with impunity when travelling on the overcrowded buses of Algerian towns (Bennoune 1999: 57). Particular targets were women in paid employment, those travelling independently and any woman in a public space without appropriate head covering. Monique Gadant writes that sexual segregation and the debate about Algerian identity tends to be 'incarnated in the roles and the spaces allocated to them and the clothes that they wear' (Gadant 1995: 100).

These attacks on women had been building up throughout the 1970s and 1980s but were the tip of the iceberg in terms of violence against women. In the early 1970s, women employed in state owned factories in Sidi Bel Abbès were stopped from going to work by men throwing stones and they had to be given police protection. Women living on their own were particular targets: in June 1989 a divorced woman living alone with her children in the southern town of Ouargla, was stoned by a mob and her house burned down. Her youngest son, Ali, a handicapped child of four was burned to death.[10] In 1990/1 (before the legislative elections) women in university halls of residence were harassed by FIS militia who imposed a curfew on them from 6.00 p.m. Anyone opposing this was 'corrected' with the aid of a whip or bicycle chains.

After the cancellation of the elections in 1992, attacks on women intensified. Amnesty International reported that armed opposition groups singled out women as special targets. One of the first cases they reported was Karima Belhadj, a twenty year old secretary at the Direction Générale de la Sûreté Nationale (DGSN) who was shot dead near her home in the Eucalyptus suburb of Algiers in January 1993. In February 1994, Katia Bengana, a seventeen year old secondary school student, was shot dead near her home in Meftah (Blida). She had received death threats for refusing to wear, and speaking out against the hijab'(Amnesty International 1997). Amnesty International wrote: 'civil servants, wives and relatives of members of the security forces, journalists, artists, women's rights activists, newspaper and cigarette vendors, hairdressers and beauticians, and many others have been the targets of death threats'(Amnesty International 1997).

There have also been many abductions, sexual assaults and rapes connected to the civil conflict, reaching a peak in the period 1995-1998. They particularly affected people living in the countryside, prompting families living in isolated areas to send their daughters to live with relatives in town.

These attacks were still continuing in 2001 (as were terrorist attacks against the general population). In July 2001, a number of women living and working in Hassi Messaoud (about 800 km south-east of Algiers) were attacked with extreme violence (some were even raped) by a group of some 300 men armed with clubs and knives in a series of punitive raids. The men accused them of being prostitutes - something the women reject. Later in the same month, three women living alone were similarly attacked by a group of men in the town of Tebessa (north-east of Algeria near the Tunisian frontier) on two occasions (*Le Monde*, 25 July 2001). This has given rise to women's mobilisations and some government initiatives, which I shall document later in the chapter.

In a society experiencing such extreme brutality, it is easy to overlook everyday domestic violence, but some Algerian women's groups point to the way in which public violence can spill over and legitimise violence in the private sphere. As a corollary to their campaigns against the *Code de la Famille*, associations have been formed to support married women with children who have been forced to leave their homes as a result of repudiation or divorce, which may be accompanied by violent treatment. The association *SOS Femmes en Détresse* estimate that 80 per cent of the calls for help they receive are from such women. Given Algeria's long-standing housing crisis with an average of seven people per household, 30 per cent of the population living in three-room apartments and 18 per cent in one room, this solidarity is essential.

Research on violence towards women has widened the definition of violence against women from domestic and sexual aggression, to a spectrum ranging from physical or moral aggression to political, institutional, economic violence, and violence related to war. The *Collectif 95 Maghreb Egalité* have conducted a survey *Violence à l'encontre des femmes*. This was undertaken in 2000 in eight regions and in 22 *wilayas*, with responses from 1,220 people. It revealed how widespread is such violence. Those most likely to be treated violently were in the age group 30-39: mainly married women. The second largest category was women aged between 20-29 years of age. The majority of people who had committed these acts were men but some 30 per cent of such acts were by women: their victims are more likely to be their children or sisters - some 49 per cent of those who mistreat children are women. Two million people aged eighteen and over had attacked members of their own family; the main victims were wives and sisters. All levels of society and all age groups are affected.[11]

Recent reforms to the penal code make it possible for associations to mount a legal defence for the victims of violence. *SOS Femmes en Détresse* are concerned with reception centres for women who have suffered violence. The association *Rachda,* of which the Deputy Khalida Messaoudi is a leading member, emphasised the need to develop grassroots work: they have started an enquiry into the circumstances of the (continuing) attacks at Hassi Messaoud (*El Watan*, 29-30 October 2001).

Another key issue related to violence against women is that of more than 2,000 women raped by terrorists. Some are cared for at the *Darna* reception centre funded by the Italians. Some women activists have argued that these women should be given the status of victims but this position is hotly debated: others argue that it is more urgent to set up a credible counter-power to push women's demands. Women's organisations emphasise the problem of a lack of hostels for people who have been attacked - especially minors who are generally treated alongside delinquents. The DGSN claim to have recruited more women police officers to help deal with this problem.

I have outlined the dimensions of the problems and challenges facing women in Algeria. Now I will survey the broader picture before looking at the actions Algerian women are currently taking.

3. Trends in the Position of Women in Contemporary Algeria

In this section, I sketch out the broad position of women in Algeria making brief comparison with other countries of the Maghreb. I take some recent figures relating to marriage, fertility, education, employment and violence against women to give some indications of their position. The broad long-term picture is optimistic.

In terms of published official demographic data we can situate the position of Algerian women somewhere between that of women in Tunisia and Morocco. Figures for Moroccan women show generally worse conditions and Tunisia, which is generally lauded for its enlightened approach to women, tends to be better, but only marginally so. Life expectancy for Algerians is 66 for men and 69 for women compared with 63 and 67 for Moroccans, and 67 and 69 for Tunisians. Since the launch of the National Programme for the Control of Demographic Growth in 1983, there has been a gradual acceptance of contraception in Algeria. However, fertility rates in Algeria are higher than in both other countries: at 4.1 compared with 3.5 in Morocco and 3 in Tunisia (UNDP 1998) - although more recent figures suggest that Algerian figures may now be nearer to 3 (Oufreha 1998). Maternal mortality rates in 1994 compared favourably with those in Tunisia (UNDP gives figures of 160 per 100,000 in Algeria, compared with 170 in Tunisia and an astronomical 610 in Morocco). More recent figures cited in the national press earlier this year found 120 per 100,000 women dying in childbirth, mainly because of a shortage of midwives (*El Watan*, 5 April 2001).

Further evidence comes in more comprehensive academic studies, such as that recently published by Kamel Kateb. He suggests that there have been basic changes in patterns of marriage running directly counter to the thrust in the Family Code (Kateb 2001). While marriage remains a near-universal institution in Algeria (almost 97 per cent of all adults have been married at some time), the average age of women at marriage is increasing - from 18 in 1966 to 25 in 1992.[12] Fatima-Zohra Oufreha's research suggests that growing numbers of women are rejecting the idea of marriage before the age of eighteen (Oufreha 1998). The difference in age between spouses is also falling, which suggests that it is becoming less common to find older men marrying younger women and then trying to dominate them. This may be related to other factors, such as the difficulties of finding suitable housing, or of associating freely with members of the opposite sex. But it also signals one way in which social control over women has relaxed. Oufreha also finds that there is a growing preference for female children: 92 per cent of Algerian women told the PAPCHILD survey that they would prefer girls to boys (Oufreha 1998). This suggests that there may be important changes in women's self-perception and the way in which they negotiate patriarchal family structures which force women to have large numbers of children in order to have boys (Lacoste-Dujardin 1986).

4. Girls' Education

Assia Djebar (1985: 11) paints a striking picture of education for Algerian girls in the 1950s:

> From the first day a girl leaves her home to learn the alphabet, neighbours cast know-
> ing glances at her, pitying her audacious father and her responsible brother. Disaster
> will inevitably descend upon them! Every educated virgin would be able to write,

would surely write 'that' letter. The time would come for her when written love would be more dangerous than forbidden love. Behold the body of the girl who gets around. Make her invisible. Turn her into a being more blind than the blind, kill her memory of the outside world. What if she knows how to write? The gaoler of a body without words - and written words get around - can finally sleep peacefully: all he has to do is keep her brothers in line, padlock the only door and build a blank wall up to the sky.

In the independence movement, there was considerable support for the education of women, even if it was to prepare her to fulfil the role of wife and mother more adequately. Cheikh Ben Badis argued 'to educate a man is to educate an individual, to educate a woman is to educate a whole family' (Bennoune 1999). Throughout the 1960s and 1970s there was a massive drive to extend education to both sexes, partly by building schools in the countryside to help access for young women. The proportion of girls with an education grew from 32 per cent in 1965-6 to 79.52 per cent in 1991-2 (Bennoune 1999: 69). Figures for female basic literacy in 1994 shows Algeria with a female literacy level of just over 49 per cent compared to Morocco's 30 per cent and Tunisia's 54 per cent (UNDP 1998).

It was at secondary level, and therefore post-puberty, that levels of female participation tended to be less impressive. Algerian government figures prepared for the UN Committee on the Status of Women (CSW) show these figures rising. Girls as a percentage of all pupils attending secondary school have now risen from 47.4 per cent of all pupils in 1992, to 52.5 per cent in 1996. Moreover, girls tend to do better than boys at their studies: they are less likely to be excluded, drop out or have to repeat school years. They tend to be younger than boys when they reach the final year of secondary education, but represented 55.3 per cent of successful candidates in the baccalaureate exams in 1996. While they excel in the more traditional 'female' subjects such as humanities and foreign languages, they also do well in the natural and life sciences, and management and economics. Figures for higher education show women's participation rising slowly. The paradox of Algeria, with its considerable regional variations, is that of a country with one of the highest levels of educated women in the Arab world, yet with relatively low levels of women in paid employment.

While the Family Code sought to regulate domestic relations, organised Islamist groups have attempted to restrict women's access to education. Educated women are more likely to work and employed women to be independent of fathers and husbands. After the FIS local election victories in 1990, there was new pressure against mixed classes and many women teachers lost their jobs. Girls were intimidated when they attempted to continue to higher education and schools began to be used for proselytism rather than education. Many associations have been established to resist these moves.

5. Employment
Throughout the world, women's employment tends to mirror their domestic role and to be concentrated in the (lower-paid) public sector. Algeria is no exception.

Women are relatively well represented in education, medicine and public administration. In the national education sector, women account for 38 per cent of employees (or 172,000 of 459,000), and in the health sector, women are 37 per cent of all employees (or 70,000 of 180,000).

Compared with Morocco and Tunisia, Algeria falls badly behind in terms of women's paid employment. Algerian women earn only 19 per cent of all earned income while Tunisian women earn 25 per cent and Moroccan women 28 per cent. Algerian women account for 27 per cent of professional and technical workers (figures for Morocco are 31.3 per cent and Tunisia 35.6 per cent) and 5.9 per cent of administrators and managers (compared with 25.6 per cent for Morocco and 12.7 per cent for Tunisia).

A central aspect of the problem of access to paid employment is how women's access to public space is contested, bound up with the idea of her escape from the control of her family. Doria Cherifati-Merabtine points out that a woman who works does so under very specific conditions and that she is always under pressure to show that she remains 'a real woman'. To work is to deviate from her projected life-project: for many women who go 'out' to work, it is the expression of the failure of her family's hopes for her life, and is often due to divorce or widowhood. The working woman is associated with the poverty of the colonial period and the words used to describe her tend to have pejorative associations. So the idea of the working woman remains an identity in construction which has to be given value (Cherifati-Merabtine 1996). Paid employment implies the dual threat of woman's visibility in public spaces but also 'it encourages processes of individualisation or financial autonomy which are associated with decision-making in the private sphere' (Cherifati-Merabtine 1996: 295).

These small advances are threatened by changes in the structure of employment due to changes linked to globalisation. In recent years, there has been an increase in poverty linked to a deterioration in public services especially in the urban centres. In 1987, Algiers had the best public services in the country, with 92 per cent of households with drinking water, 96 per cent electricity and 91 per cent linked to a mains sewer. In 1998, it had fallen back to fifteenth place with only 82 per cent of households with water, 83 per cent electricity (*El Watan*, 23-24 December 2001). Problems such as the intermittent supply of clean water and increased food prices have a direct impact on the lives of women who are expected to keep the household running, especially in increasing the double burden for women in paid employment. There has been an increase in insecure employment, which is likely to continue. The reduction of the size of the public sector is likely to affect women's employment disproportionately. With the rise of inequality and poverty, has come an increased level of prostitution (female and male). At the beginning of 2001, *El Watan* reported major increases in prostitution in all areas of the country (*El Watan*, 8 February 2001). This has been compounded by socio-economic factors, pressures on the family unit, the flight from the countryside, and the increase in unemployment and the destitution of divorced women.

6. Women's Political Mobilisations

In its evidence to the UNCSW, the Algerian government stresses that it has ensured the increasing participation of women at all levels of Algerian politics, partly as a result of the reform of voting procedures. Since 1995, proxy votes have been limited to exceptional situations. Thirteen women from various political parties were elected to Parliament in the legislative elections, in which there were 332 female candidates; they represent 3.2 per cent of the deputies elected (compared to 0.7 per cent in Morocco and 6.7 per cent in Tunisia (UNDP 1998). Seventy-five women were elected to the Communal People's Assemblies from among 1,281 female candidates; 62 women were elected to the Departmental People's Assemblies from among 905 female candidates. The Council of the Nation has nine women members, four were elected by the electoral college, and five were appointed by the President of the Republic (CEDAW 1998).

As a result, women have organised to achieve their own aims often outside the main political arena. I divide these mobilisations into two main phases, the unofficial mobilisations against the *Code de la Famille*, prior to and immediately after 1984, and the formation of legally recognised associations after the Constitutional reforms of 1989.

6.1. Mobilisations Against the Family Code Prior to 1984

Throughout the 1960s and 1970s, the periodic attempts to draft a Family Code, gave rise to women's counter-demonstrations and mobilisations. While Algeria signed up to most of the major international instruments supporting the rights of women, an important strand of conservative Islamic public opinion was constantly pressing for the application of the *Shari'a* throughout Algerian life. This struggle intensified after the Family Code was presented as draft legislation in September 1981. A women's group in Oran named *Isis* was part of a movement to organise space for women to meet and debate together, this time based on university structures. The *Association pour l'égalité devant la loi entre les hommes et les femmes* was set up in 1985, to campaign for legal equality. Street demonstrations were organised by women, giving a new visibility to women in political life, led by *moudjahidates* and comprising women trade unionists, teachers and students. Djamila Amrane writes of about a hundred *moudjahidates* who met in the *Maison du Peuple* under the protection of the UGTA (*Union Générale des Travailleurs Algériens*). Women's associations insisted that their voices should be heard and occupied the entry to the National Assembly in protest. They wrote to the President and drafted legal amendments - to no avail.

Since 1984, women's associations and political parties have been at the forefront of work for the abolition or fundamental reform of the Code. Disparate groups formed a common agenda. The *Association pour l'égalité devant la loi entre les hommes et les femmes* united some 30 organisations in a national co-ordination in December 1989, to seek the abolition of all forms of discrimination. At the same time they have called for the ratification and application of conventions guaranteeing rights of women and children, the defence of the right to work for all women and security of their employment, and the end to sexual discrimination in education (Egalité 1991, Saadi 1991: 48-9). Human rights lawyers active in Algerian politics point to the contradiction between Algerian laws which stipulate non-discrimination, its international commitments and the Family Code.

The uprisings of October 1988 prefigured the transformation of the political scene in Algeria, as the Chadli government liberalised the laws on political association in the new constitution of 1989 (Tahi 1992: 399). It became possible to set up political parties and legally recognised associations.[13] Some twenty women's associations were quickly established, mainly in the north and centre of the country, concentrating in the larger towns (Brac de la Perriere 1993). Their existence has been as precarious and unsettled as the interrupted process of the establishment of a pluralist democracy in Algeria.

These associations represent many different viewpoints, some attached to political parties, others define themselves by their autonomy.[14] In her account of the Algerian women's movement, Chérifa Bouatta (1997) identifies four major tendencies (excluding the religious fundamentalists).[15] One major division is between those who call for the amendment of the Family Code and those who want its outright abolition. The former approach attracted many women who had been involved in the UNFA but who were critical of its bureaucratic approach. Linked to these associations are others mainly engaged in social activities, operating crèches, cooperatives and workshops such as the *Association pour la défense et la promotion des droits de la femme* (Algiers) and *Association pour la promotion de la femme* (in Mostaganem and Annaba).

A second tendency focuses on the transformation of attitudes underpinning women's oppression through cultural activities such as exhibitions, cinema, festivals (*Association pour l'émancipation de la femme* [Alger], *Sakhrat en nissa* [Staouéli] and *Israr* [Constantine]).

A third strand campaigns unequivocally for the abolition of the Code and all discriminatory laws. They demand a civil code which guarantees sexual equality, bans polygamy, divorce, paternal guardianship, and establishes the equal rights in law of both parents and woman's unconditional right to employment. Organisations such as *L'Association pour l'égalité devant la loi, Égalité* (in Algiers, Oran, Annaba), *Voix des Femmes* (Boumerdés) and *Tighri net mettout* (Tizi Ouzou) are involved in information campaigns and organising debates, and support political parties, which have similar positions (Bouatta 1997: 8).

The fourth and most radical strand is represented by *Triomphe* (*L'Association indépendante pour le triomphe des droits de la femme*) formed from a split in the *Association pour l'égalité devant la loi*. It argues that women's position transcends all other concerns and eschews involvement with male structures of power except on their own terms (Bouatta 1997: 11).

The different tendencies have emphasised a variety of campaigning activities. The overarching issue has been the *Code de la Famille*, but women's associations have participated in the international agenda. Violence against women is another key priority. Given the serious pressure on Algeria's social infrastructure over the past ten years of conflict with the armed opposition groups and religious fundamentalists, not to speak of the impact of structural adjustment, women's organisations have also tended to move in to fill the gap in social provision. They also have important links with the Algerian diaspora and organise cultural and solidarity activities.

6.2. Mobilisations Against the Family Code after 1984

These have taken conventional political forms such as lobbying, petitions and demonstrations. The *National Women's Coordination* established a national forum for women's associations to establish a minimum platform in 1989. They agreed to prioritise the political demand for opposition to the Family Code as unconstitutional (Saadi 1991). They insisted on raising broader issues: that women had an unconditional right to work; that women should be able to exercise their right to vote in an effective manner and not have their votes cast by male guardians and that they should have access to a modern, scientific education.

Divisions between organisations focus on a range of issues along a continuum between radical and reformist positions. While the main division concerns the reform or abolition of the Family Code, there are further dilemmas around how broadly women should mobilise and what political compromises might be necessary in order to achieve their aims. Others 'are beginning to wonder whether they have been trapped by the abolition versus amendment argument at the expense of broader women's interests' (Bouatta 1997: 14).[16] A related set of issues focus on the relations of women's associations with political parties, given concerns that women were being used by different bodies to legitimise their actions. A number of political parties claim to support the rights of women, and to oppose the Family Code - for instance the *Parti Travailliste*, the RCD (*Rassemblement pour la Culture et la Démocratie*), the FFS (*Front des Forces Socialistes*), the PAGS, MDS (*Mouvement Démocratique et Social*).

The decision to suspend the electoral process in early 1992 rather than risk a FIS (*Front Islamique du Salut*) victory gave rise to further controversy. Although women's rights were being progressively curtailed in FIS-controlled local authorities, some women's groups wanted a direct confrontation with the Islamists, and many demurred over the suspension of elections, while others greeted it with relief.

The *moudjahidates* have played a respected role in all these tendencies, helping to legitimate the demands of women's groups in a situation where nationalism is a dominant value. After independence, many studied in a French medium, before the Arabisation of the education system. Their political and ideological milieu was the same as that of the men in governing positions but, as women, they were vulnerable to accusations of representing Western interests. Despite this, their prestige is such that their support for the women's movement has helped to discredit the Islamists' attempts to besmirch them, as being manipulated by Western imperialism.[17] Ighilahriz recounts a memory of a woman friend who was distributing lipsticks in the streets of Algiers just after the victory of the FIS in the elections in December 1991. She writes:

I didn't usually put on makeup, but on this occasion it was a way of showing that we weren't affected by the result of this first round, and that we Algerian women were going to stay fresh and beautiful. My friend went all over town with four or five lipsticks and we all put some on! (Ighilahriz 2001: 243).

There is a dilemma for women who 'have been caught between two sets of legitimacy: they cannot serve their cause as women and at the same time belong to the nation for whose very existence they have suffered' (Helie-Lucas 1993: 211). Women are caught between the frontal attacks on their right, to be present in a public space at all and their concern to maintain a unity of struggle against Islamic fundamentalism. Adopting a feminist perspective risks isolation from the masses, and any movement is forced to adopt some kind of nationalist perspective. Many associations have accepted this limitation as offering a civic option for women who are defined as guardians of tradition rather than citizens.

Although the Family Code was at the centre of women's organising, associations have not focused only on this issue. The extreme situation of violence, often focused on women, has called forth very different sets of issues and responses. Political action is very difficult in a situation where even signing a petition can lead to personal danger. Women have been forced into the forefront of fighting terrorism, because many of them have been victims, either specific targets or as a result of the killing of members of their family. It has also proved extremely exhausting and demanding at a personal level for those involved.

6.3. Mobilisations Against Violence

Violence against women is increasingly prominent on the agenda of women's organisations. Organisations such as *L'Association de solidarité et de soutien aux familles des victimes du terrorisme* have called demonstrations against acts of violence (Fates 1994). In the face of massacres leaving the survivors isolated, traumatised and destitute, associations have travelled to the scene of atrocities to identify people's needs and support the victims. Given the controversy over the authorship of violence, they see it as important to record what has happened. This is a crucial activity in any conflict like this, to record such events, reaching beyond the fog of war, which tends to obscure such dreadful events. In recent months for instance, there has been an energetic campaign to draw attention to the violence and harassment in Hassi Messaoud and Tebessa.

There are significant demonstrations around the question of the victims of violence, which hold opposing views. The National Association of Families of the 'Disappeared' (ANFD) hold weekly demonstrations in Algiers and Constantine to demand that the government provide information about missing relatives, but claim that they were not able to obtain official authorisation to function (Human Rights Watch 2001). At the opposite end of the political spectrum, a group of women organised as Families of the Victims of Terrorism demonstrate against what they see as the betrayal of the amnesty and neglect of victims under the *Concorde Civile*. There is a danger that both groups will be manipulated by different political parties,[18] and also that the issue of domestic violence (discussed in section 2) is overlooked.

In the past year there have been officially backed seminars about violence against women, defining it as a public health problem and pressing for stronger legal sanctions against such violence (*El Watan*, 4 July 2001). Khalida Messaoudi emphasised that men were waiting for women to take the initiative on this issue. The seminar developed the idea of a specialist group of women parliamentarians to take the issue forward. Women's associations are also addressing the deficiencies of state provision of counselling services for the victims of violence - unused because of lack of trust in those involved.

7. Solidarity
So far, I have considered Algerian women as though they were isolated from international pressures and influences. The significant Algerian migrant and exiled population in France maintains close links with home, and has an important impact on women's lives.

Family remittances and regular visits are extremely important for many people, offering one another a different view of the world. But many local community-based associations have responded to the isolation and the violence faced by relatives in Algeria by deciding to go beyond family obligations and to correspond on an organised basis, community to community, and to develop the idea of twinning (*Pour*, 18-19 October 1998). Their solidarity has also helped to compensate for the running down of public services. Since 1993, many children from Algeria have been invited to spend summer holidays in France, for education but also to find calm away from the trauma of bereavement, although this has not been a straightforward affair (Lloyd 1999).

Solidarity activities match the resources and concerns of people from the socio-economic groups which tend to be active in local associations, such as teachers, social workers and mediators. Although there is clearly inequality of resources, it is important to note that Algerian associations have made their terms of engagement clear. In the autumn of 1998, I conducted interviews with a *Caravane* of Algerian associations, with a very strong representation of women, who toured France to arrange long-term cooperative projects between Algeria and France. The idea for this exchange had been developed during a meeting in Algeria of the association *Tharwa n'Fadhma n'Soumeur*, based in Algiers and *Association ARCAM* of Toulouse (France). They sought to present a different view of Algeria from the violence presented by the media, which they saw as operating 'to obscure the fact of a growing civil society, but also the very creative action taking place in many areas such as culture, thought, social action and demands for rights'.[19] The *Caravane* thus aimed to show a wider public the diversity of Algerian social life, to exchange experiences and to establish real partnerships. They sought to put together packages of partners with whom to organise in a flexible, multifaceted way. They represented a wide range of groups: those collecting reading materials for children or working to defend their rights (*Le Petit Lecteur d'Oran, Association Stambouli* from Tizi Ouzou and *Fondation Belkhenchir* from Algiers); environmental groups working on arid land (*Espoir Vivant* from Tiaret and *Association de Béni Abbes*); a solidarity group for the victims of terrorism (*Djazairouna*); women's associations (*Association pour l'Emancipation de la Femme, Association des Femmes Médecins d'Oran*, and the *Association Nationale pour la Défense et la Promotion de l'Emploi*); a Touareg cultural group, and youth organisations.[20]

The organising of international solidarity has the potential to transform local community associations and deepen their international reach and experience. The *Caravane* is one of the many examples of a sustained exchange of ideas and support, which is rooted in the migrant and exiled Algerian communities particularly (but not exclusively) in France. With the help of associations from Algeria, which can ensure that solidarity is appropriate, important resources can be created from the personal skills and networks of migrant communities. They appear to be aiming at the sort of transversal organising, described by Nira Yuval-Davis in which:

> *perceived unity and homogeneity are replaced by dialogues which give recognition to the specific positionings of those who participate in them as well as to the 'unfinished knowledge' that each such situated positioning can offer... The boundaries of a transversal dialogue are determined by the message rather than the messenger. (Yuval-Davis 1997: 9)*

The international activity of Algerian associations goes beyond links with migrant groups based in the ex-colonial power. Women's mobilisations in particular have the capacity to take on a broader, international dimension. Based in Morocco, but with members across the Maghreb, the *Collectif Maghreb Egalité 95* was set up to prepare for the Fourth UN World Conference on Women in Beijing (1995) and prepared reports on the implementation of strategies adopted at the Third UN Conference on Women in Nairobi (1985). They assessed the state of ratification and application of international conventions on women's rights and formulated measures towards an egalitarian codification of the personal status and rights of the family in the Maghreb (an alternative Family Code), activities bound up with those of women's associations in Algeria.

The international Women Living Under Muslim Laws network embraces appeals for solidarity with women in prison and national campaigns against severe application of the *Shari'a,* and information swapping (Helie-Lucas 1993). International exchanges offer some women the opportunity to see different versions of Islamic society, which may suggest more positive spaces for women, challenging the view of a homogeneous Muslim world. This approach again is marked by the respect for different positions and the respect for local groups' autonomy to define their own analysis and priorities, which characterises transversal politics (Helie-Lucas 1993: 223). *Femmes Contre l'Intégrisme* have taken similar initiatives with the organisation of conferences to exchange women's experiences of fundamentalism around the Mediterranean. This approach also suggests a more open way of offering solidarity than that commonly associated with the more prescriptive, judgmental approach of some Western feminists, which is inevitably much more restricted in its scope and reach (Bourqia, Charrad & Gallagher 1996).

Conclusion

This chapter has examined the position of women in Algeria from a number of different perspectives. It is impossible to ignore the backdrop of the *Code de la Famille* and the conservative patriarchal system, and the way in which the conflict of the past ten years has concentrated in a particular way on limiting women's social role. Women have been special targets of Islamist violence because of their exemplary status in Algerian society. Although they had proved their capacity for resistance during the war of Independence, women were discouraged from taking a public place in the newly independent Algeria; instead, they were expected to put their interests after those of the wider society. This expectation of self-sacrifice is based on gender roles rooted in the needs of patriarchal society. However, an examination of demographics and women's socio-economic position reveals important changes. Algerian women are marrying at a later age, after receiving a good education, and they are having fewer children. There are signs that gender relations within the family are being renegotiated. Serious problems remain: there are high levels of violence against women throughout society, but the recognition of this as a problem by women's groups and by the Algerian authorities is a significant step forward. There are signs of considerable strain due to over-stressed public services, and women bear the brunt, either in terms of more difficult personal circumstances or in their attempts to shore up social provision through solidarity organisation.

Women's position tends to deteriorate sharply during periods of conflict. The future possibilities for Algerian women depend largely on the prospects for peace and security in the country and what kind of settlement, if any, the government makes with the Islamist opposition. Algeria's association with the European Union may help to increase pressure for the country to adhere to its obligations under international human rights provisions, and this will pose a difficult choice between the rights of women (and the reform of the *Code de la Famille*) and the position of the Islamist opposition.

Notes

1   The Algerian permanent representative at the UN Committee on Human Rights commented (20

July 1998) that the country has been involved in *'un processus de transition vers le pluralisme politique et l'économie de marché'*.

2   Cheikh d'Al Azhar in *Tahir al mar'a* 1899 (cited in Saadi 1991: 38).

3   Imam Ali Belhadj, *Horizons*, 23 February 1989, in an interview with Fouad Boughanem (cited in Saadi 1991: 17).

4   Text of the Soumman Congress, planned August 1956, and the Tripoli Programme, June 1962, in *Textes* (1976). [All translations are mine, unless otherwise stated - CL.]

5   Ben Bella's Speech of 1 May 1963 (cited in Bouamama 112).

6   Speech of 8 March 1966 (cited in Bouamama 165).

7   Reproduced in *Alger Republicain*, January 1990 (cited in Saadi 1991).

8   The UN Human Rights Committee notes that the Family Code is not in conformity with Articles 3, 16, 23 and 26 of the Covenant.

9   'The Committee is seriously concerned by the fact that the Family Code still contains many discriminatory provisions which deny Algerian women their basic rights, such as free consent to marriage, equal rights to divorce, sharing of family and child-rearing responsibilities, shared child custody rights with fathers, the right to dignity and self-respect and, above all, the elimination of polygamy' - paragraph 91 of the Concluding Observations of the Committee on the Elimination of Discrimination Against Women: Algeria, 27 January 1999. A/54/38 paragraphs 41-94, CEDAR 20th session 19 January-5 February 1999. Many Algerian women's groups insist that polygamy is largely a symbolic issue - it is not widely practised in Algeria. In the 1966 census it was only recorded as 2.1 per cent of all marriages in rural and 1.3 per cent in urban areas (see Gadant 1995: 96).

10 Khalida Messaoudi, then member of parliament for the RCD, in a speech to Swiss Radical Feminists *Service Libre d'information* No. 25, 1 July 1999, www.worldlib.org/executive/interlaken/twilight_fr.html.

11 This is corroborated by official sources: the DGSN had counted (across 42 *wilayas*) 1,439 women victims of violence, of whom 1,087 were victims of physical violence, 50 of sexual violence, 267 bad treatment, 4 murders and 31 of sexual harassment. The majority of the perpetrators were close relatives.

12 EASME/PAPCHILD survey 1999 - see Oufreha 1998, note three, for details of this survey conducted by the *Office national des statistiques* among 6,694 households.

13 Women's organisations are regulated by Law 87/16 of 21 July 1987 on non-political associations, although freedom of expression and association was formally granted in the Constitution of 1989.

14 Eleven out of the 380 members of Parliament are women at the time of writing. Of these eleven

among the most prominent are Louisa Hanoun of the Workers' Party (PT), Dalia Taleb of the FFS and Khalida Messaoudi who until recently represented the Rally for Culture and Democracy (RCD).

15 As Bouatta comments, there is little published material on Islamist women's associations. They tend to be linked closely to the Islamist political parties and to focus on a combination of charitable work with proselytism. They tend to support the Family Code because it is based on the *Shari'a*.

16 A more strategic course was adopted following the failure of a petition, in which women's organisations collected a million signatures, only to be trumped by Islamist organisations which collected three million.

17 Although Monique Gadant points out that while feminst ideas came from France, they were also disseminated through Middle Eastern newspapers in the 1930s, through the Egyptian reformist ideas of *Al Azhar*, or from Turkey in the form of Kemalist influences (Gadant 1995: 80-81).

18 *Al-Ahram* weekly on-line, 29 July-4 August 1999, No 440. www.ahram.org.eg/weekly/1999/440/re2.hm

19 Statement of *La Caravane de l'Espoir*, 1-31 October 1998.

20 Personal interviews with members of the *Caravane*, 16 October 1998 and Benabessadok (1998).

6 Rural Women in Algeria and their Participation in Economic Activity: Data Analysis

Zine M. Barka

Introduction

The active participation of women in social and economic development is an interesting topic, very often dealt with in political debates and cultural events. It therefore represents far more than women's basic right for large-scale inclusion in the country's economic, social and political activities. Many factors are favourable for a higher integration:

• The growing level of female literacy compared to former generations and the on-going increase in the number of girls attending schools (47 per cent at the primary level and 55 per cent in secondary education in 1998-99). These percentages of girls in full-time education are basic to the promotion of women's integration in active life.

• Women's willingness to take part in earning income for the household, in order to improve its living conditions, and more particularly, to increase the woman's freedom.

However, it is worth mentioning that the access of women to the job market is not an easy task. There are a number of impediments:

• Socio-cultural constraints;

• Household duties;

• Education and nursing.

Many studies emphasise 'the absence of detailed data concerning the contribution of woman to economic life compared to the overall macroeconomic indices' (Attout, Chebab & Kelkoul 1999: 5). This lack represents one of the factors that limits 'seriously the efforts made to measure the integration of women in the development process' (Attout, Chebab & Kelkoul 1999: 5).

Rather than entering into the details regarding the methods used to quantify women's participation in the gross national product in order to assess their integration in the development process, we limit our analysis to the activities undertaken by women in rural areas. In this way, we will make use of the 1996 data then, to exploit it to the full, we will analyse the results obtained in 1996 from a survey conducted by the *Institut National de Vulgarisation Agricole* (INVA). We should first mention that there exists a problem related to the under-evaluation of women's activity, partly due to an insufficient coverage of activity in the informal sector, where female activity is particularly high in rural areas. This type of activity represents 'an index of socio-economic shift' (Hammouda 1984). Let us look at the legal and statutory framework underlying women's work.

1. Rules and Regulations
The Constitution, the law and other statutory clauses guarantee the equality of Algerian women:

• The 1996 Constitution: Article 24 stipulates that 'the citizens are equal before the law, without any discrimination of birth, race, sex, opinion or any other condition and circumstance be it personal or social.' There are other articles from Chapter 4: Rights and Freedoms, which cover equality of rights.

• The 82-06 Law (27 February 1982) relating to work relationships: This law governs work relationships between the employer and employee. It states in Article 8 that 'workers have the same rights and are subject to the same duties whatever their sex and age as long as they hold the same jobs; on the basis of the same qualifications and output, they obtain the same salary and advantages for the same work.'

• Article 16: indicates that 'women at work have specific rights provided by legislative and statutory clauses which are applicable, namely those related to the general conditions of work and prevention against work related risks.' In this very specific context, the same article states that 'women cannot be employed in dangerous tasks or tasks that are harmful to their health.'

Other clauses, favourable to women at work, include the following provisions:

• Maternity leave consisting of fourteen weeks with a total acceptance of financial liability (social security);

• Nursing mothers have two-hours' leave a day during the first six months and an hour's leave for the following six months;

• The retirement age for women is brought forward by five years compared to male workers, provided that a fifteen-year period of work has been accomplished;

• Women who work and have a child under five years or suffering from a handicap (disabled) requiring continuous care, can be freed from duty temporarily (leave of absence).

We can then say that the legislative and statutory framework does not actually constitute an obstacle to the inclusion of women in the various economic activities. We shall now deal, through statistical data, with the position of women in the economic sphere, focusing particularly on the rural areas.

2. Women and Employment

Is there substantial female economic activity? Making use of the aforementioned references, we can note that the legislative and statutory framework does not make any sex discrimination, yet the low numbers of working women rather suggest the opposite. In 2000, the rate was estimated at 13.9 per cent of the active population.

The numbers of women who are eligible to do a job is as high as that of men. However, their presence on the job market remains relatively low. The gross rate of activity (Table 1) shifted from 3 per cent in 1977 to 11 per cent in 1996, representing an 8-point evolution in 20 years.

Table 1. Gross Rate of Activity in Percentage

	Men	Women	Total
1977 Census	36.6	2.6	**19.5**
1987 Census	42.4	4.4	**23.6**
1989 Survey	40.7	3.3	**22.2**
1990 Survey	41.0	3.4	**22.4**
1991 Survey	40.9	3.6	**22.4**
1992 Survey	41.5	3.8	**22.8**
1996 Survey	47.5	11.0	**28.5**

Source: Various publications of the Office National des Statistiques (ONS)

3. Activity and the Urban/ Rural Divide

The data relating to the rates of activity in urban/rural areas (Table 2) show that the participation of women in active life is relatively higher in urban areas than in rural ones (16 per cent as against 8 per cent). This discrepancy can be explained, among other factors, in terms of the high concentration of non-agricultural economic activities in urban areas and, on the other hand, in terms of an under-evaluation by the statistical survey of the various activities undertaken by women in the rural areas, i.e. a lack of reliable data.

Table 2. Rates of Activity in 1996 (Gender and Urban-Rural Divide)

Area	Urban			Rural		
	Total	Masculine	Feminine	Total	Masculine	Feminine
Rate of Activity (16 years and above)	46.2%	76.4%	15.8%	44.1%	79.6%	7.5%

Source: *Données statistiques*, N°254, Office National Statistiques (ONS)
Alger, 1er Trimestre, 1996

Table 3. Rate of Activity Per Age (1996)

Age group	Males	Females	Males + Females
16–19	50.5	9.7	30.9
20–24	81.9	20.6	52.1
25–29	93.2	19.2	56.3
30–34	96.9	14.9	54.4
35–39	96.5	10.7	52.5
40–44	96.9	8.9	54.9
45–49	95.2	7.3	52.0
50–54	91.0	4.1	49.6
55–59	80.0	4.5	42.4
60 years and +	24.5	1.7	12.7

The evolution of the activity rate of women varies from one age group to another. Table 3 shows that the three groups aged between 20 and 34 represent the highest rate compared to women of the other age groups, representing 20.6 per cent, 19.2 per cent and 14.9 per cent respectively. The highest employment is in the 20-24 age group. The rate of female activity constitutes a decreasing function starting from the age of 30, unlike that of men, which is, to a higher extent, relatively stable from 20 to 59.

4. Working Population: Characteristics and Evolution

According to the data provided by Table 4, we notice that administration and other services are the sectors that offer more jobs for women, representing 61.3 per cent and 23 per cent respectively. Industry and trade activities come in the third position and the building-industry in the fourth position. However, the agricultural sector had witnessed a low demand for female labour from 1977 to 1996, representing only 1.8 per cent.

Table 4. Distribution of Female Employment according to the Activity Sector

Activity sector	1977	1982	1983	1984	1987	1989	1996
Agriculture	5.6	3.4	4.8	2.3	2.7	3.5	1.8
Industry	17.4	14.3	15.0	13.3	12.4	11.5	7.4
Construction	2.1	1.5	2.3	3.5	3.4	3.0	1.9
Transport	3.2	3.3	2.7	3.1	2.5	2.4	-
Commerce	3.3	2.5	3.8	5.3	3.4	2.8	4.6
Administration	53.8	64.4	63.7	64.2	64.3	70.6	61.3
Services	10.2	8.8	7.7	8.3	5.4	-	23.0
TOTAL	100	100	100	100	100	100	100

Source: *Données statistiques*, N°23, ONS Alger, 1992 & N°254, ONS Alger, 1996

5. Employment and Socio-Professional Category (SPC)

Female activities still remain concentrated in specific occupations. An analysis of female occupations in relation to the socio-professional category (SPC) shows a significant increase in the numbers employed in the education sector (33.4 per cent), middle management (11 per cent) and the professions (9 per cent). Another sector in which the number of employed women is on the increase is the health care services.

Table 5. Evolution Structure of Female Employment in Relation to the SPC

SPC	YEAR							
	1982	1983	1984	1985	1987	1989	1990	1996
Teachers	28	25.7	27	25.8	26.9	33.9	34.2	33.4
Professional/ Managerial Staff	3.9	3.8	3.8	5.8	7.2	9	9.5	9.0
Middle management	8.1	10.3	10.1	13.5	12.6	11.2	9.4	11.0
White collar Staff	24.4	26.4	31.3	25.5	22.4	19.3	20.4	19.3
Non-skilled Staff	17.6	18.2	15.8	15.3	14.9	11	11	11.6
Manual workers	9.3	8.2	7.4	9.8	6.8	7.7	7.5	7.7
Others	8.7	7.4	4.5	4.3	9.2	8	8	8.0
Total	100	100	100	100	100	100	100	100

Source: For clarification purposes, this is an adaptation of the results of a survey on labour, *Office National des Statistiques* (ONS), Alger

6. Employment and Education Level

The quantitative evolution of female employment can be attributed to a number of global socio-educational factors, namely the increasing rate of female education, i.e. girls attending schools and universities. In effect, Table 6 shows better qualification and education levels of working women.

The population of working women having no educational level (illiterate) is on the decline, shifting from 21 per cent in 1985 to 13.3 per cent in 1996. On the other hand, the rate of working women with higher education qualifications has witnessed a considerable increase, shifting from 6.4 per cent to 16.4 per cent for the aforementioned period.

Table 6. Structure of Female Employment in Relation to Level of Education

Level	Illiterate	Literate	Primary	Middle	Secondary	Tertiary	Total
% 1996	13.3	1.4	9.3	22.6	36.8	16.4	100
% 1985	21.0	0.7	11.9	28.0	32.1	6.4	100

Source: ONS – EER, 1996, *Données statistiques* N°254, ONS, MOD 1985, collection N°31

7. Employment and Marital Status

Table 7 provides an illuminating account of the relationship between employment and working women's marital status. Thus, 34.08 per cent of working women aged between sixteen and more are married and 51.04 per cent single. On the other hand, out of the total number of single women, only 10.39 per cent have a job; yet 30.41 per cent of divorced or separated women have a job. The reasons for women to look for a job are clearly different. As far as married women are concerned, to work is usually a means to establish themselves, to get financial independence, and to contribute to the improvement of their households. As for widows and divorced women, working is a vital necessity in order to meet their needs and those of their families.

Table 7. Working Women and Marital Status (in Thousands)

	Working (a)	%	Total (b)	a / b (%)
Married	213	34.08	4,336	4.91
Single	319	51.04	3,069	10.39
Divorced/Separated	52	8.32	171	30.41
Widows	41	6.56	695	5.9
TOTAL	**625**	**100**	**8,271**	**7.56**

Source: *Données statistiques*, N°254, ONS, Alger 1996

It is quite obvious for non-single women who have a few children to look for a job, be it in urban or rural areas. However, in urban areas, the number of working women with four children is slightly high; whereas in rural areas, women usually stop working after the birth of the third child (Table 8).

Table 8. Classification of Non-Single Working Women According to Number of Children and Area

Number of children	Urban	Rural	National
0	10,71	12,70	11,11
1	21,83	17,46	20,95
2	19,44	28,57	21,97
3	15,48	19,05	16,19
4	13,89	4,76	12,06
5	5,16	4,76	5,08

Source: Enquête sur la Santé de la Mère et de l'Enfant, ONS, Alger, 1992

8. Female Activities in Two Rural Areas: Results of a Survey

In the rural areas, the work of women very often consists in contributing to the production process both in the agricultural sector, namely family farming, and the craft industry. In this context, working women are considered as effective economic agents, in the sense that they produce for family consumption (reducing, therefore, the household living expenses through self-consumption), but also for the selling of goods on the market.

We now move to the analysis of some data obtained from fieldwork research carried out between 1994-96 based on a sample of 292 women living in the rural areas of Tipaza and Tizi-Ouzou. The main objective of this research is to assess the contribution of women living in rural areas to the improvement of their household, thanks to their involvement in farming activities and other activities yielding extra income or simply an income to meet their families' needs.

9. The Farming Activity

Women living in rural areas can perform outdoor farming activities, which consist of many tasks.

The data in the forthcoming tables come from a multiple-choice questionnaire, in which informants can select one or more answers (consequently, the figures exceed 100 per cent). The answers are self-contained; the reading of this type of table can be done horizontally or line by line.

Table 9 provides information on female activities in farming. These activities consist essentially of market gardening, weeding, planting and harvesting. These manual tasks do not require high technical skills. Furthermore, these women take part in tree-cultivation activities (mainly harvesting) but to a lesser extent. These activities would require know-how and skills.

Working women are also more in charge of rearing sheep or goats than cattle rearing; the latter is much more capital intensive. The tasks that are the most performed by women are, in order of priority, feeding the cattle and other domestic animals, sheepfold/cowshed cleaning, shepherding. Poultry farming does not seem to be important; a few women are involved in this activity.

Table 9. Allocation of Answers According to the Type of Activity Performed

Type of Activity	Farmers	Non-Farmers	Undetermined Status	Total	
	No.	No.	No.	No.	%
Market gardening	221	14	57	292	100
Tree cultivation	117	0	0	117	40.08
Cattle-rearing	24	1	5	30	10.27
Ovine/caprine rearing	102	5	20	127	43.49
Poultry farming	31	6	18	55	18.84

Source: '*La promotion de la femme rurale*', INVA, Alger,1998

10. The Craft Activity

In addition to farming and household activities, women perform other craft activities, either for their own needs or for trade purposes. They perform weaving, pottery, sewing, embroidery and other activities.

According to the data in Table 10, the most common activity is weaving, representing a rate of 36 per cent among working women. Sewing comes in the second position with 22 per cent.

Table 10. Female Craft Activity

Tasks performed	Farmers		Non-Farmers		Undetermined Status		Total	
	No.	%	No.	%	No.	%	No.	%
Weaving	76	74.39	5	35.71	24	42.10	105	35.59
Pottery	16	7.24	3	21.43	11	19.07	30	10.27
Sewing	51	23.07	3	21.43	9	15.79	63	21.57
Embroidery	9	4.07	3	21.43	8	14.03	20	6.85
Others	18	8.14	2	14.28	12	21.05	32	10.96
Reference Population	221		14		57		292	

Source: '*La promotion de la femme rurale*', INVA, Alger, 1998

Conclusion

There are many statistical sources of information concerning female activities, but they are sporadic. Unfortunately there is not a comprehensive file of data (database) in this field of research which would gather information, normalise the concepts and definitions of the different individual situations and situations in female occupations. On the other hand, the analysis of the female activity trends, being an index of transformation and opening of the society, would be easier if the data were made reliable and published on a regular basis.

7 Frantz Fanon and Algeria:

Alienation and Violence

Naaman Kessous

Introduction: Fanon and the Problem of Alienation

Man is human only to the extent to which he tries to impose his existence on another man in order to be recognised by him. As long as he has not been effectively recognised by the other; that other will remain the theme of his actions. It is on that other being, on recognition by that other being, that his own human worth and reality depend. It is that other being in whom the meaning of his life is condensed. (Fanon 1952: 195-6)[1]

Since Algeria was born in violence, an assessment of the concepts of alienation and violence in the works of Fanon seems justified to understand today's Algeria. In so far as a consideration of the Algerian experience of nation building is concerned, an assessment of the colonial and post-colonial tensions framing it is fruitful. If we are to examine the process by which the Algerian transition from colonial dependency to post-colonial regeneration arduously comes out, we can gain rich insights from a reading of Frantz Fanon's concept of alienation. Moreover, his output on the question of violence illuminates our understanding of the processes by which the break with the colonial past is made. The concept of transition denotes a state of gestation heading for the birth of the new state of things. A certain measure of violence, Fanon claims, is inseparable from the dynamics that would lead to revolutionary change. The concept of violence is central to the Fanonian view of revolutionary regeneration: seeing colonialism as a process of adulteration, which brings the indigenous economic frameworks of labour and exchange values, as well as their corollary - the cultural and social frameworks - to a state of dysfunction, Fanon suggests that revolutionary violence is the only way for regeneration. From such a perspective, regeneration is perceived as a process of purification. The idea of purity, however, is not construed in terms of a cultural self-recuperation, but dispenses with influences from both the colonial past and the mythologising vision of the pre-colonial essence.

Coming from a participant in the Algerian War of Independence, and a theoretician of the universal colonial condition, Fanon's views had a direct bearing on the direction of the Algerian struggle and the ensuing breaking of the path of development. In the light of these issues, the present study aims to bring forth an analysis of the concept of alienation in the work of Frantz Fanon. We plan to pay particular attention, on the one hand, to his psychoanalytical background and, on the other, to the Marxist philosophical background, against which he developed his own theory of dialectical change. The study aims to clarify some of the theoretical confusions concerning the Hegelian paradigm and its relevance for Fanon's theory. For this, a review of previous studies of the subject is deemed necessary.

1. Alienation and Colonialism

To the best of my knowledge, the only study of colonialism and alienation in the works of Fanon is an essay by Zahar (1970), divided into eight chapters of unequal importance, preceded by an introduction and a foreword. We shall limit ourselves to a critical reading of the first chapter, on alienation, because it is there that the problems relevant to our subject are analysed.

There is no doubt that an examination of the notion of alienation in Fanon is the most effective way of bringing out the problematic of his work, especially with regard to a number of specific issues about which there can be, and occasionally are, overlaps as far as the significance of certain concepts is concerned. The function of a problematic is to delimit an area of issues where concepts or notions operate. It is through the articulation of the latter that answers are generally given. In view of this, a critical reading must take place, not on the level of the answers, but rather on a double level - the determination of the precise status of the concepts, and the way in which they operate, namely the manner in which they are arranged in order to produce a meaning. In this way, it becomes possible to detect the specific avenues through which the answers are conveyed.

1.1. An Exemplary Life

According to André Malraux, it is 'death which transforms life into destiny'. This applies remarkably well to Frantz Fanon's life. If we consider it from the point of view of its final impact, we shall see that it constitutes an exemplary outline of a destiny which was indissolubly linked to the ideas and the actions of an individual whose unfailing loyalty to and faith in a just cause always remained as strong as ever.

This biographical reminder, given in Zahar's essay, is necessary, because, as the author points out, Fanon's political activity ' had a powerful impact on the development of his theory, and the latter, in return, guided his revolutionary praxis' (Zahar 1970: 17).

From this biographical sketch, which is essentially a political portrait, we should remember that, following his scientific works and research in social-therapy,

Fanon, who was born and bred in a French colony, Martinique, became aware of the psychological alienation which colonialism engenders. In this respect, there is a whole section of Fanon's work which awaits further study and which comprises his strictly scientific works. Such works are scattered in specialised periodicals, and it would be useful to gather them in a single volume, if only because this would enable us to follow the birth and development of his thinking, which was always on the alert.

Fanon's medical studies, which he pursued and completed in Lyons, led him towards social-therapy, which he practised first in France, then in Algeria at the Blida-Joinville Hospital, where he was chief consultant from November 1953 to January 1956. After his expulsion from Algeria, Fanon's life became inseparable from his political itinerary, his many activities and his writings.

Thus, in a cursory but well-documented way, Zahar manages to convey a clear idea of the tireless manifestation of a many-sided, absorbing activity, which was wholly dedicated to the anti-colonial struggle and to the African revolution.

After her bio-bibliographical introduction, Zahar delineates the object of her study in a foreword. She asserts, without any ambiguity, that her starting point is a central notion in Fanon's work, viz. alienation. This way of proceeding is, indeed, conceptually daring and fruitful, because the notion of alienation, which can be interpreted in a medical sense on the one hand (mental illnesses, frustrations and complexes), and in an economic sense, on the other (colonisation, economic alienation), opens up a kind of double path towards the understanding of Fanon's work, at any rate with regard to its premises and its method. In isolating this central notion, Zahar makes it clear that:

> as far as colonialism and the struggle for national liberation are concerned, Fanon's experience is practically confined to Algeria. His analyses of racism are based essentially on his experience in the West Indies and France. Whenever in the course of his argument, colonialism is mentioned, it is primarily French colonialism. (Zahar 1970: 17)

This clarification leads the author to distinguish between two kinds of colonial policies, the English, which is governed by the principle of indirect rule and tends towards segregation, and the French, which is governed by the principle of assimilation. It is the latter which, according to the particular way in which it operates, creates the specific phenomena of alienation and frustration. We leave to Zahar the exclusive responsibility for such an assertion, which I cannot endorse, for it would imply that English colonialism did not alienate the populations of the Commonwealth; this issue, however, had better be left aside so that we can proceed to an analysis of Zahar's first chapter.

1.2. Colonialism and Alienation

The notion of alienation is so full of significance that Zahar feels compelled to resort to a terminological digression in order to consider in turn what the concept means for Hegel and then for Marx. For Hegel, it stems from what Zahar calls an objectification process: 'Hegel assumes that the human being, conceived (by him) as consciousness and thought, necessarily loses himself in the object in order to reach himself: he can be "for himself" (*pour soi*) only in becoming "other"' (Zahar 1970: 21).[2] For Marx, on the other hand, man's alienation emerges within production relations which are dominated by the capitalist mode of production: 'Marx situates the alienation of labour in the relationship between the producer and the product of his labour, and in the relationship between the worker and his own activity' (Zahar 1970: 21). With Hegel, alienation remains the process of consciousness (alienation-thought), whereas, with Marx, it is a concrete reality, which stems from the worker's living and working conditions in a social formation where the dominant mode of production is the capitalist mode of production.

After such a reminder, which had necessarily to be succinct, especially with regard to the nature of alienation in Marx's works, Zahar examines whether it is possible 'to make an effective use of the concept of alienation developed by Hegel and Marx in the analysis of colonial conditions.' In order to answer this question, the author needs a further digression, which consists in the attempt 'to determine the level of economic development in the countries described as underdeveloped' (Zahar 1970: 23). The economic description of colonial society is achieved by Zahar in three stages. First, she looks at the socio-economic consequences of colonial intrusion; secondly, she analyses the impact of the capitalist economic system on colonial society; finally, she examines the economic exchange-relationships, which characterise colonial society. In the course of this economic digression, Zahar makes use of the work of such economists as Paul Baran, Charles Bettelheim and Andre Gunder Frank, and she posits that the economic development of a colonial society is 'de-centred' ('disharmonious development') and that, as a result, it does not allow, and, indeed, ultimately renders impossible, the social integration of the individual. This impossibility, which is on the whole an objective one, is further accompanied by cultural alienation, which consists in the recognition by the colonised of the colonisers' superiority.

According to Zahar, for Fanon, it is this latter form of alienation which, inasmuch as it gives rise to a process of frustration and identification with a racist stereotype, 'distorts the vision of economic facts among the exploited and prevents them from thinking in concrete class terms' (Zahar 1970: 30).

Finally, Zahar returns to Hegel on the basis of a chapter in *PNMB* which is entitled 'The Negro and Hegel', and in which Fanon transposes into the colonial world Hegel's famous master-slave relationship in order to describe the nature of the relations which bind the coloniser to the colonised. Reversing the Hegelian process according to which self awareness has to go through the recognition of domination and the dialectical inversion of relationships, Fanon observes that in the colonial world, 'the relationship between the White master and the Black slave does not include the moment of recognition.' It would seem, therefore, that we are dealing here with a truncated dialectic, which lacks an essential element in order to operate, a frozen dialectic. The absence of recognition is attributed by Fanon to historical conditions (slavery) and to the existence of a racist ideology which is inherent in every colonial system, an ideology which the colonised internalises to such an extent that he is perturbed both in his being and in his practice. Using Fanon's own terminology, we can say that the Black slave turned away from the object (the only possibility of his liberation), i.e. from class consciousness achieved on the basis of the economic process, in order to fix the image of the White master, whom he apes and thus confirms in his domination.

This is where alienation, in Fanon's sense of the term, can be found, in a system which prevents the colonised from seeing that violence is the only way of destroying this age-long relationship of fascination into which he constantly loses himself, since he drops the substance for the shadow and gives up reality for its affected mask.

1.3. Proposed Interpretation of Fanon's Problematic

So far, Zahar's views have been presented as faithfully as possible. It is now time to put forward a few critical remarks about this essay devoted to Fanon and his work. It is possible, and indeed legitimate, to consider Fanon's work in the light of the central notion of alienation, and more especially of colonial alienation, since the whole of Fanon's writings call for such an approach, in view of the author's insistence on mentioning alienation and on analysing it. However, alienation is not a simple notion, and it is, moreover, open to a wide variety of interpretations. In view of this, Zahar's way of presenting it does not really contribute to our understanding, because all that we get is an account of Fanon's interpretation, taken *in abstracto*, after an account of the Hegelian and Marxist interpretations. It is, in my opinion, one of the most serious shortcomings of Zahar's essay, from which all others stem.

The approach, which is suggested in this study, is based on the belief that the notion of alienation, as it is used by Fanon, covers at least three different realities, which will be presented separately for the sake of clarity but which in fact overlap with one another.

The first reality covered by the notion of alienation is of a medical nature and is related to Fanon's scientific studies and to his work as a psychiatrist. It should not be forgotten that Fanon was a physician, so that in this specific context, the notion of alienation covers a reality which is pathological, observable and curable according to each case, and which concerns one or several individuals. From a very early stage, Fanon - and Zahar is right to stress this - showed a great interest in the many and diverse links between mental disorders and socio-economic realities. A number of his scientific articles clearly reveal such an interest on his part. However, what needs to be stressed is that the numerous problems raised by alienation in its diversified reality (the many kinds of mental disorders) are resolved, on this level, both in a theoretical way (as shown by Fanon's articles) and in a practical way (as shown by Fanon's therapeutic practice). It can, therefore, be asserted that, for Fanon, to consider colonial society as one which breeds mental disorders (alienation) is really to broaden, at a different level admittedly, his own early working hypotheses. One must see here a logical link and draw all the consequences by going beyond the exclusive consideration of Fanon's medical practice. This medical practice must be analysed in the light of his coherent ideological theory.

The second reality covered by the notion of alienation is of a philosophical nature and can be related to alienation as it is conceived in the writings of Hegel. We have already seen how Fanon, particularly in *PNMB*, re-introduces this notion and at the same time updates it thanks to a phenomenological problematic, itself due to the influence of Sartre, whose writings then constituted Fanon's theoretical horizon. At this stage, a deeper analysis of Fanon's problematic in the light of phenomenology would have been undoubtedly appropriate, all the more so since, in the works which followed *PNMB*, Fanon used the notion of alienation, no longer as a descriptive tool, but as a critical one, which enabled him to widen its meaning and so to extend it to the whole of colonial reality. Fanon intended his work to be a general critique of the colonial situation, and this contradicts Zahar's formal distinction between English and French colonialism inasmuch as Fanon explicitly refers to the African revolution, and it is well known that Africa was colonised by more than one imperialist power, including Britain and France.

Lastly, the third reality covered by the notion of alienation is related to the global problematic of Fanon's work, namely to his work taken as a whole, in which the notion operates both as a descriptive category and as a theoretical concept. That this notion is the key to Fanon's thought is certainly true, but one must add that it plays such a role through what it says as well as through what it does not say. For, at this third level, the notion of alienation is not at all taken in the same sense as previously, but it becomes the one element which gives a structure to a theoretical problematic and to an ideology. It is impossible fully to account for this notion by means of an internal study, because unless alienation is considered from the outside, it will inevitably refer back to itself and to the architecture of which it constitutes the most solid link. Zahar's reading remains internal to this problematic, and this is what prevents her from noticing its contradictions, especially when she articulates Fanon's notion of alienation on the identical notion which can be found in Marx's early writings, the 1844 *Manuscripts* and *The German Ideology* in the first place.

For Marx, alienation is closely dependent on the emergence of the capitalist mode of production. Alienation is, therefore, a consequence of the social and technical division of labour and is part of a real process - that of the conditions in which individuals live and work. Hence the relationship between alienation on the one hand, and the main contradiction between productive forces, means of production and relations of production on the other. By alienation, Marx designates something entirely different from the Hegelian philosophical category, even in such works as *The German Ideology*, which are not quite free from the influence of Hegel's philosophy. This means that Marx never endows alienation with a scientific status, that he never uses it as a concept. Besides, in *The German Ideology*, he already takes care to warn us that he uses the term 'alienation' for a specific purpose, viz. in order to make his remarks intelligible to philosophy. Knowing the connotations of this philosophical expression when Marx deals with it, we should display great caution when we discuss it in connection with the author of *Das Kapital*.

1.4. The Need for a Synthesis and its Limitations

At this stage, we can provisionally conclude that, with Fanon, the notion of alienation tends to be a synthesis between that same notion as it was understood by Hegel, on the one hand, and by Marx, on the other. But such a synthesis is not for Fanon a mere juxtaposition or addition, it is also a further elaboration of the Hegelian and Marxist interpretations.

In relation to Hegel, the further elaboration consists in taking account of mental disorders, frustrations and various complexes brought about by alienation, and this on a double level, that of cultural alienation and that of psychical alienation. It is worth noting that Fanon achieves this further elaboration of Hegel precisely at the point where he notes the lack of a particular element in the Hegelian dialectic. In other words, Fanon tries to provide a methodological justification for the absence of the moment of recognition in the White master - Black slave relationship. The question, which arose for him, was to explain how such an absence was possible other than through the medium of mental alienation.

In relation to Marx, the further elaboration is achieved by the awareness that colonial society, Fanon claims, does not encourage the birth of a proletariat and, consequently, that of a proletarian class consciousness. The very structure of colonial society, from the economic point of view, objectively prevents, according to Fanon, the birth of a proletariat. Fanon thus attributes the revolutionary role of this non-existent proletariat to what he calls, after Marx, the lumpenproletariat (what equates to today's 'underclass') and to the peasantry, the latter being the most numerous class in colonial society.

What Fanon was trying to achieve was the re-introduction of the dynamic of the class struggle into a process of war of national liberation. We believe that, in this respect, Fanon was confronted by two main problems and that his work tried to resolve them by resorting to two processes of transposition. The first problem was: how to widen a scientific practice and theory (psychiatry) and extend it to encompass the dimensions of social reality? The second problem was: how, in the absence of the proletariat in colonial society, to re-introduce the revolutionary dynamic of the class struggle within the context of national liberation? It is this double problem, which determines the Fanonian problematic, and it is through it that Fanon's work must be critically examined.

In the light of all that has been said so far, it appears that in the work of Fanon, the notion of alienation has enabled him to fill what had been hitherto a theoretical void, viz. the way in which the process of colonisation determines certain types of social and economic relations. However, Fanon's work raises a number of issues, which it is important to tackle, if only in order to determine the specific nature of Fanon's thought beyond the historical conditions which motivated and determined it. This should enable us to understand what has been called 'Fanonism', an ideology which is no longer solely confined to Fanon's writings, but whose relevance should be examined in relation to a global political assessment embodied in concrete political practices, such as those of the FLN in Algeria.

2. The Economic, Racial and Political Aspects of Alienation

The Marxist analysis of alienation constitutes the sub-structure of the entire theoretical and practical work of Marx, Engels and their disciples. For the indictment of a socio-economic system presupposes a global analysis of this inherent evil of the capitalist system, alienation. And the Marxist revolution, which is a continuous revolution, would have been impossible and would have lacked its foundation without the analysis of alienation. The revelation of the evil - the workers' alienation through the owners' violence - must lead to a dialectical therapeutic - the fight against the evil by the violence of the have-nots (revolutionary practice: Paris Commune, October Revolution, etc.).

Paraphrasing Lenin, we can say that the revolutionary practice of human liberation presupposes the revolutionary theory of human alienation. This applies to Fanon's evolution, both theoretical and practical. In his innermost being, Fanon experienced a double alienation - the alienation of racial minorities and the alienation of colonised nations. Like Marx before him, he evolved his theory on the basis of an observable fact, a fact which moreover he personally experienced and which guided the whole of his life. What does it consist of? It is the fact of being different. Fanon notes that, as a black person, he is different from others in the French society where he lives, or at any rate, that he is made to feel that difference.

> 'Look, a nigger!' It was an outer stimulus that startled me into awareness. I attempted a smile.

> 'Look, a nigger!' It was true. I felt amused. 'Look, a nigger!' Gradually, the circle was closing tighter. (Fanon 1952: 100)

This lived experience of the black person applies to all those whom Sartre calls 'the natives' or 'the damned of the earth', by contrast with men. For Fanon, action, supported by a clear theoretical vision, had its own further consistency and, in a dialectical way, it constantly enriched theory.

Fanon was lucid. He was suspicious of hasty judgments and of enthusiasm. In this respect, he wrote in his first work:

> This book should have been written three years ago... But at that time, the truth had a burning effect on us. Today, it can be told without passion. This kind of truth does

*not need to be thrown into people's faces. It is not intended to generate enthusiasm. We
mistrust enthusiasm... which represents contempt for man.*

And he went on to say:

*We would like to heat up man's carcass and then vanish. Maybe we shall obtain the
following result: man keeping the fire by self-combustion. (Fanon 1952: 26-7)*

Thus, equipped with a theory, which he kept enriching until 1961, Fanon
attempted, by resorting to a specific activity, to confront alienation within the
framework of the Algerian people's struggle for independence, and it was that
struggle which enabled him and his comrades to overcome all its aspects. Finally,
in answer to some of Fanon's critics, we can say that if he analysed all the aspects
of alienation, it was, however, to the economic aspect that he paid particular
attention, because it is the one which conditions all the others.

2.1. Economic Aspect of Alienation

It has been claimed, repeatedly, that Fanon's political thought was influenced by
Sartre's writings exclusively. Such an influence undoubtedly exists, and Fanon
himself would not deny it, having lived for some time in Sartre's wake and having
been one of those who best understood *Being and Nothingness*. Fanon kept his
admiration for Sartre all his life, as can be seen, among other things, from what he
told Claude Lanzmann shortly before he died: 'I would pay twenty thousand francs
a day to be able to talk with Sartre from morning till night for about a
fortnight'(Beauvoir 1963: 619).

However, although it is true that every individual, in the course of his ideological
growth, embraces at a given moment a particular ideology, it is even truer that the
same individual, if he is to go beyond the stage of childhood, must get out of the
cocoon within which he was shut, even if such a process takes place within the
framework of the very ideology he is discarding. Fanon was thus able to transcend
the Sartrian heritage. Had he not done so, he would never have joined the Algerian
maquis[3] and would never have written *Les Damnés de la Terre* (The Wretched of
the Earth).

The same applies to psychoanalysis, which had a very great impact on Fanon in
view of his medical career. Too many readers 'jump the gun', as it were, and fall into
'psychoanalysm' simply on the strength of a statement by Fanon in *PNMB*, viz. 'A
psychoanalytical interpretation of the Black Problem can alone reveal the affective
anomalies which are responsible for the complexual edifice' (Fanon 1952: 27-8). To
reduce Fanon to such a statement is to transform him into a follower of Wilhelm
Reich or Jacques Lacan.

Fanon was related to Marxism. Like the author of the *Manuscripts*, he made a
ruthless analysis of alienation, taking economic data as his basis. This analysis
represents a synthesis, which includes the psychoanalytical and sociological

notions he borrowed from Marxism. The starting point of this synthesis is an examination of the economic conjuncture. Alienation is, in the first place, economic, and all other determinations bring us back to a state of conflict, which is of an economic nature. The thesis according to which Fanon hardly mentioned this economic derivation is unfounded, because the alienation of a human being in relation to all his potentialities, especially the psychical ones, pre-supposes a fracture in the economic field to which this human being belongs. Every form of alienation is the concentrated expression of the primary alienation, i.e. of the economic alienation. When Zahar writes that 'Fanon is mainly concerned with the analysis of psychical alienation', she adds immediately afterwards that 'All colonised peoples are subject to the economic conditions of alienation, which he (Fanon) regards as the constitutive elements of the psychological phenomena of alienation' (Zahar 1970: 29). Fanon did not need to repeat what Marx had done a hundred years before him when he put forward a critique of political economy. Marxist theoretical work was his heritage, and his own field of investigation had been made possible thanks to this heritage.

Economic alienation, as it was brought about by capitalism in the nineteenth century, is the cause of two kinds of alienation: the first, the presence of racial minorities, which are economically weak and exploited, in Western societies or on the periphery of these societies, is analysed in *PNMB*; the second, the political alienation of the countries which are said to belong to the Third World, is described in *The Wretched of the Earth*. It is, therefore, correct to speak of Fanon's Marxist heritage and to endorse the following statement made by David Caute:

> *Just as... Marx roots alienation firmly in the division of labour and in class struggle, Fanon locates it equally firmly in the imperialist division of the world into poor countries and rich, exploiters and exploited, rulers and ruled. (Caute 1970: 34)*

In this perspective of global analysis, Fanon clearly posits the problem of these economically weak minorities and the numerous forms of conditioning to which they are subjected. He shows that the presence of these minorities in the 'Babylons of the North' is due to colonisation, which is itself the consequence of the development of capitalism. One of the consequences of colonialism was the destruction of the structures which prevailed in colonial societies before their enslavement. The intrusion of colonialism, which was global in its effects, and violent in its manifestations, had, as a result, the placing of African, Asiatic and Latin-American countries into the orbit of the Western capitalist system. This is what conditions the existing status quo, since nothing positive was installed to replace what had been destroyed. Conrad Schuler is right when he points out that:

> *The decaying traditional structures were not replaced. The colonised countries became hinterlands which were duly exploited by capital invested from abroad and run according to the needs of the capitalist parent-states. (Schuler 1968: 100)*

In those enslaved countries, what happened to the human beings, to the natives? They were made to submit to 'the course of history' by force. Thus an economy of subsistence made way for an economy based on the slave trade, and this, in connection with other imposed demands, laid the basis for the formation of a lumpenproletariat:

The massive expropriation of peasants from their lands, which were transformed into plantations, and the emergence of competition between the goods produced by local artisans and manufactured goods, created the conditions for the emergence of huge reserves of ruined manpower. (Bettelheim 1970: 28)

The emergence of this ruined manpower, lacking any kind of vocational training, and left on the market at the mercy of modern slave-traders, is a very important phenomenon, which extends beyond the purely economic field and becomes part of an extremely dramatic sociological context: the existence of minorities originating from under-developed countries who have come to sell themselves in the Northern mother-countries.

2.2. Racial Aspect of Alienation

The racial aspect of alienation is directly conditioned by the economic aspect. The existence, on the periphery of capitalist countries, of countries which are economically and politically dominated, and thus robbed of their wealth, has, among its many consequences, the result of displacing manpower from these countries to the industrial centres of the colonising nations. The latter develop very fast, and so require an ever-increasing skilled manpower as well as a sub-proletariat. Thus, a qualitative change occurs in the vocational training of the workers who belong to the colonising countries, as they refuse to perform 'menial' or 'dirty' tasks.

Against such an economic background, racism rears its head. The majority of sub-proletarians come from countries with a so-called coloured population. Even when such populations happen to be white, such as the Arabs, the Turks, the Irish or the Porto-Ricans, it is enough for them to be 'dark'. This racial aspect has become so acute that one tends to forget the economic factor that has caused it. When European workers clash with foreign workers, the reason is not to be sought in some kind of Kiplingese pattern - 'East is East and West is West, and never the twain shall meet' - but rather in the economic factors which are the real cause of racial tension. For example, it is primarily for economic reasons that London dockers objected to the presence of Indians in 'White Britain' and supported Enoch Powell, whose whole policy was based on hostility towards immigrants, or that a section of the working-class population in some of the Parisian suburbs is against North African immigration. The racial conflict is always secondary. It affects not only working-class immigrants, but also intellectuals and students, who are even more keenly aware of racist hatred against them because they were able to interiorise more quickly the differences which set them apart from the indigenous population.

2.3. Political Aspect of Alienation

The two phenomena, which have been described above, involve a political approach as an inevitable corollary. This was always Fanon's perspective, and his political analysis includes, as well as widens, economic and social considerations with their racial determinants.

Every form of political domination brings about a state of alienation, and this also applies to colonialism and to the refusal to grant racial minorities their political, cultural or religious rights, in other words, their autonomy. Both the economic and the political forms of domination are the result of colonialism, and in this respect, Fanon's theses on the alienation-colonialism dialectic are valid, not only for the colonised countries in Africa, Asia and Latin America, but also for such political minorities as the Basques in Spain, the Quebecois in Canada, the Irish in the UK, or the Blacks in the USA. The situation faced by these minorities is the same as that of the West Indians, with minor differences of course, in that they are all the victims of a domination founded on violence. The violence may be subtle (as in Quebec) or overt (as in Martinique), but its purpose is to deny a whole people what constitutes its originality. In all cases, there occurs economic subjugation, and above all, cultural alienation, which is embodied in the gradual disappearance of what represents the soul, the language, of the people concerned.

In this respect, the example of Quebec is particularly instructive. Are not the inhabitants white? What is more, do they not originally come from France, the main colonising nation together with Britain? And yet, the Quebecois, those 'white Negroes of America', to quote one of their members, are subjected to a form of colonialism on the part of their English-speaking countrymen, and they have to wage a desperate battle to ensure that their children will not be compelled in future to speak English among themselves. Here is a very revealing account of Quebec, which comes from a visitor who is himself from Martinique, Fanon's native land, and which shows the most sordid aspects of alienation. It is a letter, which is given here in full, sent to a Parisian weekly under the title of *Les Aliénés* (Alienated people):

> *I come from the West Indies and last June I spent some time in Quebec. I came to the realisation that, although French-speaking Canadians live in a province which is rich, huge and well developed, whereas the territories of the West Indians are small, poor and under-developed, both peoples share common psychological characteristics which are caused by a colonial situation. Here are two examples of what I would call an alienated psychological behaviour.*

> *Several Quebecois spoke to me about their fears concerning the possibility of independence for their province, arguing that Quebec (which is three times the size of France) was too small and that it needed the technology, the capital and the experience of the English-speaking Canadians and the Americans. Other Quebecois seemed to me to display a clear inferiority complex in relation to the English-speaking population, something that would shock quite a few ' metropolitan' sensibilities. They told me, just as did a number of English Canadians, that the latter were by nature more*

gifted for leading positions, that they somehow possessed qualities of leadership, that they were endowed with more initiative, a very rare quality among French-speaking Canadians. As it happens, I heard exactly the same type of arguments on the part of West Indians with regard to the Whites.

These two examples show to what an extent a colonialist system can bring about complexes of impotence and inferiority among a people, even if it is white. (Désiré 1970: 315).

This economic and political situation is typical because it enables us to understand the mechanics of alienation in their totality. A situation, which is initially economic, then political, acquires a psychological dimension at the level of individuals and gives human beings an inferiority complex, bordering on a guilt complex, because they were born into a particular race or a particular country.

History shows that a minority position is not due to racial considerations. Initially, the situation which gives rise to alienation has its source in economic and political components. The alienation of a coloured people has its roots in the interiorisation of an inferiority, which is the product of economy and history. If racial considerations were alone operative, racists would have to find reasons to account for the fact that some European nations found themselves in classic colonial situations, involving the violence of the colonisers, the gradual disappearance of the original values of the colonised, especially cultural values, and the expatriation of manpower. The case of Quebec has been mentioned, with all the violence that it involves: a similar study could be made of the situation in the Basque country and in Northern Ireland.

Fanon was always aware of the fundamental nature of economic considerations, and this can be seen throughout the whole of his work. He wrote in *PNMB* that:

If an inferiority complex occurred, it was as a result of a double process

- first, economic

- then, through the internalisation, or better still the epidermisation of this inferiority. (Fanon 1952: 28)

And, in *The Wretched of the Earth*, Fanon showed that in the course of revolutionary action aimed at disalienating a people, it was necessary to destroy by violence the economic and political structures, which are, to repeat, the basis of everything.

3. The 'Self-Fulfilling Prophecy'

In the process which leads to alienation, the important stage is reached when the individual agrees to become part of established patterns, the latter being centred on the divisions among individuals, classes, countries, nations and races, on the one hand, and the domination of one of these over the others, on the other hand. It is obvious that, at first, such patterns are not readily accepted by the colonised. But domination and the destruction of values lead the oppressed to such a state of despair and debasement that they finally acknowledge 'the strength' of their victors, who have been striving with all their might to achieve such a result.

This stage of submission can only be attained through the violence of the stronger, a mechanical violence which destroys the resilience of the individual whom it breaks, transforms into an object, and delivers to his master in a state of humility and resignation. This violence is not only that of armed force, but also and above all that of ideas, religious ideas conveyed by missionaries, and cultural ideas conveyed by the schools, not forgetting those more modern ones, which are the most pernicious and which are conveyed by the mass media, TV and the cinema in particular.

Such an ideological apparatus often leads those who are dominated to accept their fate. It is impossible at this stage not to recall the words of Aimé Césaire, whom Fanon quotes at the beginning of *PNMB*:

> *I speak about millions of men into whom there have subtly been instilled feelings of fear, inferiority complexes, trembling, abasement, despair and servility. (Fanon 1952: 25)*

Inferiority is suggested to these millions of men and women and no sooner do they accept it than they settle down into a state of the deepest alienation. To this process, which consists in the acceptance by an individual of stereotypes which distort him, we give the name of 'self-fulfilling prophecy', an expression first used by R. K. Merton in his *Social Theory and Social Structure*, and which he defines as follows:

> *a false definition of the situation evoking a new behaviour which makes the original-ly false conception come true. (Merton 1957: 423)*

In *PNMB*, Fanon describes the process of self-enthronement, which leads the colonised, or at any rate some of them, to accept racist prototypes and even, in some cases, to wear the masks of the dominators. The self-enthronement of these false clichés takes such forms that some members of the colonised nation reach the point when they hate and curse themselves for not having been born among the elect. Zahar equates this attitude to:

> *... a psycho-social process, which one must assess as one of the many possible reactions of an out-group (the colonised) to the prejudices of an in-group (the colonialists). (Zahar 1970: 36)*

In the Babylons of the North, the out-group is made up of the racial minorities who have come to sell their labour power. In the colonised countries, the out-group constitutes the overwhelming majority of the population. In this connection, Gustav Jahoda writes that:

> There does not appear to have been adequate recognition of the paradoxical fact that the mentality of many Africans, in their own country, was in some ways characteristic of minority groups elsewhere. (Jahoda 1961: 115)

This means that the members of the out-group react according to the wishes of those who belong to the in-group, and are alienated to such an extent that they do more than deny themselves, they forget themselves in a state of stupidity.

There are some forms of behaviour on the part of colonised peoples which enable us to understand the full force of the 'self-fulfilling prophecy', for example, the reactions of cinema audiences, especially children, when they watch films in which the Whites and the Blacks fight each other. When in some African regions, little Black children go and see a film about Tarzan and the Black 'savages and cannibals', they forget the colour of their skin and side wholeheartedly with the fair White hero who rules over the jungle and who embodies right versus wrong, just as John Wayne does in those westerns where he faces the 'Indian savages'. These little 'niggers' in African cinemas have the same reactions as those of the poor Whites in the Deep South in the USA.

This is not surprising, and in his examination of the attitude of little Ghanaian children towards the school textbooks written exclusively by Europeans, Jahoda remarks that:

> Schoolchildren were thus led to internalize a set of values that were in some crucial respects at variance with those to which they were exposed in their home environment; values which they heard were characteristic of Europeans, and had made them as strong, wise and powerful as they were. At the same time the children could not help being aware that these virtues were not practised by their own families and neighbours. This, naturally, was merely an indirect way of suggesting inferiority. (Jahoda 1961: 122-3)

In another passage, he looks at the reaction of African cinema audiences when they watch films dealing with Africans:

> They (the African spectators) did not identify with the Africans on the screen, but adopted to them something of the attitude European audiences would adopt; in other words, they were apt to judge fellow-Africans by white standards of 'civilized' behaviour. (Jahoda 1961: 105)

These sessions of 'collective catharsis', to use one of Fanon's expressions, lead the colonised straight to the road of complete denial of oneself and of one's culture, a road which was also taken by a number of alienated Algerians who had been persuaded by the French coloniser that their ancestors were the Gauls.

4. The Delusion of Assimilation

As we have seen, and as Marx had already pointed out in his 1844 *Manuscripts*, whose sub-title was *Political Economy and Philosophy*, alienation is a global phenomenon, whose essence is above all economic. The reification of man in modern societies, whether European or not, is much worse than anything which had hitherto been attempted, and a reification of such magnitude was made possible only thanks to the greater refinement and intensification of violence. It is for this reason that alienation reveals its most monstrous aspects only in the countries which were or still are colonised, for the means of violence which were used there are unique in the annals of history, if one excepts the extermination of the Indians in America. The aim of such violence is to enslave man with the aim of exploiting him better. Already in 1932, Wilhelm Reich could note that:

> One does not need intelligence, but only a little moral courage in order to admit that capitalist powers do not bring the colonial peoples Christian faith, clothes, ethics, for the sake of civilisation, but rather that they seek to instil into every colonised individual the mentality of the European coolie, by soaking him in alcohol in order to weaken his body and his will, so that he can be exploited more easily. (Reich 1932: 134)

In order to perpetuate their exploitation, the capitalists were compelled to seek ways and means of dealing with the liberation movements, which began to shake the structure of colonial societies shortly after the end of the World War II. It is within this perspective that one must try to assess the issue of assimilation, for this phenomenon can be studied only by articulating it around two contradictory poles - alienation and liberation. To the global phenomenon of alienation, one must oppose its dialectical negation, liberation. Why liberation? Because it, too, is a global notion, which spreads to the whole of a human being and of society.

According to Fanon, any solution short of total liberation is nothing but a delusion and a mystification. One such mystification occurred when the colonial powers offered their subject peoples assimilation through direct administration. The policy of assimilation is unsatisfactory, because assimilation is a partial phenomenon, whereas, Fanon claims, only a global phenomenon, i.e. liberation through violence, if necessary, can destroy the alienation, which was imposed by force of arms. Moreover, both time and concrete experience helped to demystify the notion of assimilation and to show that it had been thought up exclusively as a bulwark against the demand for independence on the part of colonised peoples and of national minorities in Western countries. Any policy of assimilation is vitiated from the start because of its nature and its objectives, for any recognition of the other must necessarily be preceded by the recognition of the right to be different:

> The only way of breaking this infernal cycle which brings me back to myself is to restore to the other, through mediation and recognition, his human reality, which is different from natural reality. (Fanon 1952: 196)

Assimilation leads to the degradation of human beings because recognition does not take place. The pretence of recognition, which it involves, is false and inauthentic. Any recognition which is imposed, i.e. which is operated by the person, who has initially deprived the individual of his/her freedom by force, is a mystification. It is up to the individual to recognise him/herself as alienated, to posit him/herself as someone who is different from the oppressor, and then, in the same activity, to wage the struggle for disalienation. The loss of personality was not the result of a decree: neither can this be the case for its opposite. Liberation involves battles, defeats and victories, but Fanon considers that assimilation, in an oppressing and alienating context, cannot be anything but an operation which aims at degrading the movement by which man and the people seek to regain their own original values.

However, the policy of assimilation has met with some success, both on the level of individuals and on the level of some colonised nations, and this has resulted in a worsening of alienation. Zahar writes in this respect that:

> It is by officially presenting assimilation as an ideal state, whilst it was at the same time preventing its implementation in a brutal manner, that French colonialism has given rise to specific phenomena of alienation and frustration. (Zahar 1970: 18)

Fanon had foreseen the dangers implied in the policy of assimilation. In the chapter of *PNMB* which is entitled 'The Negro and Hegel', he observed that the policy of the master towards the slave, of the White man towards the Negro, is identical to the policy of assimilation and paternalism of the coloniser towards the colonised. The slave has to wage a fight to the death against his master in order to liberate himself. He must posit himself as someone who is different from his master. Fanon argues that with regard to the colonised, especially the Negro, the illusion of assimilation, the frustration of such a mirage, the worsening of alienation, all contribute to the fact that in the dialectic of the Negro (the oppressed) and the White man (the oppressor), the Negroes, or at any rate some categories of Negroes (especially among the intellectuals), do not want to posit themselves as the antithesis of the Whites, but rather prefer to become assimilated to them.

This attempt at identification on the part of the slave is just what the master was after when he offered assimilation. Moreover, the desire for assimilation is particularly strong among the bourgeois classes and among many intellectuals in the colonised countries. Fanon gives the example of the bourgeois and semi-bourgeois groups in the West Indies who try to ape the speech of Parisian salons.

For Fanon, the consequences of such attitudes are dramatic. The fact that one fine day the White master chose to recognise his Negro slave has meant that, for the many generations that followed, real freedom was postponed, for such 'freedom' as was granted was nothing but an illusion, a catch, a mystification which placed the oppressed in a state of alienation that was worse than material dependence.

5. Permanence of Violence

We have seen that alienation (the loss of one's original values) grew worse as a result of the development of capitalism and colonialism. The point was made by Marx when he wrote in *Das Kapital*:

> *In modern agriculture, as in urban industry, the increase in the productivity and the mobility of labour is purchased at the cost of laying waste and debilitating labour-power itself. Moreover, all progress in capitalist agriculture is a progress in the art, not only of robbing the worker, but of robbing the soil... Capitalist production, therefore, only develops the techniques and the degree of combination of the social process of production by simultaneously undermining the original sources of all wealth - the soil and the worker. (Marx 1976: 638)*

Faithful to its original essence - the constant increase of capital - capitalism sought to extend the total alienation of Western man to millions of people living under other skies, and this thanks to its colonial policies. How right Lenin was to call imperialism 'the highest stage of capitalism'! With colonialism, the capitalist system has created an exceptionally refined form of alienation and has imposed it, not just on individuals (the workers), not just on a class (the proletariat), but on whole nations, on whole continents, always with the aim of benefiting those who in the West had already succeeded in de-humanising man. And it is in the colonies more than anywhere else that violence has been used in order to enslave those who are nicknamed, not 'peoples' (much too refined a term), but tribes, or as Sartre calls them in his preface to *The Wretched of the Earth*, 'the natives'. The combination of alienation and violence has led to such disastrous results as cultural alienation or a-culturation, economic alienation or exploitation, religious alienation or evangelisation, all of which have their climax in political alienation or colonialism.

Slavery was the most acute form of alienation, but after its official abolition, the process continued unabated, and in its thirst for power, the capitalist system went so far as to commit or to encourage genocide on a massive scale, e.g. the destruction of the American continent's earliest inhabitants (the Indians), or the forcible uprooting of millions of Africans who were driven away from their homelands in order to provide cheap labour in the West. In its attempt to create a new lumpenproletariat, the system has compelled those who are hypocritically called 'immigrant workers', in fact the slaves of modern times, to tear themselves away from the sun and the land they know in order to go and live in the drab surroundings of the Northern mother-countries: Porto-Ricans in New York, Mexicans in Los Angeles, Pakistanis and Indians in London, Arabs and Blacks in Paris, Irish in London or Liverpool, Turks in Hamburg. In the past, people referred to American ghettos such as Harlem or Watts; today we must speak of such slums as Brixton, Toxteth, Aubervilliers, Les Minguettes. It is in the widening of the problematic of alienation that one finds the clearest convergence between Fanon and Marx.

Conclusion

The aim of this chapter was not to present something entirely new about a topic which is as wide, as old and as controversial as alienation. What has rather been attempted here is an understanding of the mechanics of alienation by considering those writers who have devoted particular attention to the subject, Fanon and Marx in the first place. These two thinkers made an analysis of the theory of alienation, not for purely speculative reasons, but in order to use it as a basis for their political practice. Herb Gintis wrote in *Les Temps Modernes* that 'a political movement is viable only to the extent that it considers poverty, racism, war, women's oppression, economic destruction, etc. as aspects of the consequences of alienation' (Gintis 1971: 1413). Both Marx and Fanon began with theoretical research aimed at understanding reality, the better to be able to issue a rousing call for changing it. One can assert that every revolutionary struggle represents the response of the alienated to the alienation of their conditions of existence; hence the need to discuss alienation as an element of pollution of one's environment.

Such a discussion also helps to see the link between alienation and violence. Alienation represents permanent violence against man/woman within the framework of one's labour, of one's family, of one's relations with one's fellow-human beings, and this violence is ever on the increase. The case of the worker under global capitalism is particularly significant. He/she tends to lose their status as a human being in order to become a mere object in the context of a process of production, exchange and profit. The institutions of capitalism work in such a way that they reduce all aspects of social life, equality, justice, labour, technology, commodities, the community, and the environment, to mere instruments for the maximum increase of production and profits. Marx expressed the same idea when he pointed out that the only values recognised by the system were efficiency, growth, progression and profit. Such a system de-humanises man/woman, it changes the individual into an object by depriving him/her of initiative, thought and the values of life, whilst offering her/him instead the values selected by the mass media through the medium of advertising. Thus, institutionalised violence aimed at creating alienation has become our daily diet and is changing us into machines that are just good enough to consume the signs, which are imposed on them.

Man/woman can destroy the combined forms of violence which are used against him/her only by resorting himself/herself to other forms of violence in order to recover her/his unity. If alienation is still with us today, it is because mankind has yet to wage the last fight which leads to the end of dependence through the demise of the oppressors; the alternative model - letting the oppressor keep the initiative - is bound to reinforce the status quo. The countries, which were de-colonised by decree from their oppressors, are like the Roman freedmen who continued to be under the sway of their former masters. Once these countries reject paternalism and charity, they will learn from their experience of struggle that it is necessary to fight to the death in order to win the very negation of alienation - freedom.

Fanon's insistence on alienation and violence was not only to get rid of colonialism but also to create a new humanity and Algeria was to become the new nation to personify this 'purified' human being. However, one ought not to go as far as suggesting that the Fanonian theory of violence accounts for the horrific violence in today's Algeria. Is the violence we are witnessing in Algeria since the 1990s a hangover from a *pre*-Fanonian moment in Algerian history? We may want to look for an answer to this question in pre-1945 (especially the 1930s) Algeria.

Notes

1   Fanon' s *Peau noire, masques blancs* is henceforth referred to in this chapter as *P.NMB.*

2   All translations are mine - NK, unless otherwise specified.

3   By *maquis*, we designate the Algerian underground resistance.

8 The 'New Man' at the Dawn of the Twenty-first Century: Challenges and Shifts in Algerian Identity

Margaret A. Majumdar

Introduction

The question of Algerian national identity is an important issue not just for the understanding of contemporary Algerian society and politics, but also for the role which it plays as an important element in the current process of socio-economic change, political reconfiguration and ideological repositioning. The aim of this chapter is to analyse this issue, highlighting some of the contradictions, shifts and realignments that are characteristic of the way in which it has been perceived historically, before assessing the impact of present-day social processes upon its current evolution.

1. The Building of Nationhood: National Unity and Diversity

While in many ways the Algerian war of independence could be seen as a prime example of a liberation struggle inspired by anti-colonialist nationalism, the question of Algerian national identity has been problematical from the outset and remains a live issue in the present day. A number of different, and often contradictory, paradigms have been proposed, some of which have held sway at various points of time in the official discourse of the state. However, there has never been a national consensus on the identity question and all of the models proposed have met with serious challenges and dissent.

1954 marked the defining moment when at least partially and temporarily the nationalist movement came together under the FLN in what passed for a united front against the colonial enemy. The reality hitherto had been a nationalist movement split into a number of very different, usually antagonistic currents, ranging from the positions adopted by the Algerian Communist Party, the powerful nationalist movement known successively as the ENA, PPA and MNA, associated with the leadership of Messali Hadj, who was projected as the legitimate successor of the Emir Abd El-Qadir, leader of the initial resistance against the French in the nineteenth century, plus various reformist groups working for autonomy rather than full independence, and the important religious movement known as the *Oulemas*.

The FLN was essentially the creation of a group of young militants, who seized the moment to impose their leadership on these very disparate elements and to force the pace to an armed insurrection on All Saints Day, 1 November 1954. However, although it adopted the name of the National Liberation *Front*, in reality it was never conceived as a 'front' in the strict political sense. Rather than acting as an alliance of heterogeneous components, bringing together different groups, classes and parties, the FLN's strategy was to bring together all sectors of Algerian society, in a front of individuals rather than of parties, under the ideological banner of the unified nation, but through the organisational form of a *single party* (Stora 1992: 148).

The unity of the FLN was represented as the mirror image of the unity of the nation, in opposition to the previous parties and movements, which only served to accentuate and institutionalise divisions within that nation.[1] The pluralism of pre-1954 parties was seen, perhaps not unreasonably, as a factor of weakness in the anti-French struggle. The resemblance to the political ideas of De Gaulle is striking, particularly as expressed in his key speech at Bayeux in 1946, and would merit further exploration. There was a key difference, in that the nation was incarnated in the single party, rather than in the strong national leader, although this was to come later. Even more importantly, the Algerian party-nation was of course conceived as a counter-state, harnessing the forces of the nation to confront the colonial state. The hegemony of the FLN was eventually acknowledged by the French government, which recognised its monopoly to represent the Algerian people in the Melun talks of 1960 and then the Evian negotiations, which began in 1961 and led to the Independence Agreement of 1962.

Previous nationalist movements, particularly the Etoile Nord Africaine and the PPA of Messali Hadj, were consigned to oblivion. However, in spite of this united front, tensions and conflicts were never far from the surface and right through the War of Independence, internal scores were being settled, often through violent means and assassination, particularly, but not only, amongst the expatriate Algerians in mainland France.

We have so far concentrated on the nationalist movement, as constituted by those actively engaged in political and military organisations. However, if we look at the population at large, we see an even more complex and chequered picture. In its ethnic origins, it shows the traces of a constant stream of invaders and settlers, going right back to Antiquity - Phoenicians, Greeks, Romans, Jews and Arabs from the East and then Jews and Moors arriving from Spain after the expulsion at the end of the end of the fifteenth century. These were followed by Turks and then of course the French and other European settlers from the Mediterranean basin, just to cite the major groups. Moreover, all of these were grafted on to an indigenous population, known collectively as Berbers, but themselves divided into very disparate groups, claiming different origins and whose indigenous character is probably merely relative, since they in their turn almost certainly originated elsewhere, though, like the Celts, to whom some claim they are related, there is not agreement as to where this might be.

There has been much debate over the significance of this ethnic diversity for any modern understanding of Algerian national identity. After all, many modern nations, with populations of similarly diverse ethnic origins, have managed to constitute their nationhood, without insoluble difficulties, and ethnic diversity as such cannot be factored as an a priori obstacle to national consciousness.

It is certainly true that there are nonetheless different historical narratives, upon which different groups could draw to contextualise their wider social identity in the geographical space known variously as the middle Maghrib, an administrative unit of the Ottoman Empire, then as the three Algerian *départements* of France, though Algeria as such did not exist as an autonomous political unit until 1962. These include various mythologies of exile, as for the Jews and returned Moors from Spain. For some of the French in the 1920s and 1930s, it was the notion of 'Latin Africa', going back to the Romans, which attempted to rationalise the European presence. For Berbers, it was the myth of the legendary Berber warrior queen, La Kahina, and the even earlier champion against the Romans, Jugurtha. For Arabs, it was the legitimising power of the history of Islam. And for both the Arabs and the Berbers, the heroic figure of Abd El-Qadir, who, although a tribal chief whose authority never extended throughout the whole territory, can nonetheless be considered a proto-nationalist figurehead. Even in diversity, these myths and narratives have overlapped to a certain extent.

Essentially, the French found a splintered tribal society when they invaded in 1830. However, unlike the Turks who had imposed a top layer of administration to ensure the collection of taxes and other dues but had been largely happy to leave the tribal infrastructure in place, they soon began the process, which was to continue throughout their rule, of economic, social and cultural dislocation. Without going into any great detail here, this process can be broadly and briefly summarised in terms of three main aspects.

Firstly, the forcible expropriation of land in favour of European settlers, through a variety of violent and pseudo-legalistic means, led to the destruction of what had been a largely self-sufficient agricultural economy. This in turn led to the physical dislocation of tribal groups and individuals and the ultimate shift of large numbers of the rural population to towns and cities and eventually to mainland France itself.

A second significant factor was the twofold policy of social and cultural assimilation for a small minority through education in the French system and the French language on the one hand, and the marginalisation of the vast majority, by dint of their religion and languages, on the other.

The third factor related to the political sphere, through the imposition of a political ideology, based on the attractive notions of Enlightenment universalism and Republican ideals - the universal rights of man, liberty, equality and fraternity, at the same time as the real exclusion of the major part of the population from citizenship and political rights.

All of these elements combined to create further fractures and fault-lines which fashioned the particular configuration in which Algerian nationhood was to be constructed. Thus, going back to 1954 and the beginnings of the armed insurrection that was to lead to independence, we find that, apart from questions of military strategy, the FLN were faced with the key political problem of unifying a still disparate and fragmented body of people behind the banner of independence for Algeria as a separate nation.

This national identity was still fairly embryonic even at this stage, although there were a number of processes working to create the conditions for a specifically Algerian national consciousness to come into being. The dislocation of tribal society had brought people together from all sectors of the society, notably in mainland France, which was an important centre for the development of national consciousness, among immigrants who became aware of what they had in common as Algerians, what united them from a positive point of view, rather than their local and tribal differences. Just as importantly, the conditions were created for their collective self-identity through their *negative* collective definition by the French.

This embryonic nationalism had been articulated through various forms of nationalist political ideology, associated with the different strands of the pre-FLN movement. Now that the FLN had won the battle for political control of a unified movement, albeit coexisting in an uneasy and often broken truce, they needed to develop and promote a national political ideology, capable of shoring up the as yet fragile nation.

This was not going to prove an easy task. Indeed, the war was to lead to further fragmentation of the inchoate Algerian nation - the fact that a sizeable number of the Algerians, known as the Harkis, opted (more or less voluntarily according to their circumstances) to fight with the French, led to a new schism with many, up to a million with their families, fleeing the country to France at independence and others facing retribution in their homeland.

In terms of constituting a nationalist political ideology, the simple solution of a call for a return to the pre-colonial past was not available to the FLN for a number of reasons. Although French colonisation had not succeeded in wiping out all traces of pre-colonial society - far from it - the structural vestiges, the cultural traditions and historical mythologies that did still exist did not add up to a *national* heritage, given the fragmentation of Algerian society.

The solution, more or less consciously adopted, was the constitution of a nationalist political ideology based on three main elements: the French common enemy; Islam; the New Man. The Arabic language was to be added later in the post-independence period as a fourth important element.[2]

Firstly, and most importantly during the period of the war, the identification of the French common enemy proved the most powerful unifying factor for the nation.

This polarisation developed as a direct and almost inevitable consequence of colonisation.

Secondly, Islam was also to play a most important role in bringing Algerians together in this struggle. Again, this aspect developed as an almost natural product of the experience of French colonialism, given that the French state authorities had themselves defined Algerians according to their religion, in defiance of their own official ideology of secular republicanism, using Islam as the rationalisation of their inferior status. None other than Jacques Soustelle was later to recognise, in 1990, the effect of this particular contradictory stance on the specifically religious form taken by the nationalist movement.[3]

However, this should not detract from the fact that Islam was enthusiastically embraced as the mobilising factor of the Algerian national resistance, from its earliest forms in the previous century, right through the war. It certainly did constitute a major factor of cohesion, since, apart from the Pieds Noirs and the Jews, 99 per cent of the population were Muslims, including those of Berber origin. It is perhaps not surprising therefore that Islam should be consciously adopted as an integral part of Algerian nationalism, nor that it should continue to play a key role in the national ideology of the post-independence Algerian state, where it was linked with the notion of an Arab identity, in the inseparable couplet of Arab-Islamic identity. Indeed Ben Bella's first words upon his release from French custody at Tunis airport in 1962 made this orientation abundantly clear, when he proclaimed: '*Nous sommes des Arabes! Nous sommes des Arabes!! Nous sommes des Arabes!!!*' ('We are Arabs! We are Arabs!! We are Arabs!!!') (Roberts 1993: 80).

In contrast, the third element, the notion of the New Man, was even more clearly the result of a voluntarist political agenda, in which it was linked to a resolutely modernist political project, in which all references to the past were to be banished.

All of these elements were to prove extremely problematic in themselves. Moreover, the way in which they interrelated with each other was also to bring major problems in its train. Added to this, the choice of socio-economic model for the development of the newly independent country, largely based on a variant of state-directed, state-controlled socialism, was also to sit uneasily with some of the elements of the nationalist ideology. Moreover, none of these elements, either singly or collectively, bore any exclusive relation to the *Algerian* nation as such, which came to be identified with the FLN.

We shall return to the question of Algerian specificity shortly. For the moment, our main concern is the notion of the New Man, and its varying importance and content at different moments in the war and in post-independence Algeria. The next section will therefore pick out certain threads from what is a very complex, interwoven set of notions and ideological influences.

2. The New Man – His Origins in the Algerian Revolution

The concept of the New Man formed part of a deliberate strategy to found the new nation on the basis of its fundamental 'newness'. This was not about rewriting history to provide new, more appropriate myths for the emergent nation. It was rather about decreeing that history and the new nation began for Algeria on 1 November 1954, which became the founding date and myth of the national revolution.[4]

Not only did this key date provide the myth for the founding of the nation. It also provided the basis for the legitimacy of the FLN as single party and ultimately for the state which came into being at independence. In Algeria, this went even further by giving sole historical legitimacy to the original core of founders, the *'chefs historiques'* ('historical leaders'), by dint of them having been the first to launch the insurrection. Indeed, this principle has proved astonishingly resilient, even after the collapse of the FLN State as such, from the end of the 1980s and is perhaps demonstrated most strikingly in the presidential elections of 1999, when any candidate who could not lay claim to participation in this founding event was excluded from eligibility to stand.

The 'newness' of the Algerian Revolution was given theoretical backing through the notion of regeneration of the nation and the emergence of the New Man through revolutionary violence as a purifying force.[5]

Fanon was, of course, a key figure in the theorising of this idea of regeneration, which was associated with a complete break with European values, linked to an appeal to the colonised to turn their backs on Europe, which could offer nothing of use to the anticolonial struggle.[6] This was dramatically brought out by Sartre in his preface to the *Damnés de la terre* (Sartre 1961: 5-7). At the same time, Fanon warned against seeking this regeneration in an illusory return to the glories of the African past and saw the Revolution as an opportunity for the colonised to enter history and make it truly universal at last. Or, as François Maspero put it, dissociating himself from both the 'great white error' as well as the 'great black mirage' to develop a new revolutionary approach (Maspero 1970: 8).

In this of course, Fanon, while developing his own original voice, remained deeply indebted to European thinking, ranging from a revolutionary interpretation of the Hegelian master-slave dialectic to the whole development of revolutionary theory from the French revolution, through Marx, Lenin and others, as well as to the thinking of Jean-Paul Sartre, who amply reciprocates by echoing Fanon's voice in his turn (Said 1993: 237).[7]

Fanon's originality lies, at least in part, in the way in which he developed the notion of the New Man on a number of different levels.

Firstly, on the level of individuals, the overthrow of colonial domination through the violent revolutionary activity of the subjugated 'native' would overcome the alienation and dehumanisation which had made the colonised into pure body, animal or thing, described by Fanon in his essay 'The North African Syndrome', first published in *Esprit*, in February 1952, as:

> *... creatures starving for humanity who stand buttressed against the impalpable frontiers (though I know them from experience to be terribly distinct) of complete recognition. (Fanon 1970: 13)*

Or again:

> *This man whom you thingify by calling him systematically Mohammed, whom you reconstruct, or rather whom you dissolve, on the basis of an idea, an idea you know to be repulsive (you know perfectly well you rob him of something, that something for which not so long ago you were ready to give up everything, even your life) well, don't you have the impression that you are emptying him of his substance? (Fanon 1970: 24)*

Revolutionary violence would thus enable the reified colonial subjects to become *whole* men, full human beings.

Secondly, although the impact of this humanisation would be felt at the level of individuals, it would only be achieved through collective activity, as part of a national revolutionary movement. Indeed, Fanon saw the peasantry and the lumpenproletariat (mainly made up of landless peasants who had moved to the towns) as the main agency of change, in the process of bringing about the transition from the animal to the human state.

For Fanon, the process did not, however, end at the *humanisation* of the colonised through revolutionary violence and struggle and the achievement of national liberation. On the one hand, this meant seeing beyond the Algerian national revolution, to the role which this struggle was to play as the spearhead of the African Revolution as a whole. Against particularisms, he saw nationalism as a mere moment in a dialectic of universal liberation.

Along with the particular political outcomes, it also entailed going further to the emergence of a new type of human being, of significance for the progression of the species as a whole to a higher stage of being. This was not just a political project, but an anthropological, moral project, in which the aim was not just to become a Man, but a New Man, by which is meant a Better Man, in control of his own freedom and free of alienation through the harmonisation of body and soul.

> *It is a common saying that man is constantly a challenge to himself, and that were he to claim that he is so no longer he would be denying himself. It must be possible, however, to describe an initial, a basic dimension of all human problems. More precisely, it would seem that all the problems which man faces on the subject of man can be reduced to this one question: 'Have I not, because of what I have done or failed to do, contributed to an impoverishment of human reality?' The question could also be formulated in this way: 'Have I at all times demanded and brought out the man that is in me?' (Fanon 1970: 13)*

This approach posits as a basic human characteristic the tendency to measure one's achievement or humanity against the contribution one has made to the betterment of the human species.

Much of this is echoed in other thinkers and writers in the 1950s and 1960s. The ideas of the early Marx and Lukàcs, amongst others (including Nietzsche from a somewhat different tradition),[8] were taken up and developed by Sartre, for instance, who had a clear view of the progression of what he currently termed 'sub-humans' to a new type of total and fully *human* being (Sartre & Lévy 1991: 36-8). Sartre saw the history of human society as a progress towards the realisation of Man and, in the 1950s and 1960s, was a passionate advocate of Fanon's views on the redemptive power of violence, though he was later to disavow this position, claiming that he was seeing a lot of Fanon at the time, 'who was a profoundly violent man' (Sartre & Lévy 1991: 63-4).

The notion of the New Man was not, of course, a purely European phenomenon. Aimé Césaire, for instance, in many ways a father figure to his fellow Martinican, Fanon, spoke eloquently in his poetry of the 'inventions of new souls' (Said 1993: 372). But perhaps the most significant development of the notion at this time, in the context of the socialist and communist movement and prior to the Chinese Cultural Revolution of the mid-1960s, was that of Che Guevara, who extended the notion, beyond the embryonic concepts of Lenin's Cultural Revolution, to encompass all aspects, physical, social, cultural of the New Man. For Che Guevara, the creation of the New Man was just as important as the creation of a new economic and social system.

> To build communism it is necessary, simultaneous with the new material foundations, to build the new man. (Guevara 1987: 250)[9]

This entailed a fundamental break with the past:

> ... almost everything we thought and felt in that past epoch should be filed away, and that a new type of human being should be created. And if each one of us is his own architect of that new human type, then creating that new type of human being - who will be the representative of the new Cuba - will be much easier. (Guevara 1987: 125-6)[10]

> So it will be because you are Young Communists, creators of the perfect society, human beings destined to live in a new world where everything decrepit, everything old, everything that represents the society whose foundations have just been destroyed will have definitively disappeared. (Guevara 1987: 185)[11]

Guevara's notion that '... every Young Communist must be essentially human and be so human that he draws closer to humanity's best qualities, that he distils the best of what man is through work, study, through ongoing solidarity with the people and with all the peoples of the world', (Guevara 1987: 184) was also very close in many ways to Fanon's basic humanism and no doubt influenced by it.

It was a humanism, linked to a belief in the perfectibility of the human species, through constant improvement, which would lead to the formation of a new genus of humanity, linked in Guevara's case to the formation of a new social system:

Man as a wolf, the society of wolves, is being replaced by another genus that no longer has the desperate urge to rob his fellow man, since the exploitation of man by man has disappeared. (Guevara 1987: 367)[12]

But how does all this relate to the realities of the Algerian Revolution?

We would have to start by asking what was the real effect of the ideas developed by Fanon, as the man on the spot, on the national ideology promoted by the FLN. This issue has been much debated. On the one hand, there is no disputing the important role which he played in the highest leadership circles of the FLN and his subsequent status as a major hero of the Revolution, (helped no doubt by the fact that he conveniently died just before independence). At the same time, there is little real evidence that his ideas had much substantive theoretical and ideological influence on FLN policy at the time of the war, when his main input was as a publicist and ambassador for the Revolution in the wider world. There is even less evidence that his ideas carried much weight in the post-independence situation.

Nonetheless, his notion of the New Man appears on the surface to be an exception, as it is a theme which was constantly taken up throughout the revolutionary and post-independence period and even into the present day. There are two points that need to be made about this. On the one hand, the theme of the New Man takes on very special connotations in Algeria, which are quite specific to the country. On the other hand, those who refer to the New Man in Algeria at different moments of its recent history are not necessarily referring to the same thing at all.

Let us take the example of one the FLN leaders, Krim Belkacem, who, writing in the FLN newspaper, *El Moudjahid*, on the fourth anniversary of the 1954 insurrection, talks of the emergence of the New Man in terms which involved something akin to the notion of *métissage*:

Our revolution is becoming a melting-pot in which men of all walks of life and conditions, peasants, artisans, workers, intellectuals, rich or poor are undergoing a process of intermixing, which will lead to the birth of a new type of man. (El Moudjahid, 1 November 1958, quoted in Stora 1992: 162 - my translation MAM)

However, this was not a process which would lead to hybridity. On the contrary, it was more the elimination of difference, a bringing together of different elements of the nation into a single, unanimous people, in what appears to be a Rousseau-inspired vision of the nation. This was a very different message from that proposed by Fanon and could be closely related to the attempt to weld the divided nation together under the authority of the FLN, through the establishment of a single or 'mono' culture and ideology, to which all must needs subscribe.

Another variation on the theme appears in the work of several writers of fiction, in the guise of the 'First Man', though with very different content. Significantly, this is the title chosen for the posthumous autobiographical novel of Albert Camus, where it is used to describe the feelings of the boy Jacques Cormery, identifying with the pioneering coloniser embarking in 'virgin' territory, as the *premier habitant, ou le premier conquérant* (Camus 1994: 256-58). It also figures in the work of probably the most important Algerian writer to date, Kateb Yacine, though to very different effect, where the notion of the first man, as trailblazer, conquering pioneer, is explicitly rejected in favour of a concept of the land as marked by the traces of all those who have walked and worked its soil, or, as Mourad puts it in *Nedjma* (1956), *'le monde qui n'en est pas à sa première femme, à son premier homme'* ('the world which is no longer that of the first woman, or the first man') (Kateb Yacine 1981: 19-20).

3. The New Man - Stunted at Birth

Returning to the New Man and the problems entailed in his realisation in post-independence Algeria, it is probably fair to describe this New Man as stunted at birth.

One of the factors related to the on-going problematical relationship with France. Once independence had been achieved, the disappearance of the unifying effect of the common colonial enemy was to clear the ground for the re-emergence and indeed accentuation of the divisive forces splitting the Algerian nation.

At the same time, the dependence on France in many respects continued, and still does, in terms of political ideas, constitutional frameworks, general culture and language. Even the Revolution itself was commonly discussed with the French Revolution as a reference. Various phases were compared with those of the French Revolution - there was a Directory stage, for instance, followed by the comparison of Boumedienne's *coup d'état* with that of Napoleon. Even one of Fanon's titles bears the signs of this reference back to France - *'L'An Cinq de la Révolution Algérienne'* (Fanon 1959).

Partially in recognition of this fact, but more importantly, in recognition of the still fragmented reality of Algerian society, the regime which was established under Houari Boumedienne after 1965 instituted a policy of the 'nationalisation' of culture, with as one of its key elements the Arabisation of education and national life. This policy was designed to bring about a break with French colonial culture and focused on the language issue - this in a context where the use of French and its teaching in schools had actually increased significantly after the end of colonisation. It entailed the introduction of the Arabic language, which in its classical, written form was not the everyday, living language of any sector of the Algerian population.

This was to take a further step towards the 'normalisation' of Algerian society, through the attempted establishment of a homogeneous national culture, in which difference and dissidence had no part to play. The Arabisation policy also entailed the creation of a new historical myth, that of a sovereign Algerian state destroyed by the French in 1830. In stressing the existence of a continuous state of insurrection in the country since that date and up to independence, this new take on history also, paradoxically, began a process of undermining the historical legitimacy of the FLN and the newness of its actions in 1954.

Once again, this policy was rationalised in terms of the New Man. This was not the New Man as conceived by Fanon. Here it was the *homogeneity* of the New Man that was brought to the fore and his definition in total opposition to all things French. Boumedienne's definition of the New Man in the 1969 pamphlet, *Symposium d'Alger*, was very much along these lines, not so much Man as he ought to be, but Algerian Man 'as he really was', once the foreign accretions imposed by the French were rejected:

> *Any tribute to man and respect for his noblest undertaking must first involve the need to be oneself, not a man borrowed from elsewhere, but a real man, just as he has been fashioned by the history, geography, economy and blood of his forefathers. Refuting the untruths spread by colonialism and highlighting evidence of the African past and cultural presence was from the very beginning of our struggle, a task to which we gave due place and importance. (quoted in Stora 1992: 231 - my translation MAM)*

The problem was that this New Man was also an artificial construct and did not at all represent the actual diversity of the Algerian population, as they really were.

The real cultural theorist of the Boumedienne years was, however, Ahmed Taleb Ibrahimi. He was a key figure in the re-framing of the notion of the New Man under Boumedienne, for whom he served as Education Minister, then Minister of Culture, as well as in various capacities under the next President, Chadli Benjedid.

Situating his ideas within a broadly Marxist framework, in which he prioritised the notion of alienation, Taleb Ibrahimi linked the notion of the New Man explicitly to that of a Cultural Revolution as here in a passage from 1973:

> *The cultural revolution consists of working to create a new man in a new society [underlined in the text], encouraging the adoption of a new way of life more in tune with the ideals of the Revolution and geared to consolidating and furthering the success of this revolution. (Taleb Ibrahimi 1981: 219 - my translation MAM)*

Yet, during this period, Taleb Ibrahimi was also defining the New Man primarily in opposition to French cultural influence. The position that France had killed Algerian culture was one which he took, along with others such as Abdelmajid Meziane, who put forward the position that France's master plan involved the total cultural annihilation of the Algerian population (Stora 1992: 231).[13]

The Arabisation policy also had the effect of denying any specificity to the significant Berber minority. Figures like Taleb Ibrahimi and Omar Saadi, for instance, claimed that the Berbers had been totally merged with the Arabs since the eighth century. That they were not was soon to become strikingly evident and reveal that the new Algerian nation had not become a homogeneous reality. In fact, the spark was ignited, when in April 1980 the government cancelled a lecture by the writer Mouloud Mammeri on his anthology of ancient Kabyle poetry (Stora 1992: 236). This led to protests in what has come to be known as the Berber Spring, with a major challenge to what had passed, on the surface, for a unanimous public ideology (Maddy-Weitzman 2001: 23-47).

From 1980 onwards, the fiction of the nation united under the FLN State was to reveal itself as increasingly threadbare and the New Man was showing his age. The undermining of its political authority culminated in the unrest, which intensified from 1988, and then its resounding defeat in the elections of 1991, which were set aside and cancelled.

How much of this ageing process could be put down to an inherent tendency for revolutionary breaks with tradition to become ossified as part of a new tradition? There is something of this no doubt. However, the revolutionary break, conceptualised through the notion of the New Man, was flawed from the outset and, in many ways, the seeds for the Islamic revivalist movement had already been sown by the policies adopted from the start by the FLN, which was not prepared to extend the notion of the New Man to encompass the New Woman.

4. The Rebirth of the New Man

Paradoxically, the Islamic revival has also been accompanied by the rebirth of the notion of the New Man. The Islamic movement, particularly the FIS (*Front Islamique du Salut*), which developed from strength to strength from 1989, took over this particular aspect of the ideology of the post-Independence FLN.[14] This type of New Man is closely linked, on the one hand, with the restoration of a particularist identity through association with Islam and a fundamentalist return to original purity. There are some, like the cultural theorist, Ali Mazrui, who see this regression as an inevitable general phenomenon in the postcolonial cultural domain, which he contrasts with an essentially forward-driven economic sphere; for him, cultural revolutions must entail 'a marriage between revolution and nostalgia.'

> *... while the ultimate aspiration for economic revolutions in the modern world is a future-oriented ambition, the ultimate aspiration for cultural revolutions in the Third World must include a backward-oriented sense of restoration. Economic ambition is an effort to realize material well-being at a new level of efficiency; cultural ambition is the effort to realize spiritual well-being at the right depth of identity. Economic revolutions need to be effectively innovative; cultural revolutions must in part be, at least in the Third World, selectively revivalist. The latter is indeed a marriage between revolution and nostalgia. (Mazrui 1990: 244-5)*

However, although his thesis may have some descriptive validity as to what may be happening on the ground, there seems to be nothing to justify the inevitability of the process, especially since economic change is also dependent on cultural change, changes in social relations and ideology and no economic transformation is sustainable without an appropriate cultural transformation to accompany it.

In Algeria, the reborn New Man does not only hark back to a fundamentalist past; it is equally dependent on a radical rejection of foreign influence. Indeed, he is now defined primarily by a complete rupture with French influence. This was a position that had been maturing over the years, as we have seen under the Boumedienne regime and through figures such as Taleb Ibrahimi in particular, though what is now different is the denial that French colonisation was able to destroy any part of Islamic society in Algeria. On the contrary, its survival is said to be due, not just to its power of resistance, but also because of the absence of any real interaction between the two societies or nations co-existing throughout the colonial period.

In spite of these two features, one of the key criticisms levelled against the FIS by the FLN in disarray was that it was a *new* party, with no ties to the Algerian nationalist past. This was because it did not situate its vision of the national space within the parameters set by the War of Independence, but beyond in the wider Islamic *Ouma* (Stora 1992: 309). Clearly, the FIS do not see Algerian history beginning in 1954. On the one hand, it sees itself as providing a link to the *Oulema* movement of Abdelhamid Ben Badis in the 1930s, as well as to the PPA. On the other hand, one of its main leaders, Abassi Madani, was himself one of those who originally took part in the insurrection on 1 November 1954.

Moreover, it took up the theme of national unity, presenting itself as the real representative of the *'bloc indécomposable'* that is the Algerian Islamic nation. For many in Algeria in recent years, the FIS were indeed able to proclaim themselves the real heirs of the FLN, (the *'fils* of the FLN' - Roberts 1993, p. 86) complete with their own vision of the New Man.

5. The New Woman and her Exclusion from the Algerian Nation
We now finally come to talk about the New Woman and her exclusion from the Algerian Nation.

For if the New Man was in reality stunted at birth, the same cannot be said for the New Woman. Indeed, the Algerian War of Independence had a profoundly transforming effect on the lives of a large number of Algerian women, who came out of seclusion to play an active part in the war, as *moudjahidates*.[15] This was not just in a support role, providing hiding places, helping the wounded with medical care, carrying messages, weapons and so on. Large numbers of women also played an active part in the military campaign in their own right, in particular through the planting of bombs. This type of activity meant the breaking down of centuries-old religious and social taboos, of which the abandonment of traditional Muslim dress to go unveiled into European districts was just one of the more visible aspects.

It is significant in this context that Kateb Yacine, in his seminal novel about Algerian nationalism, chooses to portray Algeria as a woman, the Nedjma of the title, representing the link between the diverse strands of the Algerian nation. His vision of the new Algerian nation is as a synthesis of all the different elements which had left their mark on the land and which had voluntarily decided to commit themselves to the new nation through a national pact. Importantly, women were to be not just equal, but to have a leading role in this nation.

Moreover, this symbolic woman representing the nation is not one which is founded on origins, nor necessarily on the relationship with the land, with the ancestors or with 'roots'. Sometimes associated with the sea, as in Mohammed Dib's *Qui se souvient de la mer* [1962] (Dib 1990), the woman represents continuity at the same time as fluidity and the opening up of the possibilities of the future.[16] Kateb Yacine's Nedjma is not the mother of the nation; she is a daughter, a lover, a woman - the key agent of a national future, rather than a link to an original past.

In the non-fictional universe, however, the New Woman did not survive long, in spite of a measure of FLN rhetoric, glorifying the tortured female martyrs of the Revolution. Indeed, the battle had already been engaged, before the war was even ended, with the FLN opposing a reform proposed by the French authorities in 1959, to abolish polygamy and the rights of repudiation of women. As with the very complex issue of the unveiling of women, which was also urged on Algerian women by the French, the FLN opposition was carried forward in the name of Arab-Islamic values and in recognition of the need to defend the unifying force of religion and traditional family values as a major, if not the major, factor in cementing the unity of the nation against the French colonial power (Touati 1996: 2-3).

Since independence, there has been a steady erosion of women's rights. In the immediate post-war period, the state adopted a dual discourse. On the one hand, it promoted the education and employment of women, as part of a modernising, vaguely socialistic project of economic and social development. As we have seen in chapter seven of this volume, reliable figures relating to female employment are still hard to come by. There is some evidence that progress has been made from the low figure of 1989 where less than one in twenty women in the active population had a job, giving Algeria the lowest rate for female employment, in comparison with Morocco and Tunisia (Touati 1996: 5). We have seen that the 2000 figures suggested a figure of 13.9 per cent of employed women in the active population (chapter seven) and, in the most optimistic scenario so far, the Minister in charge of the family and women's affairs, Boutheina Cheriet, was suggesting in an interview in 2003, that women represented 18 per cent of the total labour force in the formal sector (*Liberté*, 29 April 2003). Given what remains an extremely low proportion of women who are economically active in Algeria, particularly in the formal sector, this policy cannot be considered a success, in spite of the tremendous strides made in female education.

Moreover, at the same time as it pursued this modernising project with regard to women, the Algerian state recognised, and ultimately endorsed through the lack of countermeasures, women's 'archaic' position in the patriarchal family. In spite of a constitution which gave women equal rights, this process was to culminate in 1984 in the Family Code, based on Koranic tradition, which institutionalised the unequal position of women in respect of both the family and Algerian society, and keeps them in the position of minors, in respect of both fathers and then husbands.[17]

The New Woman, so full of promise in the 1950s and early 1960s, has in effect been largely excluded from the Algerian Nation.

6. Symbolic Representations of National Identity

Of course, issues relating to national identity have found expression not only in the official discourse of the state power, but also in other outlets, including expressions of dissident ideas, as well as theoretical reflections and cultural representations of one kind and another. A number of key figures and metaphors have played a role in this representation, whether these are linked to spatial notions such as the national land and the sea or more temporal notions such as the symbolic centuries-old tree, the role of ancestors, oral tradition and memory, as well as the key symbolic figure of the Mother/Woman.

All of these figures have played a role in building up the symbolic web of a national history and project, specifically linked to the particular spatial and historical characteristics of the Algerian nation, yet transcending, on the one hand, the partial histories of individual families, tribes and clans and, at the same time, welding together a fragmented history marked by successive discontinuities resulting from invasion, conquest, war and resistance.

In all of this, the key factor of continuity has been the national space or territory, which, though it is not an undifferentiated whole but marked by diversity and differentiation in terms of geography as well as political symbolism, has nonetheless played an important role in providing the founding principle upon which any formulation of a syncretic history of the nation is constructed. The key role played by the notion of the national land has not however remained static and cannot be considered in isolation from its relationship with the sea, which is an archetypal symbol of continuity and even universalism. Whilst the proponents of *Algérie française* viewed the Mediterranean as no more of a barrier than the river Seine flowing through Paris, for the national liberation struggle it represented the frontier of the national territory and a boundary to be re-established. At the same time, of course, it also represented the route taken by the Algerian diaspora, who remained part of the nation while on French soil. The on-going importance of trans-Mediterranean ties weakens significantly the legitimacy of any concept of Algerian national identity based exclusively on a *droit du sol*.

Nonetheless, it provides a more solid basis for national identity than an approach based primarily on ethnicity, given that bloodlines may unite specific families, tribes and clans across the generations, but these ancestral ties provide continuity only at a sub-national level. Their role is nonetheless an important one in providing the web through which the transmission of fragments of the collective memory and shared cultural elements takes place, to become woven into the stuff, which constitutes the real, material diversity of the national fabric.

At the end of the day, however, the nation can only be defined as an abstract entity if it takes shape through a political project, with its own political memory and legitimacy.

7. The Political Model of the State

It is clear that the national project forged through the independence struggle and the later project to construct the national state as a homogeneous Arab-Islamic entity have now run their course and that a (re)-definition of the specificity of the Algerian nation is being called for, in harmony with its relationship to its territory and history, described by some as an 'Algerian Algeria', as well as its relationship with the wider world, but, most essentially, in terms of a political model which all its citizens can accept, and which gives priority to the relationship between the nation's state and its citizens.

Algeria's fall from its perceived leadership position as a beacon of change half a century ago has indeed left it in a sorry state. However, the problem has perhaps to be recognised for what it really is, not as how it is often perceived. In other words, it is misleading to view the present crisis as one of the national identity. After all, Algerians know who they are. However, there is a real discordance between the nation as it really is and the political machinery available to it to develop a national project for the future, which is capable of carrying its citizens with it. If anything, it is a crisis of citizenship.

On the one hand, the amalgam of a homogeneous political nation based on the French modernist model, legitimised by a key founding historical event, the Algerian Revolution, and its fusion with a supposed homogeneous supra-national culture, based on religion and language, as part of the wider Arab-Islamic world, has proved largely unviable. On the other hand, the challenge represented by the Islamist movement to official State nationalist ideology now appears discredited after a decade of bloody violence, but also because it has seemed singularly incapable of forging a concept of the nation which is inclusive in terms of women and also in terms of allowing space and real citizenship to the various regionally and culturally diverse components of the Algerian population.

There now appears to be a greater willingness to explore the possibility of the construction of a synthetic nation, based on the inclusion of these different elements. This has not been lightly conceded but is the fruit of the determined resistance on the part of Berber and women's movements, as well as the refusal by the young people who form the majority of Algeria's population, 70 per cent of whom are less than 25 years old, to accept the continued endorsement of the status quo by the threadbare reference to the historical legitimacy accorded by participation in the liberation war (*Le Monde*, 18 March 2002). Increasingly, the artificial monolithic model of Algerian national identity has come under attack, to such an extent that those in power can no longer ignore the challenges that this resistance represents.

There is evidence of a number of harbingers of change in the way the nation might be redefined to represent the heterogeneity of the Algerian people and its past. For instance, previously shunned political figures who had been airbrushed out of history are now resurfacing in publications, conferences and other media in the public domain. Tlemcen airport has been renamed after Messali Hadj and Setif University has been named Ferhat Abbas University. A major conference on Saint Augustine, highlighting his role as a major constituent figure of Algeria's national past, was held in Algiers in 2000 and attracted the participation of President Bouteflika.

Moreover, following pressure by women's groups and movements, the present Bouteflika regime has promised to rethink the family code, although at the time of writing nothing concrete has yet emerged (Lokmane 2002). A similar breakthrough is promised on the Berber issue, with the avowed intention to accede to some of the demands of the Kabyle-based movement for linguistic and cultural recognition, as formulated in the El-Kseur platform, but also to take on board its wider demands for real democracy and citizenship (*Liberté*, 13 March 2002). Indeed, Tamazight has now been given recognition as an official language. However, this new approach has yet to be reflected in any real break with the pattern of unrest and repression, which has become the norm.

Thus, while there is some evidence that re-thinking has been taking place, this has yet to be endorsed in a clear-cut commitment to a new vision of the nation in the official discourse, as well as the concretisation in practice of a new relationship between citizens and state. For this to be achieved, major changes in the political culture will be required and will no doubt be won, rather than conceded. However, without this fundamental transformation, it is inconceivable that the human resources represented by the citizens of Algeria will be fully engaged in the on-going economic, social and political development of the nation. Their participation is a vital ingredient for its success.

Notes

1   '*L'unité incarnée par le FLN est l'image de l'unité nationale. Pour le Front, l'acte d'adhésion ne fait qu'incarner la nationalité, tandis que l'adhésion aux anciens partis ne réalisait qu'une division factice et stérile de la nation*' (Stora 1992: 149).

2   The question of language and Arabisation is dealt with by Mohammed Miliani in chapter ten.

3   '*Rappelons que la situation imposée aux Algériens au temps de la colonisation française était la suivante: devenir citoyen français, c'était renier son appartenance religieuse. Ce refus de citoyenneté (qui considère pourtant la religion comme une affaire privée), cette application d'un faux modèle de la République, provoqua l'essor d'un mouvement indépendantiste, à base*

religieuse et ethnique, et la guerre avec le dénouement que l'on connaît' (quoted in Stora 1992: 287).

4   *'L'événement prend valeur de mythe fondateur: en ce jour aurait commencé, ou recommencé, l'histoire de l'Algérie par la volonté de quelques hommes faisant table rase du passé. Désormais, c'est le 1er* novembre 1954 qu'il faut commémorer, et non pas la proclamation de l'Etoile ou du PPA (en 1926, 1937)'* (Stora 1992: 149).

5   *'La 'révolution algérienne' fut vécue par ses inspirateurs et ses dirigeants comme l'acte fondateur d'une ère nouvelle. Les initiateurs de 'novembre 1954', on l'a vu, se proclamaient en rupture absolue avec le passé. Ils n'entendent pas construire, dans le cours de la guerre, d'images globales et unificatrices d'un mouvement précurseur. Ils établissent la croyance de la rupture radicale qui séparerait la nation algérienne, 'régénérée' par la violence révolutionnaire, de l'ancienne société coloniale. Ce faisant, ils font repartir l'histoire du nationalisme algérien du point zéro'* (Stora 1992: 151).

6   See also chapter eight of this volume for a discussion of Fanon's ideas.

7   See also (Said 1993: 323-32) for a discussion of Fanon's theoretical input beyond the national question to the politics of human liberation in general.

8   See (Roberts 1993: 82), on the importance of Nietzsche for the conceptualisation of the Algerian Revolution.

9   From 'Socialism and Man in Cuba' (1965).

10 From a speech, 'Duty of Revolutionary Medical Workers' (20 August 1960).

11 From 'What a Young Communist should be' (10 October 1962).

12 From 'Letter to José Medro Mestre' (26 February 1964).

13 For a discussion of the influence of Taleb Ibrahimi and Algerian political discourse in the mid-sixties and early seventies, see (Benrabah 1999: 93-6).

14 (Cf. Stora 1992: 308-9): *'Image dépassée aujourd'hui que ce type de militant nationaliste, prêchant avec force arguments populistes le refus des inégalités sociales, prédisant un monde meilleur par l'élimination de la présence étrangère, promettant la pureté d'une action à entreprendre par un retour aux sources? Non, c'est elle que l'on retrouvera dans le mouvement islamiste qui monte en puissance en Algérie, dès le début de l'année 1989.'*

15 See chapter six of this volume.

16 For a more detailed discussion of the role of the sea/woman and its relationship to the nationalist struggle, see Majumdar 1999.

17 See chapter six in this volume.

9 Languages Policy in Algeria: Between Convergence and Diversity

Mohammed Miliani

Introduction

For a decade now, Algeria has frequently been on the front pages of international newspapers - more often than she wanted to be. Happy news or events have not constituted its lot. The constant images of murderous fundamentalists have pervaded the writings of journalists always in search of bloody accounts or macabre statistics of death tolls. However, what is totally absent in the perceptions of people abroad is the formidable struggle of the civil society, though embryonic, against the ever increasing invasion of nepotism, ignorance, preferential treatment in political, economic, social and educational domains. Such a positive image is ignored by the international press more interested, in its majority, in the bloody killings and the growing importance of fundamentalism. Sensationalism is still the name of the game. The crises the country is experiencing are varied and somehow extremely difficult to solve. Not least of the problems society endures, is that of languages and the policies meant to organise, legislate or rank them. The management of languages has often been taken over by politicians who have never called upon the citizens to express their views about what concerns the latter most, and what is ultimately highly personal, though it involves, paradoxically, decisions at higher levels in the decision-making spheres.

Language policies have run counter to the existing linguistic processes (assimilation, learning cultures, cross-fertilisation), which are nonetheless natural, more complex and far from being completed. Nearly 40 years after independence, the cultural crisis has ended with serious identity problems, at least for the youth. Within state institutions (schools, universities, administrations, companies), people are still subjected, unwillingly, to language reforms, more like guinea pigs. In such an area of the public domain, the citizen is yet to be given freedom, if not his rights. Transition, from a postcolonial country to a modern one, seems to be taking a long time, helped in this by makeshift policies or partisan reforms in all sectors.

1. A Multi-Facetted Crisis

Today's events and the present social instability can in no way be explained in political terms only. The crisis the country is suffering from is in essence political, economic, cultural and social. Politically speaking, after an interlude of socialism until the late 1980s, the transition towards a more democratic system seems to be taking more time, while the costs are high. The political crisis is essentially due to internal struggles within the national movement, to the frequent intervention of occult lobbies (Aziz & Taibi 1995), and to the political blockage of open and democratic discussion on sensitive issues. The present phase is still confused due to the co-existence of a multi-party system and a reigning political philosophy advocating uniformity of thoughts and views. However, the philosophy of the one-party system seems to prevail despite the presence from the 1990s of a plethora of parties from one extreme of the political spectrum to the other, with a host of Islamic/Islamist parties. The political philosophy of the one-party regime lingers on in the sense that proponents of paradigms of convergence are legion. Thus, the supposed unifying term of *qawmiyya* (or *Umma*) supra-nationality, one Great Arab Nation, though unidentifiable, takes precedence over its antonym, *wataniyya* (nationhood, Lacheraf); though the latter is more focused, realistic and more in line with the majority's perceptions and attitudes.

Economically, the transition from a state-controlled economy to a market-oriented one is far from being over. On the contrary, the various planned reforms (privatisation of state-owned companies on a large scale, management of the increasingly moribund public sector, and direct foreign investment) have not yet found an environment (social, economic and legal) propitious for a harmonious development. Thus, the reforms of the code of commerce are somehow behind the decisions in the economic sector. Apart from the oil industry, which amounts to 95 per cent of exports, economic life seems to have come to a halt. Households' revenues have decreased in the last ten years (a loss of 25% in real terms). The number of unemployed has rocketed from 853,000 in 1987 to 2,359,000 in 1997 (Mekidèche 2000). The proportion of public finance devoted to education has shrunk from 25.2 per cent of the budget of the State in 1987 to 17.39 per cent in 1997, while the needs have increased substantially. This has been accompanied by the 'fragilisation of the systems of social security, the increase of poverty and the deterioration of health and education public services' (Mekidèche 2000: 24).[1] Furthermore, the nearly deceased state-controlled economy has generated a general feeling of compulsory state charity for all, along with the obscuring of people's duties, while their rights are more often expressed through trade unions more obsessed by the sharing of the oil income, than by the development of the country's system of production.

Socially, the population seems at a crossroads, with no objective to realise. Individualism has finally had the upper hand over communalism. Social and moral values have disappeared while the necessary systems of reference for creating meaning are non-existent. Their absence offers no markers for judging worth, or for assessing group or individual actions. As a system of reference, history is yet to be written. It is still a process which is hostage to numerous falsifications. Mainstream history has adopted a reductionist approach to historical events, while holding a number of Algerian nationalists up to public opprobrium. Furthermore, the numerous crises and tensions have not reduced the confrontational aspect of modern history, nor pushed people to accept their own past. Things are still too explosive and sensitive. The country as well as its leaders are either intentionally amnesiac, selectively blind, or ashamed of the heterogeneous voices from within while advocating homogenising policies. Many historical events before colonisation, during the revolution and after independence, are still kept as secrets, or have remained unsolved because of the controversies surrounding them. The result of such a malaise has led to a great social instability of which the youth are the first victims. Social values (e.g. work, respect and honesty) are less and less part of people's agenda. Economic and social survival by any means is the motto of a good majority, and a keyword to avoid economic poverty and cultural or social destitution. This has become fashionable but to the detriment of the long-lasting and more valuable status of citizenship: individual interests and profits are always put before the community's welfare. Previous social practices developed along the lines of a strict social code of ethics have been replaced by new ones impregnated with individualism, always conflicting with the *res publica*.

Culture is another domain in total shambles. The failure of the management of culture by state-run institutions has precipitated the disappearance of long and well-established culture-oriented bodies. Worse, numerous reforms have led to a progressive cultural shrinkage. The Algerian cinema is non-existent. Music has become '*kofr*' (sin) - that is why 'raï music' was accused of being dirty, not to be listened to by families. Theatre is embryonic. Literature, in French or Arabic, is not as thriving as it used to be. Furthermore culture is being managed by administrators, not creators. Language, as a cultural manifestation (language is culture), has not escaped unscathed from all types of manipulation (political, social or educational). Very often decisions implying the management of languages or dialects have not taken into consideration the parameters rooted in the social reality of the country. Mainstreaming, as it is understood in this country, i.e. the ironing out of all idiosyncrasies characteristic of the Algerian society, has been on the political agenda for decades now. All decisions concerning the management of languages, rarely their development or their promotion, have involved the pruning of any element not concerned with the Arab-Islamic dimension of the country. What was ignored was the richness of the acquired heritage of centuries of contacts, tensions and commerce with other civilisations. The language situation of the country is therefore a tangled one, partly due to the number of dialects and languages in contact, but mostly because of the manipulation directed towards them. Besides, the diglossic dimension of the country (presence of a high and low variety of Arabic: the language of the Koran along with the Algerian dialect) has added to the complexity of the language situation, already problematic with the presence of French-Arabic bilingualism.

It is at school level that the rift is most distressing. The young seem to be torn between the 'language of the mother' and the 'language of the school'. Their psychological stability is at stake, not just because of the complex sociolinguistic context, but also the various discourses developed by the adults' biased views about which native linguistic variation to use (Classical Arabic or the dialect), or which foreign language to teach (French as the existing language of the colonisers, or English as the 'language of science and technology'). School has become a living laboratory where the language problems are posed, where tentative answers are experimented with, but where no lasting solution is likely to be found because of the divided positions of decision-makers. However, it seems that the real problematic centres rather round the dichotomy between language of knowledge and medium of instruction. If Arabic often has the position of the latter, it rarely assumes the role of the former, particularly in scientific subjects:

> *Reality in the educational system in Algeria is crystallised mainly round the search for equivalencies between school contents and the linguistic means to teach them, that is to say to teach through a medium contents that are alien to it. (Sebaa 1996)*

Such a debate has up to now been avoided by the authorities, even 'educationalists', who hope for more from the incantatory effect of the language, and the affective impact on people, rather than the real advances of the language itself, hence the gap between the pedagogical intentions (use of Arabic as a medium of instruction), and its actual limits (scientific content expressed in other languages).

In the overall sociolinguistic picture, the indigenous languages or dialects, namely, on the one hand, Berber and its varieties, and on the other, the regional Algerian dialects are being squeezed in ghettos, a process used in order to do away with ethnic or wider demands for cultural identities or rights always roughed up by political manipulative actions. The sociolinguistic situation is such that it is highly difficult to make sense out of the linguistic mess developed by awkward decisions and makeshift plans. Besides, the linguistic situation is:

> *... a fluctuating reality, crossed by latent and underlying conflicts (sometimes declared) and on the way to being completely changed by the effects of a complex centralising and voluntarist cultural policy, by the intermingling of societies in presence of their representations, their domains of use but also in the real practices of locutors... (Taleb Ibrahimi, K. 1995: 25)*

Such is the state of affairs in an Algeria shaken up by this multi-facetted crisis which is very likely to endure in the face of the lack of concern on the part of the decision-makers. Worse, their decisions which run counter to nature, due to some 'cultural blindness and/or political alibis' (Miliani 1997), are developed by their partisan views, or at times, their messianic visions of themselves as redressers of wrongs. This is no less the case with the reforms dealing with languages (at school level, the administration or the environment), which can lead one to predict difficult days ahead, if not more social fracture and anomie. A complete picture could be given by providing an account of power relations in the country, so often underlined as the key issue in Algeria. However, we can only briefly mention the problematic issue of power, authority and legitimacy. If the first one exists, and is felt at all levels, authority is nearly non-existent, while legitimacy of the different bodies is yet to be found. Indeed:

... the successive governments since October 1988, have failed in their reform efforts because they did not have authority (...) by authority I am not referring to power, but rather to legitimacy, which implies necessarily the consent of the governed. (Addi 1995: 137)

It is true that reforms can hardly succeed if the citizens are not made aware of the general interest of bringing in change. Reforms using only power, are always fought against, aided in this by the lack, at times, of legitimacy of the authority in power. Success of the reform is therefore rarely guaranteed.

2. The Sociolinguistic Context

Following independence in 1962, the country had to face several urgent challenges. It undertook simultaneously the transformation of the economic, political and social system, and also a cultural revolution. Political independence could not have been complete without the latter. The problematical issue was simple: either keep the status quo or refer to a mythical past to justify future actions. The latter path was chosen. Besides, in order to conquer and assert the Algerian personality, the Arabic language was revived. Of course, Arabic was to be reconfirmed in its role as national language. Arabisation, or the generalisation of the use of Arabic to all sectors of the economic, political, educational and social life of the country, was the third aspect of the triptych advocated by the nationalists as well as the Muslim reformists (the *Ulema*). The other two were: 'Algeria is our land and Islam our religion'. The real problem in the country is not to decide whether Arabisation must take place or not, but how to Arabise. However, the policy of Arabisation has given rise to recriminations and discourses that were frequently related to the defence of an existing social position or acquisition of a new status, hence the fight for singling out Arabic from the other vernaculars, as the only means for social and political promotion. Holding such views were two shapeless groups, not always identifiable, represented in the traits of Arabophones against Francophones. This simplistic division is not always verifiable because of people's own strategies and concerns, not to speak of their ideologies. The struggle between these factions seems to be at the level of personal motives. One can even say that the gap between the groups is more profound because it involves personal interests for the future, and the idiosyncratic societal projects they want to live in:

The present conjuncture characterised by a struggle between two social projects has issued, among other things, from this identity crisis, in the sense of a search for the self due to a destabilisation of markers, of integration symbols (stage of desymbolisation?) and, subsequently, to an attempt at the establishment of markers and to new symbols (stage of symbolisation or re-symbolisation). It is obvious that this transformation of old symbols provokes painful convulsions, as does any delivery. (Dourari 1997: 29)

It should also be pointed out that more than any other world language, Arabic benefits from a quasi-idolatry on the part of its users because of its close relationship with Islam:

... Arabic remains, in spite of the quest for modernity officially proclaimed in the fundamental texts of the country, prisoner of its theological references. (Rouadjia 1991: 120)

This is why the work on the language (corpus planning), its modernisation, and its development have not been systematically undertaken because of the sacred halo around it put there by the language users who consider the language more than a tool for communication. One of the logical outcomes is that scientific terms are difficult to translate into Arabic. Transliteration has been used for a long time as a leeway to solve terminology problems. Arab linguists have created Modern Standard Arabic in order to avoid being accused of tampering with the sacred Koran, while this new language could be made more modern, and thus transformed.

After independence the French language was systematically attacked as 'being the language' of the colonisers, and as such was rejected. And so were those who mastered this language accused of belonging to an illusory party: *Hizb Fransa*, party of France. Talking about the Francophone elite, Nait Belkacem, in charge of the High Council for the National Language created in 1981, described them in the following terms:

They are orphans of culture, neither oriental nor westerner (...). They are unstable disabled persons one must treat. (quoted in Madi 1997: 119)

Nowadays, French has been given the status of foreign language, just like English, Spanish or German. The linguistic situation is not in favour of the French language. Because of education, larger and larger numbers of Algerians are developing their knowledge of Arabic. However, French-Arabic duality will continue to be a reality in the decades to come. What was not a 'doctrinal bilingualism but a circumstantial one' (Taleb Ibrahimi 1976: 98) is not in favour of Classical Arabic either that is practised only in schools or situations where writing is involved. However:

... French-Arabic opposition has warped the debate over the relation between language and politics, language and culture, and finally language and freedom (is there such a thing when languages are planned through decrees and laws accompanied by coercive means?) (Miliani 1997: 58-9)

The linguistic and cultural situation is then more complex for it is not just a linguistic but also a cultural melting pot. The result is a society torn between its once flourishing past, and the urgent need to keep up with modernism, a task Arabic is trying to undertake. Nevertheless, a hard fact will continue to characterise the society: the Algerian will remain prisoner of his past, seated between two languages (because he does not master any of them correctly: state of semi-lingualism), and two cultures, affected by a disabling linguistic schizophrenia due to the critical predominant discourses held by proponents and adversaries about all vernaculars and languages.

The linguistic situation is even more muddled because of the existence of two forgotten protagonists: Algerian Arabic dialect and Berber. In the former case, the problem is that Classical Arabic is not the language of everyday communication, while the Algerian dialect is sometimes very far from the original. Furthermore, in everyday speech people borrow from French, and even Spanish in western Algeria (visible in the language of fishermen: the technical jargon and the names of fish varieties).

In the case of foreign languages, English is receiving an extra push from the authorities because it is said that it is not only a tool for international communication, but also a means to keep abreast of modern technological and scientific research. However, the extreme attention it is getting from all decision-makers is not always devoid of hidden interests or second thoughts. In fact, excuses and alibis of all sorts are found to squeeze French out of its position as privileged foreign language. Motives for selecting or rejecting one language or another, are varied and not always based on objectivity. Thus, struggle for power can very often explain decisions that were unrealistic if not absurd.

As far as people's perceptions of foreign languages are concerned, English is the most valued one. As for French, it is frequently perceived as an integral part of the sociolinguistic trait of the country, even if it is still in the eyes of the older generations the language of the colonisers (another slogan put forward by the anti-French language group).

Beyond the interests of a handful of decision-makers, the languages problem seems not to be in the public domain. As in any other sociolinguistic context, the language practices and rules of language use in particular discourse communities, depend mostly on the language that imposes itself in a given register. It is only men's speculative handling of what is ultimately natural, that ends up complicating the sociolinguistic environment. The intervention of the state through laws and decrees has generated dissatisfaction among all citizens, and even an upheaval in 1988. Neither the Francophones nor the Arabophones are satisfied with the state of affairs. Both groups have experienced or fostered reforms that went from one extreme to another: i.e. a concession to the proponents of a quick Arabisation, or an adhesion to the ideas of those in favour of a bold foreign languages policy with French in the forefront of the demands. In any case, the ultimate problem is a cultural one characteristic of a country in search of harmony:

> *What is at stake is then the identity of a people, that is to say its survival or its disappearance, and the failure of our cultural model lies essentially in the 'political management' of the linguistic question. (Madi 1997: 126)*

The sociolinguistic context is therefore very intricate, but made all too complicated, if not explosive, because reforms are not cumulative, i.e. they do not benefit from each other. Reforms are always preceded by a *tabula rasa* as if nothing has pre-existed. They are often introduced to get rid of previous ones. However, the language practices (code switching; code mixing; borrowing) have established naturally their own rules of use undisturbed by the globalising ideologies.

3. Languages Policies and Reforms

Algeria remains one of a small number of countries where language planning is at its most extreme. The state-led reforms have frequently taken sides with lobbies, or followed conjunctions of circumstances, instead of a resolute approach to one of the greatest challenges the country has to face. On the contrary, the history of language policies and reforms shows backward and forward movements, even pauses, in the movement towards the solving of the language problems. There were even cases when governments issued a law, just to freeze it a short while after, under the pressure of not always identified forces. Pressure groups from all sides have frequently been instrumental in the launching, repeal or freezing of a law or decision.

Language policies and reforms have usually mirrored the struggle for power at the highest level. They were also the expression or claim of a given group in power. This has in no way contributed to offering a greater stability for the state to face challenges which are far more pressing and no less delicate. Besides, the state's interests are never identified and rarely taken into consideration by the reforms decided, which are often ill-prepared, or undertaken in a hurry.

To give an account of all policies and reforms that dealt with language problems, boils down to a list of decisions, laws and decrees for or about Arabisation, always conceived in opposition to the teaching or use of French or in total negation of important endogenous and exogenous parameters. The other languages and vernaculars are either concealed (Spanish, German), praised to the extreme (English), or downgraded (the mother tongues: i.e. Berber, Algerian Arabic). This way to proceed has always been the decision of a handful of decision-makers. The population has never been associated in the process.

From the start, the various political programmes (Tripoli Programme 1962) or reference texts (Charter of Algiers 1964) agreed on two action-plans: first, Arabisation of all sectors of the economy, education, environment and administration because, as was stated by the late President Boumedienne:

> ... without the recovery of this essential element, which is the national language, our efforts will remain vain, our personality incomplete and our entity, a body without a soul...(quoted in Doucy & Monheim 1971: 214)

Originally, the process was undertaken with the view to recovering national identity long denied by the colonisers, and to salvaging the country's heritage of the Arab-Islamic civilisation. Arabisation was the third facet of the Algerian Revolution. The other two were industrialisation of the country, and implementation of the agrarian reform. The second point in the national agenda was the development of foreign languages:

... this process of total recovery of the national language and its necessary adaptation to all the needs of the society do not exclude a firm encouragement to the acquisition of foreign languages. (National Charter 1986)

From here, the readings and interpretations of the aforementioned legal documents were different, idiosyncratic if not biased. If everyone agreed on the main objectives concerned with languages policies of the state, they disagreed on a number of parameters closely linked to the process: the means to assemble in order to succeed, the speed with which to proceed, the institutions (political, educational, social or economic) concerned by the language policy, and the priorities to determine and monitor. The change the language(s) policies were supposed to bring was supposed to be quantitative but also qualitative. Unfortunately, only the first aspect was taken care of, hence the partial failure of the policies. Arabisation is not just a question of increasing the number of users of Arabic, it also involves improving the competence of these users, and at the same time working on the language (*corpus planning*, Kloss 1969) in order to allow it to enter certain registers, mostly scientific. Nevertheless, Arabic seems to find some difficulty in adjusting to the jargon and neologisms, innovations introduced in a number of sciences. Besides, the challenges put out to all protagonists were not met with success. More often than not, it is the individuals' own interests and views that dictated the slant the policies took, at times, contrary to the reasons of state. In the long run, this generated a feeling of frustration and a kind of despondency in the face of the primacy of groups' or individuals' interests over the majority. The other misinterpretation, often done on purpose, concerns the close link some people establish between Arabisation and fundamentalism. This is too simplistic an attitude because the correlation between both is not evident at all. However, such a stand developed some kind of inertia provoked by extremists of all tendencies.

The first event concerned with Arabisation to date is undoubtedly the 1976 Constitution. It stated unambiguously that Arabic was the official language, while French was declared to be a foreign one. If the interpretation can only be univocal, the content of the proposal was judged to be one-sided. 'Which type of Arabic should be official and national? (Classical or dialectal Arabic)', and 'why cannot French be considered as a second language?' were two recurrent questions asked by certain protagonists against such extreme Jacobinism (centralised democracy). It goes without saying that both sides had good points from which they developed their particular discourses. If for the first question one can easily point out that what is needed, in the case of corpus and status planning, is a linguistic norm, which Classical Arabic alone, not the Algerian dialectal Arabic, can offer, this does not mean that Classical Arabic could be used for communication purposes. Classical Arabic is nowhere the language of communication in the Arab world. This is more the domain for the dialect. As for the second question, many have criticised the lowering of the status of French, an eminently political choice, whereas this language could have been considered as a 'war booty' (as described by the writer, Kateb Yacine). On the contrary, people developed an allergic attitude towards French, as if its rejection could mean the beginning of better days.

The second question calls upon another one: 'can Algeria afford to lose the advantages of mastering an international language (French) for the benefit of another world language it is far from controlling (English)?' Should it not be practical and productive to adopt a more realistic policy towards a harmonious language planning? For reasons that are not evident, decision-makers have always privileged an extreme view of the status and place of the French language in the overall language policy of the country. However, only a non-Francophile or non-Francophobe attitude could solve the transitional phase French (as far as its status is concerned) is bound to go through.

The second event to date is the creation of the Academy for Arabic in 1986, a necessary means to face the challenges Arabic is expected to take up. However, this coincided with the cancellation of the teaching of Spanish, German and Russian at the Middle School level, a decision the impact of which had not been assessed beforehand. In the meantime, many teachers were made redundant, while others had to teach either French or English, without any initial training or competence. At *lycée* level, the same languages became optional, on an equal footing with music and drawing. The consequences are even more serious because the university departments where these languages were taught stopped getting the substantial student enrolment they had previously. Today, these departments are moribund. Worse, beginner classes have opened since, and BA degrees were henceforth awarded with no concern for the ultimate competence. All this is of course contrary to the heralded political slogans in favour of the teaching of foreign languages. If the languages are present, the policy about them lacks coherence and realism.

Then in 1991, came the Law on the Generalisation of Arabic. Some said too late, others that it was late but still welcome. However, pros and cons have been raised by proponents of and adversaries to this law. The former group felt that that was the only means to ensure a safe development of the language, and a way to give the language a more stable position than they felt it had. The latter group posited that this law spelt catastrophe because that meant the ostracism of a large contingent of highly skilled cadres. The subsequent brain-drain towards foreign countries was first caused by this 'villainous law' as it was labelled by the Francophones. The movement against the law was such that the following year, the late President Boudiaf froze it. There was a lull of four years before a new Law on the Generalisation of the Use of Arabic was unearthed in 1996 under the pressure of the 'Baathists' (panarabist movement in vogue in the Middle East under the impulse of Iraq) who were more in favour of the shapeless Great Arab Nation, and for whom total Arabisation should be undertaken quickly at any cost:

> *'Algerianity', as specific nationality and culture (...) is therefore fought against to the sole profit of an Arab supranationality and of a so-called Arab Islamic civilisation, but where only the Arab feature is underlined. (Dourari 1997: 29)*

Parallel to the process of Arabisation, an important reform was introduced before the latter event. It is the inclusion in 1993 of the English language in the fourth year of the primary schools. This decision was somehow unpopular, because it looked more like the reduction of the spreading of the French language than an attempt at solving pedagogical or scientific problems. All motives (e.g. English as the language of international communication, and the language of science and technology) were put forward to justify something that was in essence political. Very often, the pupils were forced to register in English classes. Years after, this policy is a total fiasco. The sorcerer's apprentices' experimentation has ended with more destabilisation of the young due to clashes of ideologies, rarely the outcome of a debate of ideas:

> *Perceived as the hypostasy of identity, language has become the point of impact where ideas and feelings of men in search of landmarks, of distinction, meet to confront each other, in a multilingual society not officially recognised as such. (Dourari 1997: 20)*

This seems not to be the last chapter of the language saga of the country. If by common assent, Arabic is the medium of instruction, the status of English and French is not yet settled. A committee instituted in 2000 by the President of the Republic (Commission Nationale de la Réforme de l'Education) is trying to come up with an adequate response to the management of languages at school level. The results are not yet known but already contested because it is said that the proposals are more in favour of one particular political line.

A brief assessment of the language reforms launched up to now shows the high instability that characterises the overall management of languages in contact. This continuing instability seems to get worse as time goes by. Any new reform increases the social, political, educational and/or cultural crisis more than it lowers the tensions between the various protagonists. More often than not, the reforms are focused on a particular problem. They are rarely undertaken in a systemic way, hence, the image of an educational non-system one gets of the educational sector. Besides, educational policies give the feeling that tampering in education, as a policy, is more frequent that is generally admitted. Partisanship rules language problems more often than not, the result of which is a chronic crisis, which gives the impression that transition will last. The language problem is also a debate between concerns for the 'national', on the one hand, through the paradigm of convergence advocated by the proponents of the one-party regime, and, on the other, concerns for the welfare of 'individuals' that underlie the uniformity of identity of citizens. The latter movement makes room for diversity of languages, thoughts and cultures.

The many language reforms undertaken since independence have often taken the route of convergence, of uniformity of thought towards the development of a culture of sameness. The rare voices of dissent calling for diversity are those who belong in their majority to the culturalist/berberist movement. The latter's claims and demands, as opposed to the state's eradicating enterprises against all sorts of idiosyncrasies, among which is the Berber characteristic of the country, have always insisted on the preservation of such traits. What is then at stake is the future of Algerian society. The choice is therefore Cornelian, and the proposed societal projects at opposite ends. They can even be described as top-down (more convergence) and bottom-up (more diversity) approaches, which can only give two different policies. The first one is more concerned with nation building, at the expense of regional, ethnic, group or individual claims. Whereas the second policy is a blueprint for more individual, specific, distinctive identities. Nation building processes are being implemented in order to do away with postcolonial Algeria, and to transform the country into a modern one. On the other hand, movements for more individualism are also seen as a prerequisite for a democratic country.

The preceding discussion poses the problem of authority (of the state) versus the individuals' linguistic rights, in a word: democracy, if this means equity in all domains and mutual respect. Besides, what is also at stake is a problem of modernity, a stage the country must go through in order to leave its postcolonial status. Furthermore, democracy has become 'the unavoidable prerequisite of modernity' (Sebaa 1997: 25). Indeed, if people's language of communication is downgraded, or made useless, one is then faced with attempts at reducing people's freedom of expression. Berber groups whose claims are for their mother tongue to be given a higher status, fight for their linguistic rights. Besides, they do not always identify themselves with the implemented cultural policies that look for monolithic entities and where Arabic is the only dominant variable. It is true that the Arab trait is often overemphasised to the detriment of non-Arab features. This is often felt as hegemonic attempts to reduce a community's right to exist as such, while it has its place in the mainstream of the Algerian society.

The development of a true participatory democracy demands that the state proceeds differently in the management of all languages, whether indigenous or foreign. Exclusion or ostracism can in no way be a means of dealing with such thorny problems. Participation of all citizens is then the key answer to the resolution of the problematic issue of language planning.

An overview of all reforms dealing with languages shows the state's concern for nation building at any cost. Thus, the paradigm of convergence pervades all decisions that were/are taken in such a domain. Very little freedom is given to a majority of language users, developing very often a linguistic schizophrenia because of sanctions or coercive means used to implement not always popular policies. Language policies have always been undertaken with speed, not allowing thorough analyses that could predict long-term impacts. Fundamentalism has not sprung up suddenly in a society known for practising an Islam (Sunnite) that is extremely tolerant. It is at school level that matters went uncontrolled:

> *Prepared from the lycée by a meticulous religious education punctuated by long hom-*
> *ilies concerning moral 'and the Islamic manners', these young persons will, in their*
> *majority, be well-disposed to listen to the Islamic sirens. (Rouadjia 1991: 127)*

Out of realism and not pessimism, one can predict that the language problem will go, for a while, from one extreme to another, following the swing of power between political forces. Therefore:

There cannot be a conclusion to the problem of language management because of the complex nature of the Algerian linguistic context and the everlasting absence of reason and rationality in the latter's management. If worldwide, the trend is to encourage, develop and/or maintain multilingualism, in Algeria, one foresees, by dint of time, an emergence of a monolingual society if the present process of political and educational 'unilingualisation' of the people is carried on. (Miliani 1997: 62)

The process of Arabisation has up to now not followed realism, nor even common sense, that must preside over the debates that are taking place around such sensitive questions. In the face of world economic globalisation, the country must at least keep its identity and not proceed to an identity globalisation. What must be found is a balance of the nation and state-building processes, with people's individual freedom and linguistic rights. It is highly improbable that individuals, especially Berberophones, will relinquish their ancestral rights to use their mother tongue. On the other hand, the state must also, as a challenge, try to cement the various cracks in the national identity not in a coercive way, but with more participation of individuals. Hence, the importance of establishing a progressive participatory democracy in cultural matters where people will renounce with time their individual identity and long-lasting idiosyncrasies. Coercive means can only generate confrontational attitudes of citizens or groups. Something the state has not understood is that pushing individuals to do things they do not want to do might lead to extreme positions and views. One posits as an axiom that there will not be any definite and real democracy if people's linguistic liberty (Barthes) is not protected en route towards the building of a modern state.

Notes

1   All translations are by the author.

10 Global Sport and Local Identity in Algeria: The Changing Roles of Football as a Cultural, Political and Economic Vehicle

Mahfoud Amara

Introduction

Quandt (1998) points out that the Algerian case is sufficiently rich and complex that it cannot be reduced to a single grand explanatory scheme. Ultimately, a historically based analysis of the role of sport (particularly football) in Algeria in the colonial and postcolonial period, which includes a discourse on political and national identity, is deemed essential to the understanding of contemporary sports policy in Algeria.

Sport was mobilised throughout the history of modern Algeria for different purposes (see Table 1). It has also reflected the struggle for transformation of Algerian society, from state *dirigisme* and socialism to political pluralism and a market economy, and on the field from amateurism to 'professionalism' or at least 'non-amateurism'. As a reaction to the growing media exposure and cultural flows transmitted by satellite TV channels and the impact that the global sport industry is having on local sport culture (on and off the pitch), and as a consequence also of the economic crisis, the failure of development projects, and the existence of heavy foreign debts, sport, particularly football is moving toward a market oriented economy, as part of general government strategy to reduce public expenditure and create new sources of revenue for sport. Previously prohibited because of its neo-liberal, and neo-imperialist associations, 'professional sport' is recognised today as the 'norm'. However, it remains to be seen what form this norm will take.

In terms of structure and focus, the study divides the development of football in Algeria into five stages from the colonial era to the present day. These five periods are the foundation of the Algerian national sports movement (1920-54), football in the Algerian revolution (1954-62), Socialism, sport and the nation building project

(1962-80), the economic crisis and football (1980-92), and football, democracy and the political crisis (1992-2003).

Table 1. Football as a Cultural, Political and Economic Vehicle

1926-57	Colonialism and Algerian Nationalist Movements	• Sport organised in terms of ultra-nationalist and European groups (representing cultural richness) • A colonial tool for integration • A privileged site used by nationalist movements for individual liberalisation and an instrument of subversion or political expression and rejection of colonial oppression
1954-62	Algerian revolution	• Integrated as a part of dynamic break with colonial society • Sport (football, heritage of the colonial power) used for the internationalisation of the Algerian cause
1962-88	FLN state	• Sport as a tool for nation state building • Externally, tool for national representation • Internally, an important element for political legitimatisation and integration into socialist and popular values of the nation (social positivism) • Strengthening friendship and co-operation with other socialist countries • Amateurism era
1988-92	Economic crisis and pluralism	• Increased interest in sport spectacles • An arena for political agitation and social protest or rejection of social inequalities • End of amateurism
Since 1992	Market economy	• Commercial sport?

1. The Foundation of the Algerian National Movement of Sport

As an example of colonial sport, we can cite football, which according to Alfred Wahl (reported in Dine 1996: 178) had developed in a spectacular manner, in France and *outre-mer* after World War I. In the beginning, teams were organised in Algeria in terms of ultra-nationalists and European groups (Spanish, Italian, Maltese and Jewish), reflecting the Mediterranean representation and cultural richness of Algerian society under the rule of the French Republic. The local population was not part of this social representation by the colonial power of Algerian society, and a true hostility was expressed by European settlers regarding the participation or access of the local 'indigenous' population to sport. The participation in sport was strictly reserved for European citizens (Fates, Y. 1994: 29). Algerian 'indigenous' people were not considered as citizens but 'subjects', and therefore they did not have the same rights as Europeans (settlers and state officials). According to the civil law, built on the values of French revolution, citizens' rights of freedom of thought, of speech and media, or the right of assembly and to found associations, did not exist for non-citizens. Because the majority of non-citizens were in the 'indigenous' category, they were not allowed to create their own associations or to have access to organised sport activities.

Meanwhile, as a result of a rapid increase in the level of competitions and profit, some clubs, which until then, had been composed mainly of European players, were forced to recruit talented 'indigenous' players without taking account of their ethnic origins. Some of these players were very successful and played as professionals in French teams and were even selected to play international matches with the French national team. These include players like Mekhloufi (St Etienne, 1958) who was selected to play with the French national team four times, or Brahimi (Toulouse, 1957) once, and others like Bouchouk who played for Toulouse in 1957, Ali Bennouna (Sete, 1934), Ben Bouali (l'OGC Nice, 1954), Ben Ali (Bordeaux, 1941), Firoud and Bentifour (l'OGC Nice, 1954), Bouchache (Le Havre, 1959), Salem (Sedan, 1961) (reported in Fates, Y. 1994: 34, from *Actualité de l'immigration*, 26 April, 2 May 1989).

Integration of 'indigenous' individuals into football was not only for players but also for administrators. As part of the colonial authority's policy of 'reconciliation', the presidency of Union Sportive Franco-Musulmane Setifienne (USS) was awarded to Ferhat Abbas, the leader of UDMA and supporter in his early political activism of *assimilation*. Lanfranchi & Wahl (1996: 123) suggest, according to the evidence of some *'pieds noirs'* that:

> In the case of Algeria, football formed a privileged space where the two communities mixed...Were not Albert Camus, the goal keeper for the young Racing Universitaire d'Alger and Ahmed Ben Bella, who had played professionally for Olympique Marseille, the most eloquent proof of the autonomy of sport?

However, the majority of Algerian 'indigenous-Muslims' wanted to found their own Muslim sports associations, sometimes without the consent of the colonial authorities. Mouloudia Club d'Alger (MCA)[1] was the first Muslim club to be created in 1921, with six sports sections, including football, basketball, volleyball, athletics, swimming and boxing. It was followed by others, in Constantine in the east and Oran in the west. Muslim clubs became the place for the formation of national movement leaders and a place for a wider political mobilisation. In this case, football or *'l'héritage de l'occupant'* described also by Fates, Y. (1994: 29) as *'ce corps étrange'*, was used as a means for the affirmation of Algerian society in resistance to colonial cultural hegemony, in its own field. The process of absorption and then transformation of football by nationalist movements is interpreted by Hannerz (1991), as being a form of 'creolisation' of a global culture. The periphery in this situation takes its time transforming or adapting metropolitan culture (football) to its own specification.

The majority of the names of 'indigenous' clubs started with the words *Club Musulman*, or *Union Sportive Musulmane*. Islam was a fundamental element and symbol of differentiation (between Muslim and non-Muslim clubs). Additionally, a considerable number of Muslim football clubs, to express their nationalist ideology and identity, adopted as their team colours, the colours of the 'non recognised' Algerian national flag, which were green, white and red. To protest against the massacre of 45,000 Algerians on 8 May 1945, Guelma (a team in the Constantine region) played (and still do) with black kit (Fates, Y. 1994: 32).

A description of the national space by Hussein (1997: 167) could be applied to define the role of Muslim sports associations during the colonial era. Sports clubs were in a way a space for identification, a symbolic place for gathering, and a manifestation of certain signs of community and religious acknowledgement or 'reconnaissance'. They were also a space for political messages, created by a collective voice, addressed to outsiders, and intended to be heard by the colonial power. This specific niche (sports club) was necessary for the social sustenance and expression of the Muslim indigenous population.

To reduce the influence of the so-called fanatics, nationalists and 'trouble maker' clubs, the colonial authority ordered the incorporation of three Europeans in the list of players for Muslim clubs, which wished to play against Europeans. This new rule did not stop confrontations on and off the pitch, between supporters of Muslim clubs (supporters of national independence) and supporters of European clubs (of colonial society). Football matches had become an occasion for political expression, rejection of the colonial oppression and nationalist demonstrations, all over the country. Philip Dine suggests that nationalists' movements, mainly PPA and, later on, FLN, had transformed football from a colonial tool of integration and reconciliation to a tool for political agitation (Dine 1996: 181). The letter sent by the *Préfet* of Constantine, dated 22 December 1937, addressed to the General Governor of Algiers, reflects this perfectly:

> *...For almost four months, indigenous nationalist propaganda, represented by the PPA (Algerian Popular Party) has been evident...*
>
> *Those set of ideas and doctrines delivered to a frustrated and ignorant population have resulted in a high-excitement of minds and provoked a particular 'need of expansion' within the young population, which could explain recent incidents... and regrettable manifestations that could result in compromising order and public security...*
>
> *During the match played on Sunday 20 February 1938 between JSD (Jeunesse Sportive Djidjlienne) and Union Sportive de Biskra, one minute of silence for the memory of ' 6 indigenous people killed on 6 February in Biskra' was ordered by players from JSD...*
>
> *In stadium terraces, a political agitation was directed by M. Khalef the local leader of the PPA. (In Rapport de la PRG, Archives d'outre-mer, Aix-en-Provence, reported by Fates, Y. 1994: 29 - original text in French, translated by the author)*

2. Football and the Algerian Revolution 1954-1962

According to Lanfranchi, starting from 1954, football had an important place in the FLN strategy (consciously or not) for armed struggle. An example was the decision to announce publicly the resort to armed revolution, which was made in Switzerland in a spectacular manner, in a conference held during the final of the football World Cup, organised in that country. On 26 May 1957, Ali Chekal, a former president of the Algerian Assembly, and a firm supporter of colonial society and the indissoluble link between France and Algeria, was killed by Ben Sadok, during the French Cup Final (Lanfranchi 1994: 71).

Fates points out that after the maturation of the national movement, when the FLN took over its role as the sole leader of armed revolution for independence, sport had to be integrated as a part of a dynamic break with the colonial society. As a consequence, the FLN ordered 'Muslim Clubs' in 1956 to stop all sports activities and join the ALN troops to fight against the colonial power. However, by 1958, the FLN understood the role that sport and particularly football (the most popular game in the world) could play in the internationalisation of the Algerian cause and decided to create a national revolutionary team. They gave orders to all Algerian professional players, playing in different teams in the French league, to join the Algerian national team of 'fighters' (Fates, Y. 1994: 33). Ten players, among them Mekhloufi and Zitouni, who were internationals and certain to be selected for the World Cup in Sweden, responded positively. Political leaders of the FLN welcomed the engagement and political positioning of Algerian players, which was seen as a patriotic decision that put 'the independence of the homeland before any other interests' (*Le Monde*, 22 April 1958, reported in Lanfranchi 1994: 71). Members of the FLN team, described as political militants and ambassadors of the Algerian revolution, under the leadership of Mekhloufi[2] (named by Boudjedra 1981, as '*le footballeur de la révolution*', in a novel dedicated to the FLN team), played and won successively (exactly fourteen matches), in a number of countries regarded as future allies of the Algerian republic (Lanfranchi 1994: 71) namely the Soviet Union, China, North Vietnam, and Arab countries.[3]

> *Scoring an average of four goals a game and winning many of their games, the FLN team embodies the inescapable momentum toward victory of the liberation movement itself. (Lanfranchi & Wahl 1996: 122)*

The response of the international football authorities, represented by FIFA, was to ban all Algerian players who agreed to join the FLN team. This decision was extended to all national teams, which played against the FLN team. For example, in 1958, the Moroccan Federation of Football was simply excluded from FIFA, following a demand from the French Federation, after Morocco's friendly match against the FLN team (Lanfranchi 1994: 71).

Dine states that the FLN in giving orders for indigenous clubs to withdraw from the colonial division (and stop their sporting activities in 1956), and requiring the return of professional players playing in French clubs, and their joining the FLN team had transformed football into a tool of nationalist agitation. This was further compounded by the bombing of a stadium in Algeria, and the execution of personalities who were supporters of colonial society and *Algérie Française* during a football match (i.e. Ali Chekal) in French territory (Dine 1997: 181). Nonetheless, it should be noted that the French authorities also used the stadium during the revolution (previously seen as a place for reconciliation and ethnic integration), as a tool of oppression, in an effort to destroy Algerians' (logistical) support for the revolution (e.g. the massacre of innocent members of the population in 1955 in Skikda).[4]

According to Fates, the FLN succeeded through its national football team in insuring an honourable participation in international life, by accomplishing a high quality of sporting performance and thus becoming a model for other revolutionary movements around the world fighting for their independence (e.g. the Palestinian national football team). Fates continues by stating that the phenomenon of sport participation was an efficient diplomatic instrument for the acknowledgement of the Algerian cause by international society (Fates, Y. 1994: 33).

3. Nation State Building, Socialism and Sport

Westernisation, socialist ideologies, secularism and the colonial phase have all influenced the modernisation of newly independent countries, particularly those in Arab countries like Egypt, Algeria, Morocco and Tunisia, where the appropriation of the colonial model of sport was accepted without any form of criticism or adaptation (Fates, Y. 1994: 37). According to Fates, the appropriation of the dominant model of sport was seen as a necessity, taking into account the multiple uses of sport as an element for political, social and cultural recognition. The adoption of this universal language (sport) was accumulated by the adhesion[5] of newly independent countries, during the 1960s, to the homogeneous laws, which regulate the functioning system of international sports movements and international federations. The latter were regarded as being an effective arena for future international treaties and conventions between north and south, east and west (Fates, Y. 1994: 37). In Algeria, sport as with other sectors of the society, like education, industry, agriculture, was seen by the FLN party as a real instrument that may be used: (a) externally, as a tool for national representation of the Algerian model of socialism and development; (b) internally, as an important element for political legitimisation. The FLN-state, as part of its policy for nation state building and development, had given to sport a privileged position, to serve the political formation and mobilisation of the masses, in order to maintain a social balance and stability for the political system. To continue with the process of total rupture[6] with the colonial past, after a short period of transition, the FLN-state, through its legislative system had set up a new 'Algerian' model for pedagogy and socialisation, known as the 'sport-education community'. It aimed at establishing, through the practice of sport, a moral and civic education (without any sexual distinction) and preparation of the younger generation for productive work, discipline and total integration into socialist, democratic, and popular values of the nation. With the participation of schools, sports clubs,[7] local communities, student and workers' trade unions, the objectives were concerned with the foundation of a new method of insertion within the political system, which may serve in the formation of political attitudes based on patriotism, citizenship and *civisme*, building what Fates described as a 'social positivism' (Fates, Y. 1994: 64). For this reason, a considerable financial investment (thanks to oil and gas income) was made by the state in the development of mass sport and the organisation of physical education, in training of new PE teachers and specialised sport technicians. This investment was also directed to maintaining the sport's facilities, inherited from the colonial era, and the development of new massive Olympic-scale infrastructures (e.g. the 5 July Stadium in Algiers) symbolising what is known as 'political gigantism' (*El Watan*, 30 November 2000). The aim was to host major events at national and international level such as the African, Arab and Mediterranean games, which according to Giulianotti & Finn (2000) serve to legitimise a specific state model of political administration. Other facilities were also built throughout the country (particularly in big cities), in an effort to combat centralism and 'regionalism'.

Those reforms were reinforced by new legislation[8] for physical education and sport (P.E.S) designated to all sectors of the society, and representing the essential base for national sports activities, in total compatibility with the general politics and ideology of the state (Ministry of Sport and Youth, *Assises Nationales sur le sport,* 1993). One of the most important sectors concerned with those reforms was school, where the participation in sport reached, according to ministerial estimation, 89 per cent. The promulgation of the new code for P.E.S, defined as an educational system fully integrated within the national system of education, was projected to facilitate the normalisation of sports activities and combat the inherited colonial social discrimination. More importantly, it aimed at the development of a real policy for sport, through the co-ordination, organisation and funding of different types of sport practices at different levels. Additionally, it was projected to fulfil the following obligations:

• Generalisation of PE and sport at school, university or work places, as well as in the community and within the National Popular Army;

• Encouraging specialisation in the formation of future sport coaches and technicians;

• Elaboration of a new system for detecting young talent;

• The mobilisation of necessary resources for developing the sport and physical education system.

(*Actes, Assises Nationales sur le sport,* 21-22 December 1993)

In respect of the ideals of international socialism, expressed in operational terms as 'strengthening friendship and co-operation, promoting understanding and supporting the struggle for peace and democracy and eliminating western influence' (Hazan 1987: 251), Algeria and other African and Arab (socialist) countries[9] developed a strong sporting relationship with the USSR and other socialist regimes from the Eastern block (which shared the same ideals). Those relations included receiving Soviet specialists, experts, coaches, doctors and sport administrators, sending students and athletes to physical education institutes and joint training programmes, providing financial aid and sports equipment, and finally exchanging sport delegations (Hazan 1987: 255). According to different Soviet sources discussing Soviet-Algerian sports relations, in 1982 the number of Soviet experts in Algeria had reached seventy, which is estimated to be the largest in Africa, many of them former top athletes such as A. Sergeyev (Wrestling) and Eduard Makarov (Football). This could be explained as due to the geo-strategic importance of Algeria (an Arab, Muslim, African and Mediterranean country) for the USSR's international politics. Those close sports relations had an impact on the general sport policy orientations (for historical, ideological, and political reasons) of the FLN-state. Ten years after independence, Rachid Mekhloufi, the symbol of patriotism and ambassador of the Algerian revolution, and the then coach of the Algerian national football team, was criticised by state officials for his professionalism and his method of coaching, which was seen as being too (French) European (Lanfranchi & Wahl 1996: 125). Finally, not able to convince state officials, he was dismissed and replaced by a Romanian coach,[10] regarded as having more realistic and socialist method of coaching. This decision was explained by Lanfranchi & Wahl as part of the FLN-state post-independence policy to negotiate the universalism of football, which had to be reflective of the state ideology (socialism).

It could be argued from the above that Fates's thesis regarding the adoption of the universal language of sport and the western European model of sport, which in his view happened without any form of negotiation or resistance, was not totally applicable to all cases. This becomes clear if we take into consideration the impact of socialism (a Western ideology) and anti-Western influence, in addition to Pan-Africanism and Pan-Arabism, on the general policies of newly independent countries like Algeria. This type of resistance and local response, even without real challenge to the well-established (Western) mode of organisation and practice, could be interpreted as being a form of superficial heterogeneity (see Hall 1993, cited in Houlihan 1994: 360).

4. Economic Crises and Football

Fates argued that there was a correlation between the economic crisis resulting from the consecutive fall in oil prices and the American dollar (reaching respectively 10$ and 7FM)[11] and the increased interest in sport spectacles. According to Fates, interest in sport, particularly football, had increased to become even a presidential domain. The President condemned the failure of the Algerian football team in the African Cup in Egypt 1991. He gave strict orders for the Ministry of Sport to intervene directly in changing the president of the football federation. The Ministry of Sport and Youth declared that the Algerian team's victory against West Germany, in the 1982 football World Cup in Spain, had achieved more in terms of service to the nation than the work of any other Algerian ambassadors in their positions around the world. This victory also achieved, internally within society, a sense of mobilisation and nationalist feeling, never gained before by the FLN-state. In 1986, the preparation of the national football team, for the World Cup in Mexico, was seen as being an effective ideological tool to be used by the state for finding new ways of distraction and preoccupation that keep the population away from daily realities (Fates, Y. 1994). In the same vein, Giulianotti & Finn (2000: 257) point out that 'football provides the pretext through which the "imagined community" of fellow nationals, may be reached and unified, via the match's mediation on television, radio or print'.

Because the spectacle provided by the national team became politically important internally and externally, the participation of professionals (seen during the socialist era as being against state ideological lines) became an imperative, 'demanded' by all citizens. Some of those players, because of their high popularity, were favoured in a variety of ways (free tickets, financial compensation, etc).

> *Algerian people need some emotions that have to be procured at any price. There is no event that could provide this emotion in equal manner to sport spectacles (...) In Algeria, the streets are empty on three types of occasion: at the moment of breaking the fast during Ramadan; broadcasting of national football team matches; and during the final episodes of certain popular TV series. (Fates, Y. 1994: 51 - original text in French, translated by the author).*

However, popular mobilisation achieved by international competitions, does not apply to national domestic games. The end of the 1980s had seen the starting of a state population mobilisation and repression cycle. State owned media, particularly newspaper and other security reports had shown that violence, for the season 1987-8 only, at different stadia in Algeria, had caused (officially) the death of three people, 365 injured, 127 cars damaged or completely destroyed, with 516 persons arrested. For the 1988-9 season, the same sources indicated 478 injuries, 127 cars damaged, 451 persons arrested.

Football stadia, after twenty years of independence, were transformed again into an arena for political agitation and social protest. Chikhi states that:

> *The sport stadia were next to register the heats of social discontent. At every football match, there were riots and youth demonstrations. The youth came from varying backgrounds, but they came together at regular intervals to poke symbolic fun at the high and mighty, sending up highfalutin official pretensions to morality in irreverent doggerel. In good time, such demonstrations were duly stigmatised as a threat to social harmony and unity. (Chikhi 1991: 220)*

Football matches have become the only occasion for thousands of young people to gather and shout openly against the regime and the bourgeois (called also *nouveaux riches*) and to present their social (also regional, cultural and political) demands. By asking for houses, immigration to Europe or Australia, and legalisation of drugs (sometimes in the presence of high state officials and

President), young people have used stadia to express their rejection of social inequalities, state authoritarianism and FLN hegemony. By doing so, young generations (consciously or not) became according to Fates, the actors for historical acceleration and democratic transformation.

5. Football Democracy and Political Crisis

It was a period when Algerian football had been affected by the same influences as those which Mignon (1994) describes in the French football league at the beginning of the 1990s. It is not a form of Americanisation (diffusion of American culture in Canada, or England), but another version of globalisation specific to Mediterranean football culture, which is called 'Italianisation'. The sign of this new wave coming from southern Europe did not concern the style of football played on the pitch, but it was more about supporter style (slogans, songs and symbols) and supporter behaviour, particularly in Algiers (a Mediterranean city). This may be due to the growing interest of the Algerian public TV channel and newspapers in European football, expressed by the increasing time reserved for live broadcasts, reportage and other coverage of news from the major European Leagues (the Italian league in particular, one of the most powerful leagues in Europe). It coincided with the launch of Champions' League in its new lucrative form, with more clubs, more competition and therefore more broadcasting hours. Another factor was the growing popularity within Algerian households of satellite television channels like TF1, France2 and Canal-plus, which in addition to offering longer hours for the broadcast of sporting events (including live matches, documentaries, analysis), were (and still are) seen as a means to break down the geographic isolation that Algeria was living in because of new restrictions imposed by the European Union regarding the visa delivery system. Satellite channels were also perceived as another alternative for Algerian families to express their freedom of choice to watch other programmes instead of the Algerian 'controlled' channel, which had become in their eyes another tool used by the regime for political and media manipulation.

Meanwhile, it needs to be mentioned that the 'Italianisation' of supporter behaviour in Algeria did not reach the stage of what Giulianotti & Finn (2000) refer to as a 'dislocation of national identity' when talking about the impact of the football industry on new football consumers in Asia and North America. It consists, in the Algerian case, of both local connections with their own national and club stars in addition to 'post-national' identification with European football stars made 'familiar' by the global football media and trans-national merchandising companies (see Giulianotti & Finn 2000). Mouloudia Football Club (MCA), the oldest football club in Algeria, known for its historical role in the formation of the nationalist movement and resistance against colonial hegemony, was given the name of 'Juventus' by its supporters. Algiers Union Football Club (USMA), the other popular and rival club, was given the name of 'AC Milan', and its stadium, Bologhine, the name of 'little San Ciro'. The effect of this 'Italianisation', was extended to the name of popular players and coaches: for example, Ifticene, the coach of USMA, was given the name of 'Capelo', the famous coach of AC Milan.

On the other side, Lazizi, the defender of Mouloudia, also an international player, was given the name of 'Baresi', the famous defender of the Italian national team. The other impact of this new culture, was the development of club supporters associations, transformed by their active members (mainly unemployed) into small enterprises, involved in organising trips to attend away games, the sales of different clubs' souvenirs (in the same manner as in Roma and Napoli) including badges, stickers, photos, and posters. Also in evidence was the sale of all sorts of flags and replica kits of major European professional teams e.g. Napoli, Roma, Liverpool, Milan and Barcelona exhibited by supporters at every sporting event (see Figure 1).

Football support is no longer an 'end' in itself, but a medium for the consumer to buy safely and successfully into global popular culture. (Giulianotti & Finn 2000: 266)

Off the pitch, because of the steady devaluation of the Algerian currency, privatisation and decentralisation of national co-operatives (the major sponsors of big sports clubs in Algeria) followed by the rise of unemployment, an unprecedented development occurred in the Algerian football. This development could be described as the beginning of the unofficial movement toward 'professionalisation'. It was unrecognised by the state but accepted within football clubs and it concerned the rapid growth of both transfer fees and salaries that represented the only source of revenue for some players and coaches whose positions as employees[12] in national co-operatives was no longer guaranteed.

Figs. 1 & 2. Crowd Attending a Football Match in Algiers, Illustrating Supporter Behaviour and Type of Clothing (Photo taken by Algerian New Press Agency)

At the same time there was a clear will by political parties to take over sport, particularly football (the most popular sport) for political and ideological purposes, what Giulianotti & Finn (2000) consider as the appropriation of football for service in counter-cultural (regime) resistance. Stadia became arenas for political mobilisation, and demonstrations of force for electoral campaign meetings. Inter-urban football tournaments organised during national or religious occasions in different cities were used to display symbols in favour of political, ideological and cultural claims[13] of different parties (FIS in Algiers, and RCD in Kabylie region).

6. Conclusion

Will football play the role of an economic vehicle now that Algeria is moving from a planned economy toward a market economy? The Algerian government which has financed sport since independence in 1962, now encourages the movement of sport from amateurism to professionalism, as part of a policy to reduce the size of the public sector, in order to address growing financial problems. This partial financial disengagement of the Algerian government was initiated in 1999 and it is intended that it will be completed within a period of three to five years (*Liberté*, 27 January 1999). The change in the status of football is designed to serve as a first experiment with professional sport in Algeria and may be extended to other sports, namely handball, volleyball and basketball. It will also open doors to other commercial opportunities and will bring obvious changes such as the arrival of sports agents, a professional players' union, television revenue and the potential creation of thousands of new jobs related directly or indirectly to the practice of professional sport. This evolution, which, it is envisaged, will transform sport to an important sector in the national economy, will require careful management and organisation. It necessitates an increasing amount of financial and personal support. Additionally, it needs a political system (and a policy system in general) and development strategies, which determine how existing resources are used and applied to sport (Dunning, Maguire & Pearton 1993) - in other words, the country's readiness to apply resources to the furtherance of high-performance sport. Such resources may include finance, control over legislation, specialist knowledge, legitimacy, manpower and equipment (Houlihan 1997: 19).

Thus, in order to understand the transformation of sport to professional status in the Algerian context, it will be important not only to consider the transformative capacities of state and society, but also the impact of such a transformation on wider society, which may have implications for the capacity for further transformation (i.e. development of democratic skills, management and marketing).

Notes

1 MCA was also popular within European elites (particularly from the Algerian Communist Party), favourable to the self-determination of Algerian society.

2 In April 1958, Mekhloufi abandoned the French national team preparing for the World Cup Finals in Sweden and instantly became an Algerian national symbol. A few months earlier he had been part of a French team, which won the world military football competition in Buenos Aires on the French National Day, 14 July 1957 (Lanfranchi & Wahl 1996: 119).

3 The FLN Team won 43 of its 57 matches scoring 244 goals (Chehat 1987, reported in Lanfranchi & Wahl 1996).

4 Following the decisive success of the ALN in Zone II, north of Constantine, in the large-scale attacks mounted on 20 August 1955, the colonial police and army reacted with massive repression, massacring thousands of civilian Algerians (Bennoune 1991: 71).

5 This adhesion did not happen without conflicts and a certain radicalism (for political and ideological reasons), which led sometimes to a situation of crisis (GANEFO games, black September 1972, boycotts of 1968, 1972, and 1976 Olympic Games).

6 Total rupture was not achieved, if we consider the number of teachers and sport technicians formed in France in the 1970s, according to western, secular and modern models of teaching and pedagogy.

7 The majority of clubs were directly sponsored by national corporations, like Electronic Tiziouzou, Mouloudia Oil of Algiers and Oran, Union of Sonalgas, Plastic Setif...

8 The national sport movement was still organised under the colonial law of sport dating from 1901, extended by decree 66-354 on 10 July 1963, until the appearance of the new *ordonnance* on sport and physical education, No. 76-81 on 22 September 1976.

9 Estimated at 30 for the period between 1960s and 1970s (Hazan 1987: 258).

10 The Algerian team, trained by the Romanian, suffered defeat after defeat, without making use of the service of Dahleb, or Karim Maroc, who like Mekhloufi had opted for professionalism (Lanfranchi 1994).

11 Almost all Algeria's export receipts were paid in US dollars. The devaluation of this currency reduced the value of Algerian exports by three times between 1985 and 1991 (see Dillman 1997).

12 Some of the national corporations in addition to being the official sponsors of the sports clubs, offered salaries and positions as employees for some top players and coaches.

13 For example, the pursuit of the recognition of *Tamazight* (the Berber language) as an official language by the government.

11 The Development or Redevelopment of Tourism in Algeria

Jeremy Keenan

Introduction

Algeria is one of the few countries in the world to have a massive but almost totally undeveloped potential for tourism. This is particularly unusual given the country's unparalleled natural assets and its proximity to Europe, the world's largest tourism market.

If we were engaged in the process of actually developing Algeria's tourism industry, we could talk endlessly about Algeria's extraordinary natural assets: her 1,000 kilometres of Mediterranean coast, the Atlas Mountains and the many distinct ranges within them, and the immense diversity of her Saharan regions contained within 6,000 kilometres of desert border. To these we must add her rich and diverse cultural heritage. We would be dealing with a country with which few others could compete.

Whether Algeria would ever want to follow the example of other Mediterranean states and receive five million, ten million, or perhaps even more foreign tourists a year is quite another question. Given the downside that such volumes would bring, one hopes that the country would never think of developing its potential on such a scale (even if it were able to do so). But it is debatable whether Algeria has at any time given much more than a passing thought to the serious development of this potential. Allied to this is the complex economic question of what contribution tourism could make to the national economy, bearing in mind that hydrocarbons already constitute some 95-98 per cent of the country's not inconsiderable foreign earnings.

At present, however, Algeria is not going to be able to develop a tourism industry until it has resolved its overwhelming internal problems. These problems are not just economic;[1] they are also profoundly political. Not only is Algeria's political crisis seemingly insoluble, but - even to many Algerians themselves - it is incomprehensible.

To talk about the development or redevelopment of a tourism industry in Algeria (except perhaps in the south) must therefore remain a largely theoretical exercise, at least for the immediate future. Even if the country wished to develop such an industry, the prevailing political - and, to a lesser extent, economic - conditions preclude it.

In this paper, I restrict my remarks and analysis to the south of the country, namely the Wilayas of Tamanrasset and Illizi, which cover the regions of Ahaggar and Tassili-n-Ajjer. The reasons for doing so are as follows:

• The nature of tourism development in the north, being orientated to the Mediterranean coast, the Atlas Mountains and earlier civilisations (e.g. Roman ruins, etc.) is completely different from the nature of tourism and tourism development in the south. In terms of infrastructure, the tourism product and its marketing, the two regions have little in common other than that they fall within the same national boundaries.

• While the development of tourism in the north is predicated on a solution to the country's political crisis, this is not quite so much the case in the south where there has been a significant redevelopment of tourism since mid-1999.[2]

• The current redevelopment of tourism in the south is merely the latest phase in an intricate history of tourism development in the region since the 1960s. This enables us to provide a fairly clear analysis of the nature of tourism development in the region over a 40-year period, along with the key economic, political and social issues to which it has given rise. More importantly, it enables us to say much about the positive and negative implications that certain types of tourism development will have on the region - and, in a tangential way, the country as a whole.

• Although the scale of tourism in the south is small, when measured simply in tourist numbers (we are talking in terms of thousands, not even hundreds of thousands), the current and/or future redevelopment of tourism in the region (following its cessation between the years 1992-1999) is likely to become the focus of considerable international interest. Southern Algeria is likely to be seen over the next decade or so as something of a 'global model'. Because Algeria is coming into the tourism business late, it has a golden opportunity to get it right. If it gets it right, Algeria will be seen as presiding over one of the most significant success stories in the development of sustainable tourism. If it gets it wrong (which is much easier!), it will be damned as the architect of a major environmental catastrophe. Furthermore, whichever way the south develops will have a significant impact on the way in which any future development of Algeria's huge potential in the rest of the country will be perceived and hence realised. In short, because of Algeria's 'topsy-turvy' nature, the south, perhaps ironically, is likely to become the leading edge in any future development of Algeria's potentially enormous tourism industry.

1. The Tourism Product and the History of Tourism in the South since 1962

For those who do not know the country, it is helpful to summarise what it is about the south, in terms of its assets, which enables it to offer not merely a diverse tourism product, but one that is unique within the world.

Also, if we are to understand the present nature of tourism development in the south, the critical issues that currently surround the industry and the sorts of issues and policy decisions which will ultimately determine whether Algeria presides over a global success story or an environmental catastrophe, it is helpful to have a clear understanding of how the industry has developed over the last 40 or so years.

1a. Southern Algeria's Tourism Product

The major tourist attractions of Ahaggar/Ajjer are:

Prehistoric Rock Art

The Tassili-n-Ajjer has been described as 'the world's greatest collection of Prehistoric Art'. The best-known sites are in the Tassili above Djanet (e.g. Jabbaren, Sefar, Tamrit, etc.) but extensive rock art (paintings and engravings) are found throughout most of the Tassili ranges and much of Ahaggar.[3]

Other Archaeological Attractions

The region is rich in other archaeological attractions, most of which are less obvious and not so well known, except to the 'specialist'. These concern predominantly Palaeolithic cultures, notably of the Acheulean, Mousterian and Arterian periods.[4] For such 'specialists', there are a number of interesting sites such as in the Tadrart and in and around Erg (formerly Lake) Tihodaine.

Mountain Trekking/Climbing

The various mountain ranges of Ahaggar, notably Atakor and the Tefedest, (also Tassili) are well known to rock climbers/mountaineers. They also offer some of the most fantastic mountain trekking (on foot and/or camel) in the world, especially because of the unique geology of Atakor (basic and acid lava together), the old (pre-Cambrian) exposed granites, and the extraordinary rock formations (wind and water erosion) of the Tassilian sandstones.

The Tuareg/Nomadic Life

Many visitors are/were still drawn to the region because of the almost legendary 'blue-veiled' warriors of the Sahara - the Tuareg. Their social life and culture has changed considerably, but they are still a 'tourist attraction', especially within the context of their 'nomadic' lifestyle, etc.

Unique Geology, Flora and Fauna

Both Ahaggar and Ajjer present the tourist with dramatic landforms. In Atakor these stem from the unique pattern of vulcanicity, overlying the exposed pre-Cambrian granites. The old sandstones of the Tassili offer equally dramatic scenery. In addition the great range of microclimates, extending up to almost 10,000 feet in Atakor, and the position of the region between Mediterranean and Sahelian climatic belts provides an extraordinary range of flora as well of fauna, especially bird (migratory) life.

The 'Desert Experience'

Within the context of modern-day tourism, especially the 'escape' from Europe, the 'desert experience' (sand, mountain, oases, camels, nomads, etc.) is becoming part of the 'package' scene. This is typical of much tourism in Morocco and now (once again) in Libya. Algeria has the potential, because of Ahaggar/Tassili and its greater range of environments and tourist attractions, to become the centre of the Maghreb's tourist industry.

Religion

The life of the French priest, Charles de Foucauld, who lived amongst the Tuareg at Tamanrasset and at his hermitage on Assekrem during the early years of the last century and was murdered at Tamanrasset in 1916, has increasingly become the focus of religious pilgrimage-type 'tours', notably from France, especially around Christmas and Easter.

In short, Ahaggar and Tassili are not only the most splendid of all the Sahara's many regions, but on a world scale they can count alongside only a handful of other such uniquely endowed regions.

1b. History of Tourism in Southern Algeria

The French Era - up to Algerian Independence

Prior to independence (1962), travel and exploration in the region were predominantly French based and organised. They focused on many of the above, with the inclusion of numerous motor car 'rallies' etc. The prehistoric rock art and mountaineering were probably the two main attractions of the region at that time. Archaeological 'visits' took off after the publication of Henri Lhote's account of the discovery of the Tassili Frescoes in the late 1950s.[5] Following his example, thousands of tourists (mostly French) came to the region and collected 'souvenirs' (namely artefacts, etc.). The widespread archaeological looting and damage to the region dates from this period. It has not stopped.

Post-Independence

Since 1962, tourism in the Algerian Sahara has fallen into four distinct phases: the

1960s and early 1970s; the late 1970s up to the late 1980s; from the annulment of the 1992 election to March 1999; and from 1999 to the present. Let me briefly summarise these four phases:

Phase 1: The 1960s and Early 1970s

Following independence in 1962, a small stream of 'foreign' travellers, many traversing the Sahara, passed through the region. In addition, a few European companies, mostly small and private, ran 'adventure' type holidays to the region. The best known of these in the UK was probably Minitrek. These predominately small companies ran treks through both Ahaggar and Tassili, sometimes as tours in their own right, sometimes as part of larger trans-African tours.

Although the flow of tourists through the region in the late 1960s and 1970s was small in number (a few thousand per annum), and not of any great significance to the country in terms of foreign earnings, it was absolutely critical to the region at the time. The reason for this was as follows.

The local Tuareg nomads were put under great stress in the years following independence when most of the pillars of their economy collapsed:[6]

• Slavery was abolished;

• Land was made free to those who worked it, (thus denying Tuareg access to most of 'their' former gardens);

• Caravan trade to Niger (exchanging salt for millet, the basic foodstuff of the Tuareg at that time) came to an end as a result of a combination of border controls, deteriorating terms of trade and mechanised transport.

• There was little work;

• Long-term drought hit the region.

Nomadic society faced a prolonged crisis, with many nomadic Tuareg trying to resist the inevitability of settling in the cultivation centres and working the land themselves.

The small numbers of tourists travelling through Ahaggar at that time provided a trickle of cash income into the camps. Although small in overall amount, this source of income was vital to the preservation of the nomadic (semi-nomadic) economy during those years. The importance of tourism (camel trekking, etc.) at that time was and still is recognised by the Tuareg themselves as having been critical to the maintenance of the nomadic milieu. Largely for that reason, tourists are looked on positively and welcomed by Tuareg of almost all hue (nomads, townspeople, etc.). The importance of this small-scale tourism to the survival of the nomadic community during those years cannot be overestimated.

Phase 2: Up to the Late 1980s: The First Stages of 'Mass Tourism' and Environmental Degradation

In terms of numbers, the 'high point' of tourism in the region was the late 1980s when an average of some 15,000 tourists (foreign travellers) were visiting the Ahaggar-Tassili region each year.

However, it should be noted that the impact of tourism across the region was not uniform. The 'socio-economic' impact of tourism on the two 'sides' of the region (Djanet/Tassili and Tamanrasset/Ahaggar) during this period, as in the 1960s and 1970s, was significantly different. There were two main reasons for this. One was that the nomad population (Kel Ajjer) of the Tassili was not only much smaller than Ahaggar (Kel Ahaggar), but it had sedentarised earlier and more readily, being concentrated mostly in Djanet itself (and a few other small centres such as Tamdjert, Iherir and Illizi). The second reason was because the economies of the two towns, Djanet and Tamanrasset,[7] were rather different. Whereas the economy of Djanet was based almost solely on tourism, that of Tamanrasset, being a major administrative, commercial and military centre (especially after 1991), was more diverse. Thus, while tourism had a more direct impact on the economy of Djanet than Tamanrasset, its socio-economic impact in Ahaggar was more widely felt due to the redistribution of tourism revenues amongst the outlying nomadic population.

The key feature of this second phase of tourism development in the south was that by the late 1980s some of the worst manifestations of 'mass' tourism, notably serious environmental degradation, including significant and irreversible damage to rock art sites, were becoming apparent. Indeed, the nature of tourism development was becoming so potentially damaging to the region that a major international conference, attended by 75 participants from sixteen countries, was held in Tamanrasset in November 1989 to formulate policies and draw up plans for an alternative, environmentally sustainable form of tourism. One of the conference's proposals was to establish in Tamanrasset an international centre for sustainable and responsible tourism. Because of Algeria's troubles, the project remains stillborn.

Phase 3: The Onset of 'Crisis': 1992-1999

The policies advocated at the Tamanrasset Conference were quickly consigned to history as the onset of Algeria's crisis in 1992 brought a complete cessation of tourism to the region. Tourist numbers fell from an average of 15,000 per year to a few hundred. The impact of this cessation has been as follows:

a) In Ahaggar
Prior to the onset of Algeria's crisis, there were approximately 40 tourist agencies in Tamanrasset. Some of these (probably at least half) were little more than front windows hoping to catch the passing tourist.)

As a result of the crisis, virtually all tourist agencies have closed. By 1999-2000, less than ten were still nominally in business, but effectively dormant. Only about half of these were in a position to handle more than a small handful of tourists.[8]

The impact on the surrounding 'nomadic' population would have been devastating, had it not been for the government's 'National Parks Policy'.

The Park Policy: In 1987, Ahaggar (Hoggar) was designated a National Park. By September 2000, the Park employed 550 people:

- 48 as *chefs de poste;*

- 452 as *agents de conservation;*

- 50 as office workers and drivers.

Most (if not all) of the *agents de conservation* (guardians) are 'nomadic' Tuareg.

According to my calculations, they are earning around DA 7,000 per month . (c. £70), depending on dependants etc. This comes to a total annual payment of £462,000; most of which is going into the 'Tuareg-nomadic' milieu. Although many in the region currently see the Park very critically as 'failing' in terms of its environmental conservation agenda, the Park's 'social security' policy has almost certainly saved the nomadic elements of the region from being driven into severe poverty. Such an outcome would almost certainly have had severe political repercussions, which could have taken the form of Tuareg 'revivalism', as seen in both Mali and Niger (with rebellions and much bloodshed) and/or their more sympathetic attachment to rebellious 'bandit' elements which have been prevalent in much of the Central Sahara in recent years.

Further government assistance to nomads has taken the form of issuing all nomadic families with a large tent. Small amounts of assistance have also been given by the local administration on such occasions, as when some 250 camels were killed by falling on ice in the high mountains of Atakor.[9]

b) In Tassili-n-Ajjer (Djanet)
The impact on Djanet has had more direct consequences on the town and its commercial sector than on the region as a whole, which is largely devoid of a nomadic population. According to the office for the Tassili National Park, its 80 wardens (*gardiens du Parc*) are no longer employed by the Park. I am under the strong impression that this almost total collapse of the tourist economy at Djanet has led to a certain out-migration of people, looking for work elsewhere - i.e. around Illizi and further north (in and around the oil fields etc.). Several have almost certainly moved across the border to Ghat and environs in Libya where mass tourism has restarted in earnest.[10]

The impact of the cessation of tourism on the region has been more complex and unexpected than we might at first think. It might reasonably be assumed that the loss of an entire industry, bringing some 15,000 tourists to the region each year, would have had devastating socio-economic consequences. Without in any way wanting to diminish the seriousness of this loss, we should bear in mind a number of 'less negative' outcomes.

Firstly, while most tourism agencies have been put out of business, many of them were 'fly by night' operators who were themselves major contributors to the problems of mass tourism.

Secondly, the loss of some 15,000 tourists a year on both the 'urban' and 'rural/nomadic' economies has not been as damaging as might have been expected. Although Djanet's commercial sector, with its dependency on tourism, was affected severely, Tamanrasset's post-1991 boom, caused by the town's increased administrative, military and commercial importance, has partly compensated for the losses caused by the collapse of the tourism industry. Similarly, the 'social security' dimension of the National Parks policy has averted a widespread socio-economic disaster within the nomadic milieu.

Finally, and perhaps most important in the longer run, the cessation of tourism saved the region from any further serious environmental damage. A decade without tourism has given people time in which to think about what sort of tourism is now needed. It is the outcome of this reflection to which policy-makers should now pay heed.

Phase 4: The Regeneration of Tourism Since Autumn 1999

Abdelaziz Bouteflika's appointment as the country's president in March 1999 was met with a sense of cautious optimism that the country's 'crisis' might soon be resolved. This more optimistic mood was reflected in the number of foreign visitors to Tamanrasset reaching 900 by the end of the year, of whom about half came through Djanet as part of the Tassili circuit.[11] A report put out by Algerian sources in the summer of 2000 claimed that the number of tourists passing through Tamanrasset had risen to 2,000 by the end of July 2000. This figure was almost certainly exaggerated, although there was definitely a slight increase over the previous year. Further statistics provided by official sources indicate that the number of foreign visitors/tourists to the region in the tourist season October 2000-April 2001 reached almost 8,000.

2. Comments on the Nature of Current Tourism Development in the South

While the return of foreign visitors to Southern Algeria is to be welcomed, several cautionary notes should be heeded.

The 'Massaging' of Statistics

Firstly, the statistics themselves are highly questionable. Neither the precise source of these statistics nor their method of compilation is clear. Foreigners who do travel in Algeria will know that the country has inherited and kept much of what was bad about the 'ancient' French system of administration, particularly its obsession with *chiffres* - many of which are quite unnecessary. In Tamanrasset, as in other parts of the country, at least five sets of 'statistics' are compiled for different branches of the administration: the police, the Director of Tourism, the Customs, the Wali's office, etc. Local tourist agencies place little faith in 'official' figures, believing them to be a crude form of double or triple accounting to give a more favourable impression of what is happening in the country. According to local agencies, Tamanrasset received 880 tourists between October and the end of the year 2000. If we assume that the new Pointe Afrique and Cross Air Charter flights (which, in the first case, ran weekly from December 2000 and, in the second case, fortnightly from February 2001) carried approximately 100 passengers per flight, then we can estimate some 2,200 more arrivals between January and April. If we accept the official figure of nearly 8,000, then it means that some 5,000 visitors must either have travelled overland or by regular Air Algérie flights in the first four months of the year. That was almost certainly not the case.

Having myself travelled in the region twice during this 'season', I would be more inclined to agree with the local tourism agencies who put the number of tourists for the season at a much more realistic figure of about 2,500-3,000.

The 'Politicisation' of Tourism
Secondly, the release to the media of such highly dubious 'official' statistics reflects the government's own current desire to increase tourist numbers in order to show that Algeria is a 'normal' country. One can easily sympathise with the government's politicisation of tourism in this way. It is particularly frustrating for the Algerian government to be confronted day after day with bald statements from foreign governments saying that Algeria as a whole is unsafe for tourism. That is certainly true for the north of the country, but not for the extreme south. I have repeatedly placed myself on public record during the last few months, saying that Ahaggar and Tassili are almost certainly the safest regions for tourists in the entire Sahara.[12] No country likes to hear of its regions being spoken of as 'another country', but, in many respects, Algeria's south is 'another country' compared to the north.[13]

3. What Type of Tourism Does Algeria Wish to Develop in the South?
While recognising that Algeria's current promotion of tourism, notably in the south, is primarily for political rather than economic reasons, the emphasis being placed on tourism statistics, no matter what their validity, raises my third and most important comment, namely: what type of tourism does Algeria wish to develop in the south?

The 1989 Conference in Tamanrasset recognised the dangers of 'mass' tourism that were beginning to become manifest in both Ahaggar and the Tassili. The

Conference drew a line in the metaphorical sand. Algeria's crisis, not any change of policy, stopped that line being crossed. All the signs now are that tourism in the south is about to be redeveloped along exactly the same lines as in the late 1980s.

This is not surprising. Not only is the government keen to portray rising tourist figures as some sort of index of 'returning normality', but many short-term business interests in the region are desperate to use this opportunity to make up for the lean times of the last decade.

The last year or so has shown all the signs that the industry is not simply redeveloping where it left off in the late 1980s, but that this redevelopment, encouraged by both the government's use of tourism statistics as an index of returning 'normality' and businesses desperate to make up for the lean times of the last decade, is along even more rapacious and even less sustainable lines.

The dangers of mass tourism that were developing in the late 1980s were clear for all to see, and were spelt out at the Tamanrasset conference. The increasing shift away from camel-based to 4WD-based tourism was threatening the nomadic milieu. Serious and irreversible environmental degradation, including the vandalism and looting of archaeological sites (especially rock art sites) was becoming widespread; and indigenous/local business interests were becoming increasingly marginalised as a result of the 'muscling in' of external business interests (*les gens du nord* and foreign tour operators).

The temporary cessation of tourism did not allow the environment to recover. That is because most of the damage inflicted in the 1980s - graffiti and other vandalism of rock art, the 'looting' of archaeological sites; litter (most of which does not degrade in this environment); damage to vegetation, etc. - is irreversible. The lesson that has been learnt by some of the more far-sighted people in the region is that one of the world's greatest natural environments, a world heritage site, and the country's greatest asset (along with its hydrocarbons), was temporarily saved from further damage by the cessation of tourism. It is imperative, for Algeria's own sake, that this lesson is now heeded.

In Algeria's current state, when the government has its hands full with seemingly more urgent and pressing matters, this is not as easy as it sounds. Understandably, it is easier to pass the buck to existing local or international bodies and institutions, such as the National Park, UNESCO, etc. But, for reasons which are too lengthy and detailed to be gone into here, this will not work. The National Park, in spite of the lip service that is paid to environmental conservation, is failing in that primary role. UNESCO, on whom so many have faith, has itself failed abysmally in other areas.

Algeria's south now has a window of opportunity to redevelop its enormous and unique tourism potential along the guidelines of the 1989 Tamanrasset Conference, namely - away from a tendency towards 'mass' tourism and towards an environmentally sustainable tourism.

But, to quote one leading tour operator in the region, there is no point in developing tourism: it has been developed; the 'limits' have been reached. Tourism in the region does not need to be 'developed': it now needs support in the form of environmental protection policies (and their implementation), training agencies, tax concessions and other financial support/credit schemes.

The idea that 'limits' have been reached is most clearly expressed in terms of such things as water and waste. The current drought, more the norm than the exception, means that there is not enough water for the current hotels' showers, let alone for the building of new hotels that are hardly needed. As for waste management, the predominant flora around Tamanrasset is now the plastic tree, which flourishes in the immediate desert hinterland of the town (it calls itself a 'city'). The surrounds of the town, such as the Oued Sersouf, Source Chapuis, Imlaoulaouene, etc., once tourist attractions in their own right, are now disgusting and dangerous health hazards.

In addition to the constraints on the growth of tourism in the region provided by such things as the limits on water supply, waste disposal etc., there are several other 'limits' which have to be considered, namely: the number of trained cameleers, guides, park wardens etc. In short, the future development of tourism in the region must not and cannot be reckoned simply by the simple and crude statistic of the number of hotel beds available.

Current developments, notably the *Partenariat* agreement between the French and Algerian governments of 30 January 2001, plans for new hotels, the encouragement of ever more charter flights (although not in themselves bad), the failure of the Direction of the National Park, are all indicative of the absence of any strategic planning, either short or long-term. On the contrary, all the signs are pointing towards a headlong rush to the sort of mass tourism that has led to an environmental catastrophe in the bordering Acacus region of Libya. Over the last winter/tourist season, 45,000 tourists visited the region. The environmental damage was catastrophic, including the vandalism/looting of some 40 rock art sites. Such 'looting' and vandalism has already spilled over into Algeria's far richer sites. Five years of tourism on the scale seen in Libya's Acacus region could lead to the destruction of one of the world's greatest heritages. If that is allowed to happen, the implications for Algeria will be serious. Not only will she have to bear an enormous burden of blame, but the country will probably never be able to develop its full tourism industry potential or become a global leader in the development and management of sustainable tourism.

4. The Solution - Towards the Development of a Strategy for Sustainable Tourism

In a climate in which numbers and money are all-important, let me give one simple economic illustration of how sustainable tourism in the region could be developed. The notion of sustainable tourism is used in its simplest terms: to meet the economic, social and associated needs and long-term interests of the local/regional population while conserving the region's delicate environment and cultural heritage.

The greatest assistance in developing such a strategy, ironically, may be the fact that the crisis in the north will not allow large-scale tourist development in the area (i.e. with insurance/liability cover) for the immediate future - possibly longer. Such sustainable tourism must be based on low volume (numbers of people), high value tourism. No limit can be put on numbers at this stage, nor should such a limit be desirable, quite apart from the near impossibility of enforcing it. But, to get an idea of what locals themselves are thinking, the numbers that were coming through the region in the late 1980s were 'quite enough'.

Being on an international route, it is probably impossible to control traffic passing through Tamanrasset. However, as the region comprises two Parks (Hoggar and Tassili), it is relatively easy to regulate access and movement within the region. More important than sheer numbers, is the quality and type of tourism on offer. Local tourism agencies would prefer to see small, high-paying groups of tourists, which can be offered high level personnel service: i.e. accommodation - gîte/camping of a desired quality; camel trekking with experienced 'guides'/cooks/personnel attendees, etc.; four-wheel drive tours to specific sites with camping and associated 'high quality' facilities provided (i.e. a combination of 'adventure/culture/educational/relaxing - getting away' type holidays).

Such tourists would be paying a 'premium' price for the 'uniqueness' of Ahaggar/Tassili - c. £1000 per week, i.e. analogous to prices paid for similar type tours in other parts of world. Concession rates could be paid by students, educational, scientific groups, etc.

Such tourism has major economic benefits to the region in that this form of tourism can be managed by indigenous tourism agencies (i.e. those based in and operating in the region) rather than foreign-based tour agencies. This is vitally important for the regeneration of tourism as it means that the bulk of the money paid by tourists goes to local agencies, not to foreign operators, as is still mostly the case. Local agencies would require agents in the client countries (France, Germany, UK, Switzerland, etc.), but external agents, including flights, insurance, etc., need not be more than a maximum of 50 per cent of the cost structure. This means that at least half the money being paid by the tourists is going directly into the local agency. At present, as in other global markets, this is often as little as 10 per cent, especially where hotels and other facilities are also foreign/externally owned.

Some degree of help/protection will be needed from the Algerian government - partly to protect local/regional interests from the endemic corruption within Algeria itself and the usurpation of local business interests by *les gens du nord*, and to help with the establishment of bona fide agents, etc.

The major economic benefit of this type of tourism is that it is very 'labour intensive'. Very roughly, a single tourist requires the support of at least one full-time employed attendee. For example: a group of six people on a two-week tour in the region requires the employment of at least two drivers (ideally three vehicles), one cook, one cook's assistant, one guide, one camp support staff. If any camel/donkey treks are involved en route, which is likely, then camel/donkey hire plus cameleers etc. are required.

To take this illustration further: if a group of twelve, on a two-week tour, pays £1,000 per head per week (including use of scheduled Air Algérie flights), with 50 per cent going to local operator, then local operator receives £12,000. Of this amount, about £8,000 will go to the local agency for infrastructure costs (e.g. vehicles, gîte maintenance and depreciation), overheads (e.g. fax machines, office and staff, etc.), local taxes, fuel and food supplies, camping equipment, etc. Approximately £4,000 will go directly to employees and associated suppliers. Thus, taking the present economics of the Park Policy (i.e. c. £462,000 'social security' payment), then 115 such trips (i.e. roughly 1,400 tourists per annum for two weeks each) would inject the same amount into the local (employee) network. If the tour agency is included, then the state's expenditure is met by only 38.5 such trips in a year with only 462 tourists. How does this compare with current 'package' tour operators?

Taking current tours and prices being offered by 'mass' tour operators from France and Switzerland operating charter flight package tours into the region, it is estimated that at least three times as many tourists would be required to inject the same amount of income into the local economy. These rather rough calculations indicate that this would require around 2,300 people to come on 7-8 day tours to the region. On their present schedules etc., this would require around 25 weekly return charter flights (based on 100 per flight).

The above figures are estimates, but they give an idea of the enormous financial/economic viability and benefits of such forms of environmentally sustainable forms of tourism development compared with the current trend towards mass tourism as being developed under the new Partenariat agreement with French and Swiss-based operators.

At present, there is no overall plan for the development of sustainable tourism for this region. This is urgently needed, and could be provided at very low cost by external and completely independent agencies that have long and intimate knowledge and experience of the problems of the region.[14]

Sustainable Tourism and the Political Stabilisation of the Region

Sustainable tourism in Ahaggar-Tassili can only be developed through the close integration of the tourism industry and the nomadic milieu. This is expressed in the frequently expressed local dictum:

No nomadism without tourism: no tourism without nomadism.

If the nomadic element is excluded from this development, as was beginning to become the case in the late 1980s and is becoming prevalent again now, there are two serious political consequences.

The first is that such exclusion will play into the hands of Islamic 'fundamentalist' movements, or their equivalents, as has been seen in Egypt, where the consequences for the tourism industry and the national economy have been disastrous. In southern Algeria, such exclusion is more likely to see young men being attracted to 'banditry', 'smuggling' and so forth, which is widespread across much of the central and southern Sahara, and which poses serious threats to states within the region, and especially to Algeria as the richest of the Saharan states.

Secondly, the ultimate protection of the environment, and in particular the cultural heritage (rock art, other antiquarian sites, etc.), can only be assured when local people see it not merely as part of their heritage, but as part of their future, as their own asset, over which they have control and through which their and their families' economic futures can be assured.

Conclusion

Algeria wants to be a normal country. Amongst Saharan states, 'normalisation' currently involves the vandalism and destruction of the cultural heritage. To see how this is being affected, one need look no further than the damage being inflicted on prehistoric sites in Libya's Saharan regions or to Morocco's extensive prehistoric rock art adjoining the Draa Valley. So, let Algeria become 'abnormal' by using its unique Saharan assets to develop a sustainable tourism, which can become a beacon of such development to the rest of the world.

Algeria has a choice, which is neither difficult to make nor expensive to execute. Either it can pick up the cudgels of the 1989 Tamanrasset conference and become a world leader in the development of sustainable tourism, or it can allow the present trends towards mass tourism and environmental degradation to continue and be held responsible by both its own citizens and the international community for what will inevitably become a major environmental catastrophe. In fact, Algeria has no choice.

Notes

1 Algeria is ranked 122 out of 123 countries in the world in terms of openness - behind only Myanmar.

2 Although a few more headlines like those relating to the Berber unrest and associated demonstrations against *le pouvoir* of April-May 2001 will almost certainly put an end to this.

3   The oldest rock art dates from a maximum of 13-12,000 years BP, which is when the last (Würm) Ice Age ended and the Neolithic period began.

4   Roughly 250,000 BP through to 18,000 BP.

5   Published in France under the title *A La Découverte des Fresques du Tassili*, the book was translated into English and published by Hutchinson & Co. in 1959 under the title: *The Search for the Tassili Frescoes: The story of the prehistoric rock-paintings of the Sahara*. The book has been reprinted several times since its first publication.

6   For a detailed analysis of these events, see Keenan 1977.

7   Current populations: Djanet c.15,000; Tamanrasset c.100,000 - including military.

8   The National Park Post at Mertoutek (in the Tefedest) epitomised the disaster that overtook the region. There, not one single tourist signed the Park register between 1993 and November 1999, when three Spaniards, followed by myself, entered the region.

9   The date of this rather bizarre event has been given by local informants as the winter of 1996.

10 This same trend has occurred in Ahaggar where Tuareg have moved to Mali. Their entry into Mali has been facilitated by the fact that the Kel Ahaggar gave sanctuary to Mali Tuareg during the recent Mali uprising.

11 Source: local authority.

12 I myself take tourists to Tassili and Ahaggar: Given the political instabilities (including unmarked mined areas), I would be disinclined to take tourists to many parts of Mauritania, Niger, Mali, Chad, Libya, Sudan or even the Egyptian Sahara.

13 One of Algeria's lesser-known statistics is that it is further from Algiers to the country's southernmost border than it is from Algiers to London.

14 Suggestions would be the London-based International Institute for Culture, Tourism and Development in collaboration with University College London's (UCL) Institute for Archaeology, the latter being the only centre in Europe equipped with the requisite skills and experience in this field, as well as detailed knowledge of the region.

12 Perspectives From a Major Foreign Investor – British Petroleum's Investment in Algeria

Dai Jones

Introduction

The following paper is a view through the eyes of British Petroleum (BP) at what is happening in Algeria in terms of developments in the oil and gas industry in the country and how our partnership in Algeria with the State Oil Company Sonatrach is being built. Given the level of interest in the Algerian oil and gas market place and in our projects in particular, our perspective on the challenges and opportunities ahead should be extremely valuable to the current debate.

1. BP's Journey So Far

Well before the merger with Amoco and Arco, BP was leading the UK investors in Algeria. Indeed, after the signature of the In Salah agreement with Sonatrach that took years of negotiations, BP initiated unique marketing in Algeria.

Using specifically the 'Social Investment' concept, BP offered scholarships to Algerian students to the UK, donated educational material to schools in the Sahara and participated in social improvement projects, like the very successful water supply to In Salah town (where BP's main gas project is).

As a result of BP's merger with Amoco in 1998 and the acquisition of Arco in 2000, BP has become the number one foreign investor in Algeria with more than $4.5 billion (oil at Rhourde El-Baguel, gas at In Salah and In-Amenas). BP has already invested some $1.5 billion. For the next three years, BP will invest $3 billion more, when the development of the gas projects takes place.

Clearly it has been a very exciting time for BP in Algeria and it remains an exciting time for the oil and gas industry.

Oil prices have stabilised after a period of volatility and the increased robust nature of prices has stimulated the continuation and the initiation of significant international projects in the oil and gas business. A word of caution, though, is in order, for how long this stability will last is always uncertain!

There is a powerful consumer driven shift to the use of natural gas. Gas consumption has grown by more than 50 per cent in the past two decades and has become the fuel of choice, particularly for power generation, due to its abundance, efficiency and environmental benefits. This shift is further supported by the current projected growth in world gas demands of 2 per cent per annum (which translates into about 1.6 tcf[1] per year). Southern Europe is a major component of this growth.

Natural gas is progressively changing from a local or national market business into an international one. Gas trade has been growing by about 9 per cent per annum for the last twenty years through international pipelines and LNG[2].

Europe is a major component of this growth. Europe's member states account for only 2 per cent of world gas reserves, however 80 per cent of the world reserves are within a reachable distance to Europe. In this context, there are two components to Algeria's stated hydrocarbon objectives:

• To increase its base reserves and production capacity;

• To increase natural gas export capacities.

The strategies, which were outlined to achieve these objectives, were based on partnership with foreign oil companies and included the following:

• Intensification of exploration efforts;

• Development of new oil and gas fields that have not yet been exploited;

• Enhanced oil recovery projects.

Algeria is very well positioned on the supply side to meet a healthy portion of this growth in demand. As the second largest country in Africa and the tenth largest in the world, it has the advantages of an abundance of hydrocarbons and its proximity to Southern Europe. With Algeria's existing gas transportation infrastructure, it makes it a natural and attractive supplier of low cost gas to Europe. Algeria's remaining gas reserves are estimated at around 3,800 bcm[3] with a reserves to production ratio of around 50 years. Approximately 90 per cent of Algeria's exports go to Europe, representing 25 per cent of European consumption.

BP's Algerian projects in partnership with the state oil company, Sonatrach, are expected to play a significant role in the further development of Algeria as an international leader in the oil and gas industry.

BP was first active in Algeria in the late 1970s and has maintained an active presence over the last decade. In combination with recent acquisitions and mergers, the subsidiaries that make up today's BP Algeria have been active in Algeria for an even longer period.

BP is pleased that through our partnership with Sonatrach on three major projects, we are working with Algeria to meet its set hydrocarbon objectives through their set strategies.

Turning to BP involvement in Algeria, we feel fortunate to be in partnership with Sonatrach who have tremendous experience in oil and gas operations, technically skilled staff and a strong track record, not only in finding oil and gas but also in developing, transporting and marketing it.

BP is the largest foreign oil company now active in Algeria, and the largest investor in the country, with three major projects:

1. In Salah Gas;

2. In Amenas gas condensate development; and

3. Rhourde El Baguel EOR[4] project.

The In Salah Gas project is a world class project which will open up the gas rich areas of the Western Sahara to new developments and deliver needed gas supplies to Southern Europe. The project entails the development of seven proven gas fields that lie between El Golea and In Salah, in the centre of Algeria. This new production will come on stream by 2004, to supply growing gas markets in Southern Europe. The project is unique among Algerian contracts in that it covers both joint development of the reserves and joint marketing of the gas to customers. Other competitors are now starting to follow this lead and structure partnerships along similar lines. The overall cost of the project is estimated at some $2.7 billion, with production of nine billion cubic metres of gas per year, continuing until 2027. In Salah Gas is strategically important for Algeria, as it opens a new region for production, by means of a 500-km pipeline linking the area to existing gas export infrastructure which leads to Spain and Italy, and will increase annual Algerian export gas production by about 15 per cent.

The In Amenas project relates to the development of natural gas and gas liquids from four wet gas fields in the In Amenas area of the Illizi basin in south-east Algeria. The contract is a more traditional production sharing agreement with BP taking its remuneration in the form of condensate and LPG[5] and Sonatrach taking the gas. Development cost is expected to be around $800 million to first gas production in 2005 and $1.2 billion over the life of the twenty-year contract. The new development will produce and process about twenty million cubic meters of wet gas per day and have an average daily production of 50,000 barrels of condensate and LPG.

Rhourde El Baguel is a development using enhanced oil recovery techniques on an existing oil field. REB is a giant oilfield estimated to have over three billion bbls[6] of oil in place. The PSC[7] was signed in 1996 with Sonatrach for this EOR project on a field that had been originally discovered by Sinclair in the 1960s. Sonatrach has recently farmed in for a 40 per cent equity share and we look forward to the significant contributions that this enhanced partnership may bring. More than $1.2 billion have been invested to date with the goal of increasing the production to about 120,000 barrels of oil and liquids per day. The field lies close to Sonatrach's first, and still most significant, oil field at Hassi Messaoud, in northeast Algeria.

2. The Importance of Algeria?

Algeria's current gas export infrastructure capacity stands at about 65 bcm/a[8] with the expectation that it will reach more than 85 bcm/a by 2010. Gas exports reached about 60 bcm/a in 2000, with projection for it to reach 85 bcm/a by the year 2010.

With the additional gas production of 9 bcm/a from In Salah and up to 7 bcm/a from In Amenas, BP, in partnership with Sonatrach, will be contributing significantly to the goal of growing Algeria's gas production capacity. Export gas production from In Salah alone will add approximately 15 per cent to the export supply capacity, and will contribute significantly to meeting the ever-growing demands of the European energy markets.

These are exciting times for BP in Algeria with two major gas projects underway that will contribute significantly to Algeria's gas export capacity by some 30 per cent. We are keen to remain at the forefront of Algerian gas development, as Algeria's own gas strategy adapts. We are committed to a strong future working with our partners Sonatrach. We are grateful to the Sonatrach management, for working with us constructively to provide a solid foundation to build a strong partnership between our company and Algeria. We believe that Algeria has a major role to play in providing needed energy supplies to Europe. We believe this could be done in a way that can address the issues of a liberalised EU market and the security of supply - two very politically charged issues.

Responsible liberalisation is key. The liberalisation process is a highly interconnected process and therein lays one of the key policy problems in Europe. It is easy for policy makers to pull on the levers that they can reach and leave the ones they cannot reach alone. Out of reach in European terms means politically too difficult. A good example of the levers they can reach is the destination clauses, which are present in long-term contracts between the EU member states and Russia and Algeria.

Over time, these clauses will cease to be an important part of the commercial agreements in a liberalised market. But today they are a reality - an important reality for those countries that do not fall under the EU laws and regulation and which have been fundamental suppliers of Europe energy needs over many years. This highlights the importance of proper and timely consultations between the EU and producing countries on this issue, rather than resorting to competition law. The solution will come through dialogue and a combination of geo-political compromises and commercial negotiations rather than the courtroom. This will allow Algeria and its partners to move forward, focusing on increasing sales and new business development opportunities.

The move in Europe towards a liberalised market will be good for producers such as Algeria, as the UK experience has shown. The impact of this move on current and future projects will be significant. However, it is the effectiveness of the transition, rather than the end product of full liberalisation that we need to pay attention to. How this transition is managed will govern the pace of growth in Europe, the ability to meet market demands, and investor confidence in new developments as producers.

Back to In Salah specifically, the construction of the 500-km 48-inch pipeline will open a new region for further gas production linking this area to existing gas support infrastructure currently connecting Italy and Spain. This new transportation network will be significant in the further development of more distant gas reserves and further enhance the national development plans for an increase in gas production and export.

In addition to the reserve enhancement, increased export capacity, and further development of the critical infrastructure, all of these projects will contribute to the development of work and employment for the Algerian oil and gas sector. This translates into increased revenue generation for the Algerian nation.

The last decade has been an exciting one for the expansion of the oil and gas industry in Algeria. Opportunities for exploration opened up and partnerships with various international operators enjoyed some tremendous success. International oil and gas companies operate on an increasing global scale and search out the best opportunities worldwide. Investment must always be based on an assessment of risk versus potential reward. The areas that are the most competitive and attractive to the foreign investors will succeed while others will not.

Algeria has been working over the last decade to create an environment that is attractive and conducive to large scale and long-term investment. It is imperative that this environment is maintained, nurtured and adapted to the ever-changing global market conditions and competition. This is a challenging venture but one that is essential for Algeria to take on and progress in order to be able to compete globally.

We at BP are working with Sonatrach to combine cooperative leadership with technological advances and economies of scale to develop a competitive Algerian business that creates further opportunities. Bigger is not necessarily better unless it affords the opportunities to improve competitiveness through cost savings and improved efficiencies. Given the magnitude and the commonalties between our projects, we see great opportunities to build on the synergies that these projects provide to improve our overall business.

To that effect we are working closely with Sonatrach to identify these areas of mutual benefit that range from a common organisational structure to sharing the logistics, equipment, contractors, and much more. This concept would also benefit synergies between partnerships on other projects in Algeria.

It is not easy. It requires vision and the ability to think differently from the conventional practices of the past. It requires collaboration, consultation, teamwork and above all, clear and effective communication. BP and Sonatrach have recognised this challenge and the unique opportunity it presents and are working to achieve the obvious commercial rewards. This is a true indication of the recognition of the mutual interest of both partners and the Algerian State reflecting on a new pattern of relationship between Sonatrach and international investors built on trust and mutual benefits to all involved.

In the past, foreign investment traditionally translated into initial capital investment, ongoing operating costs and a harvesting of benefits from the project. BP's involvement does not; it goes much further. Our 'Invest in Algeria' programme takes into account our commitment to differentiate ourselves from our competitors in how we do business in Algeria. We believe that it is the right thing to do and is ultimately good for business and the communities we live in.

This programme has many facets but its main goal is not just a financial commitment to the oil and gas projects but an overall sustainable investment in programmes that benefit individuals, the communities that we live in and the Algerian nation as a whole. This is reflected in some of our ongoing programmes that are highlighted below.

We have a recruitment and development programme, which we call our 10-10-10 programme. This is BP Algeria's national employee recruitment and development programme. Our goal for 2001 is to recruit 10 professionals with up to 10 years experience, sponsor 10 students undertaking undergraduate or postgraduate studies, and to recruit 10 new graduates. We hope that at least one of the experienced professionals will be able to join our leadership team within the year. It is expected that those recruited will be developed within the wider world of BP, as well as within the Algeria business unit. This will allow them to gain company wide expertise that they can utilise, either working in Algeria or elsewhere in the world.

In the communities where we live and operate, BP is undertaking a social investment programme designed to bring immediate benefits to communities in southern Algeria and provide longer-term sustainable opportunities. Projects include English language training, the provision of fresh water and solar power systems to remote communities in the Sahara desert, encouragement for small enterprises and international cultural exchanges.

This programme is still in the early stages and is evolving but we believe that it has been successful so far. It is important to design a programme that is in harmony with partner and state objectives and takes into account the real needs, without inadvertently creating a culture of dependency or imposing any conflicting values. We believe that we share the same vision with our partners and we believe that it is the responsible way to conduct business for both our shareholders and the communities where we work.

3. The Future Vision of BP in Algeria

We are continuing to build the foundation for our business in Algeria. It is a strong, broad foundation but it is critical that we construct it soundly. We are actively engaged in progressing our current projects as an efficient Algerian business, in a way that is both constructive and conducive to further development.

The initiatives that we are engaged in to enhance the business climate and viability of project synergies increase our confidence for the future in Algeria. These do however need to be brought to fruition in order to increase the attractiveness and competitiveness of Algeria on the global investment market. Real confidence comes from a consistent industry-wide track record of successful developments and a sound and reliable business climate. Investment always entails risk but the mitigation of this risk and a stable and secure business environment is essential in the attraction of future investment.

Great potential exists in Algeria and BP hopes to be in a position where Algeria successfully competes for our future limited investment. We remain open and willing to work with our partner, Sonatrach, to explore new horizons that we hope will enhance Algeria's future. We will deliver on our current commitments.

Conclusion

The thing that stands out from all the experience we have had, is the real impact global oil and gas market trends have on Algerian business and how Sonatrach and BP need to be able to get from where we are today to where we need to be, quickly enough to both create and capture the new business opportunities nationally and internationally.

We know change is good in the long run - but the change phase in Algeria seems very difficult at times, because there are always issues around contract terms, costs, tax and legislation. Our experience has not always been positive but we have learned from our experience and have tried to improve quickly.

For a company like BP, the ability to learn and change quickly is very important. We are an adaptor that seeks to resolve changes quickly and efficiently. This is still our ambition, but we underestimated the practical realities of these changes in Algeria, where change does not come easily!

Nonetheless, changes are still progressing and this is only a progress report on our journey of major investments in Algeria.

There is much more to do, many question still to be answered, but we see a more dynamic future for international business investments being created in Algeria.

Notes

1   tcf: trillion cubic feet (of gas).

2   LNG: Liquified Natural Gas.

3   bcm - billion cubic metres (of gas).

4   EOR - Enhanced Oil Recovery.

5   LPG - Liquified Petroleum Gas.

6   bbls: barrels (of oil).

7   PSC - Production Sharing Contract.

8   bcm/a - billion cubic meters a year (of gas).

Bibliography

Abdeladim, L. (1998), *Les Privatisations d'entreprises publiques dans les pays du Maghreb: Maroc-Algérie-Tunisie*, Algiers: Les Editions Internationales.

Abdul-Rahaman, A. S. (1998), 'Public Sector Accounting and Financial Management Systems in the Context of Socio-economic Development: An Empirical Study of the Volta River Authority in Ghana', *The International Journal of Accounting and Business Society*, 6: 1, pp. 68-94.

Adamson, K. (1999/2000), 'French Political Economy in 1840: Evidence from Algeria. An Exploration of the Writings of Blanqui, Enfantin and Bugeaud', *Journal of Algerian Studies*, 4/5, pp. 21-44.

Adamson, K. (2002), *Political and Economic Thought and Practice in Nineteenth Century France and the Colonisation of Algeria*, Lampeter/Lewiston: Edwin Mellen Press.

Addi, L. (1995), *L'Algérie et la démocratie*, Paris: Editions de la Découverte.

Amin, Q. (1970), *Tahrir Al-Mar'a (The Emancipation of Women)* [1899], Cairo: Dar al-Ma'arif.

Amin, Q. (1995), *Al-Marat al Jadidah (The New Woman): a document in the early debate on Egyptian Feminism* [1900], Cairo: American University in Cairo Press.

Amnesty International (1997), *Algeria: Civilian population caught in a spiral of violence*, London: Amnesty International.

Amrane, D. (1991), *Les Femmes algériennes dans la Guerre*, Paris: Plon.

Amrane-Minne, D. (1999), 'Women and Politics in Algeria from the War of Independence to Our Day', *Research in African Literature*, 30: 3, pp. 62-77.

Annisette, M. (1999), 'Importing Accounting: the Case of Trinidad and Tobago', *Accounting, Business & Financial History*, 9: 1, pp. 103-33.

Argyris, C. & Schon, D. (1996), *Organisational Learning II*, San Francisco: Addison-Wesley.

Attout, N., Chebab, T. & Kelkoul, M. (1999), *Femme, emploi et fécondité en Algérie*, CENEAP/FNUAP.

Aziz, M. & Taibi, Y. (1995), *Algérie 2000, Scénarios d'Evolution*, Tunis: Imprimeries MAN.

Balia, P. & Rulleau, C. (1978), *La Stratégie de Boumedienne*, Paris: Sinbad.

Barro, R. & Lee, J. W. (2000), *International Data on Educational Attainment: Updates and Implications*, CID Working Paper No. 42.

Barthes R. (1978), *Leçon inaugurale de la chaire de sémilogie littéraire du Collège de France*, Paris: Seuil.

Beauvoir, S. de (1963), *La Force des choses*, Paris: Gallimard.

Belkaoui, A. R. (1994), *International and Multinational Accounting*, Chicago: The Dryden Press.

Benabessadok, C. (1998), 'Des républicaines debout', *Différences*, September, pp. 4-5.

Bennoune, M. (1988), *The Making of Contemporary Algeria, 1830-1987*, Cambridge: Cambridge University Press.

Bennoune, M. (1991), 'Socio-Historical Foundation of the Contemporary Algerian State', in A. El-Kenz (ed.), *Algeria: The Challenge of Modernity*, London: Codesria, pp. 41-89

Bennoune, M. (1999), *Les Algériennes, victimes de la société néopatriarcale*, Algiers: Marinoor.

Benrabah, M. (1999), *Langue et pouvoir en Algérie: histoire d'un traumatisme linguistique*, Paris: Séguier.

Béraud, A. & Faccarello, G. (2000), *Nouvelle Histoire de la pensée économique 3: Des institutionnalistes à la période contemporaine*, Paris: La Découverte.

Bernis, G. D. de (1966), 'Industries industrialisantes et contenu d'une politique d'intégration régionale', *Economie appliquée*, 3-4, pp. 415-73.

Bernis, G. D. de (1968), 'Les industries industrialisantes et l'intégration économique régionale', *Economie appliquée*, 1, pp. 41-68

Bernis, G. D. de (1970), 'Quelques observations au sujet des biens d'équipements dans un processus général d'industrialisation et de développement national fondé sur la transformation des hydrocarbures', paper presented at Colloque des Economistes Arabes, Algiers.

Bettelheim, C. (1970), *Planification et croissance accélérée*, Paris: Maspero.

Blanqui, A. J. (1840), *Algérie. Rapport sur la situation économique de nos possessions dans le Nord de l'Afrique*, Paris: W. Cognebert.

Bocage, D. (1985), *The General Economic Theory of François Perroux*, Lanham: University Press of America.

Bosworth, B., Collins, S. M. & Chen, Y. (1995), 'Accounting For Differences In Economic Growth', paper at conference 'On Structural Adjustment Policies In The 1990s: Experience And Prospects', Institute Of Developing Economies, Tokyo, 5-6 October.

Bouamama, S. (2000), *Algérie: Les Racines de l'Intégrisme*, Brussels: EPO.

Bouatta, C. (1997), *Evolution of the Women's Movement in Contemporary Algeria: Organization, Objectives and Prospectives*, Economics Research Working Papers No. 124, Helsinki: World Institute for Development.

Boudjedra, R. (1989), *Le Vainqueur de coupe*, Paris: Gallimard.

Bourqia, M., Charrad, M. & Gallagher, N. (1996), *Femmes, Culture et Société au Maghreb: Femmes, Pouvoir Politique et Développement*, Casablanca: Afrique Orient.

Brac de la Perriere, C. (1993), *Les Associations algériennes ayant pour but la promotion des femmes*, Algiers: FNUAP.

Brenner, R. (1977), 'The Origins of Capitalist Development: a Critique of Neo-Smithian Marxism', *New Left Review*, 104, July-August, pp. 25-92.

Burlaud, A. (1995), 'Plan Comptable et transfert de technologie', in *Ecole Française de Comptabilité. Melanges en l'honneur du Professeur Claude Pérochon*, Paris: Foucher, pp. 97-101.

Callier, P. & Koranchelian, T. (2002), *The Sources And Institutional Underpinnings Of Sustained Growth In Algeria*, Washington DC: World Bank.

Calori R. & De Woot, P. (1994), *A European Management Model Beyond Diversity*, London: Financial Times/Prentice Hall.

Camus, A. (1994), *Le Premier homme*, Paris: Gallimard.

Cartwright, J. (1999), *Cultural Transformation - Nine factors for Improving the Soul of your Business*, London: Financial Times/Prentice Hall.

Castells, M. (1998), *End of Millenium*, Vol. III, *The Information Age. Economy, Society and Culture*, Oxford: Blackwell.

Caute, D. (1970), *Frantz Fanon*, London: Fontana.

CEDAW (1998), *Algeria: Initial report of States parties under art. 18 of the Convention on the elimination of all forms of discrimination against women*, 1 September, New York: United Nations.

Chandler, J. & Holzer, H. (1981), 'The Need for Systems of Education in Developing Countries', in A. J. H. Enthoven (ed.), *Accounting Education. Economic Development Management*, Amsterdam: Elsevier North Holland.

Charte Nationale (1976), Algiers.

Cherifati-Merabtine, D. (1996), 'Femmes-travailleuses: une identite dans la tourmente', in N. Benghabrit-Remaoun (ed.), *Actes de l'atelier Femmes et Developpement*, Oran: CRASC, pp. 40-62.

Chikhi, S. (1991), 'The worker, the prince and the fact of life: the mirage of modernity in Algeria', in A. El-Kenz (ed.), *Algeria: The Challenge of Modernity*, London: Codesria, pp. 191-225.

Corbett, J. (1987), 'International Perspectives On Financing: Evidence From Japan', *Oxford Review Of Economic Policy*, 3: 4, pp. 30-55.

Corbett, J. & Mayer, C. (1991), 'Financial Reform In Eastern Europe: Progress With The Wrong Model', *Oxford Review Of Economic Policy*, 7: 4, pp. 57-74.

Crainer, S. (1996), *Key Management Ideas: Thinkers That Changed the Management World*, London: Financial Times/Pitman Publishing.

CSC/PCN (1973), *Rapports de Présentation*, Algiers: Ministry of Finance.

De Soto, H. (2000), *The Mystery of Capital. Why Capitalism Triumphs in the West and Fails Everywhere Else*, London: Bantam Press.

Denison, D. R. (1990), *Corporate Culture and Organisational Effectiveness*, New York: Wiley & Sons

Désiré, R. (1970), 'Les Aliénés', *Le Nouvel Observateur, 23-11-1970.*

Dib, M. (1990), *Qui se souvient de la mer* [1962], Paris: Editions du Seuil.

Dillman, B. (1997), 'Reassessing the Algerian Economy: Development and Reform Through the Eyes of Five Policy-Makers', *Journal of Modern African Studies*, 35: 1, pp. 153-174.

Dine, P. (1996), 'Un héroïsme problématique - le sport, la littérature et la Guerre d'Algérie', *Europe*, 806-7, pp. 177-85.

Djebar, A. (1985), *L'amour, la fantasia*, Paris: Jean-Claude Lattes.

Doucy, A. & Mounheim, F. (1971), *Les Révolutions algériennes*, Paris: Fayard

Dourari, A. (1997), 'Malaises linguistiques et identitaires en Algérie', *Anadi, revue d'études amazighes*, 2, June, Université de Tizi Ouzou, pp. 20, 29.

Dressler, D. & Carn, D. (1969), *Sociology: the Study of Human Interaction*, New York: Alfred A Knopf.

Dunham, A. (1930), *The Anglo-French Treaty of Commerce of 1860 and the Progress of the Industrial Revolution in France*, Ann Arbor: University of Michigan Press.

Dunning, G. E., Maguire, J. & Pearton, E. R. (1993) (eds.), *The Sport Process: A Comparative And Developmental Approach*, Champaign, Illinois: Human Kinetics.

Egalité (1991), 'Les Luttes de femmes en Algérie', *Nouvelles Questions Féministes*, 16-18, pp. 17-28.

Emerit, M. (1941), *Les Saint-Simoniens en Algérie*, Paris: Société d'Edition, Les Belles Lettres.

Enfantin, B. P. (1843), *La Colonisation de l'Algérie*, Paris: P. Bertrand.

Enthoven, A. J. H. (1973), *Accounting and Economic Development Policy*, New York/Amsterdam: Elsevier North Holland.

Enthoven, A. J. H. (1979), *Accountancy Systems in the Third World Economies*, Amsterdam: Elsevier North Holland.

Fanon, F. (1952), *Peau noire, masques blancs*, Paris: Editions du Seuil.

Fanon, F. (1959), *L'An V de la Révolution algérienne*, Paris: Maspero

Fanon, F. (1970), *Toward the African Revolution*, (*Pour la Révolution Africaine* [1964], Paris: Maspero), trans. Haakon Chevalier, London: Penguin.

Fates, F. (1994), 'Les associations de femmes algériennes face à la menace islamiste', *Nouvelles Questions Féministes*, 15: 2, pp. 51-65.

Fates, Y. (1994), *Sport et Tiers Monde*, Paris: Presses Universitaires de France.

Frank, A. G. (1967), *Capitalism and Underdevelopment in Latin America*, New York: Monthly Review Press.

Frank, A. G. (1998), *ReOrient. Global Economy in the Asian Age*, Berkeley/Los Angeles: University of California Press.

Frank, A. G. & Gills, B. K. (1993), *The World System. Five hundred years or five thousand?*, London/New York: Routledge.

Gadant, M. (1995), *Le Nationalisme algérien et les femmes*, Paris: L'Harmattan.

Gerschenkron, A. (1962), *Economic Backwardness in Historical Perspective*, Cambridge, Mass: Harvard University Press.

Gintis, H. (1971), 'Contre-culture et militantisme politique', in *Les Temps Modernes*, 295, pp. 1404-1428.

Giulianotti, R. & Finn, G. (2000) (eds.), *Football Culture: Local Contests, Global Visions*, London: Frank Cass.

Godfrey, A. D., Devlin, P. & Merrouche, C. (1996), 'Governmental Accounting in Kenya,

Tanzania and Uganda', *Research in Governmental and Non-profit Accounting*, 9, JAI Press, pp. 193-217.

Godfrey, A. D., Merrouche, C. & Devlin, P. (1999), 'Local Governmental Accounting in Algeria and Morocco', *Research in Governmental and Non-profit Accounting*, 10, JAI Press, pp. 201-34.

GSE (1971), *Charte de l'Organisation Socialiste des Entreprises*, *Ordonnance* no. 71-74, 16 November.

Guevara, E. C. (1987), *Che Guevara and the Cuban Revolution. Writings and Speeches of Che Guevara*, ed. by D. Deutschmann, Sydney: Pathfinder.

Hammouda, N. E. (1984), 'L'activité féminine: un indicateur des mutations socio-économiques', *Statistiques*, 3, April-June, pp. 29-35.

Hannerz, U. (1991), 'Scenarios for Peripheral Cultures', in A. D. King (ed.), *Culture, Globalisation and the World System*, Basingstoke: Macmillan, pp. 107-128.

Harrison, R. (1993), *Human Resource Management - Issues and Strategies*, Wokingham/Reading MA: Addison-Wesley.

Hazan, A. B. (1987), 'Sport as an Instrument for Political Expansion: The Soviet Union in Africa', in J. M. Baker & A. J. Mangan (eds.), *Sport in Africa. Essays in Social History*, London: Africana Publishing Company, pp. 250-71.

Helie-Lucas, M. (1993), 'Women's struggles and strategies in the growth of fundamentalism in the Muslim World: From Entryism to Internationalism', in H. Afshar (ed.), *Women in the Middle East, Perceptions, Realities and Struggles for Liberation*, Basingstoke: Macmillan, pp. 206-226.

Hirschman, A. O. (1981), *Essays in Trespassing. Economics to Politics and Beyond*, Cambridge: Cambridge University Press.

Hofstede, G. (1984), *Culture's Consequences: International Differences in Work-Related Values*, London: Sage.

Hofstede, G. (1991), *Culture and Organisation - Software of the Mind*, New York: MacGraw Hill

Houlihan, B. (1994), 'Hegemonization, Americanization, and Creolisation of Sport: Varieties of Globalisation', *Sociology of Sport Journal*, V: 11, pp. 356-375

Houlihan, B. (1997), *Sport Policy and Politics, Comparative Analysis*, London: Routledge.

Human Rights Watch (2001), *World Report 2000*.

Hussein, M. (1997), 'L'individu postcolonial', in L. Barbulesco and A. Meddeb (eds.),

Postcolonialisme, décentrement, déplacement, dissémination, Paris: *Débale 5 & 6*, Maisonneuve and Larose, pp. 164-174.

Ighilahriz, L. (2001), *Algérienne*, Paris: Fayard/Calmann-Lévy.

Jahoda, G. (1961), *White Man*, Oxford: Oxford University Press.

Jensen, R. E. & Arrington, C. E. (1983), 'Accounting Education: Turning Wrongs into Rights in the 1980s', *Journal of Accounting Education*, 1: 1, pp. 5-18.

Johnson, J. (2001), 'Niger: Economic Growth & HRM and Development', paper at international conference 'Advancing Knowledge Development in African Business', 4-7 April, Washington DC.

Jones, C. S. & Sefiane, S. (1992), 'The Use of Accounting Data in Operational Decision Making in Algeria', *Accounting, Auditing & Accountability Journal*, 5: 4, pp. 71-83.

Kamoche, K. (2000), *Sociological Paradigms and Human Resources: An African Context*, Aldershot: Ashgate.

Kaser, M. & Allsopp, C. (1992), 'The Assessment: Macroeconomic Transition in Eastern Europe, 1989-1991', *Oxford Review of Economic Policy*, 8: 1, pp. 1-13

Kateb, K. (2001), *La Fin du mariage traditionnel en Algérie? 1876-1998*, Saint-Denis: Bouchène.

Kateb Yacine (1981), *Nedjma* [1956], Paris: Editions du Seuil

Keenan, J. (1977), *The Tuareg: People of Ahaggar*, London: Allen Lane

Keenan, J. (2001), *Sahara Man: Travelling with the Tuareg*, London: John Murray.

Kloss, H. (1969), *Research possibilities on group bilingualism: a report*, Quebec: International Centre for Research on Bilingualism.

Lacheraf, M. (1988), *Ecrits didactiques sur la culture, l'histoire et la société*, Algiers: ENAP.

Lacoste-Dujardin, C. (1986), *Des Mères contre les femmes. Maternité et patriarcat au Maghreb*, Paris: La Decouverte.

Lambert, T. (1996), *Key Management Solutions*, London: Financial Times/Pitman Publishing.

Lanfranchi, P. (1994), 'Rachid Mekhloufi, un footballeur français dans la guerre d'Algérie', *Actes de la recherche en sciences sociales*, 108, pp. 70-5.

Lanfranchi, P. & Wahl, A. (1996), 'The Immigrant as Hero: Kopa, Mekhloufi and French Football', *The International Journal of the History of Sport*, 13: 1, pp. 115-27.

Leibenstein, H. (1989), 'Organisational Economics and Institutions as Missing Elements in Economic Development Analysis', *World Development*, 17, pp. 1361-73.

Lin, Z. & Deng, S. (1992), 'Education Accounting in China: Current Experiences and Future Prospects', *The International Journal of Accounting*, 27, pp. 144-77.

Lloyd, C. (1999), 'Transnational mobilisations in contexts of violent conflict, the case of solidarity with women in Algeria', *Contemporary Politics*, 5: 4, pp. 365-377.

Lokmane, S. (2002), '8 mars. Au-delà du folklore', *Liberté*, 7 March.

Maddy-Weitzman, B. (2001), 'Contested Identities: Berbers, "Berberism" and the State in North Africa', *Journal of North African Studies*, 6: 3, pp. 23-47.

Majumdar, M. A. (1999), 'Le Silence de la mer', *Bulletin of Francophone Africa*, 14, pp. 75-88.

Marx, K. (1976), *Capital* Vol. 1 [1867], Harmondsworth: Penguin.

Maspero, F. (1970), 'Editorial Note', in Frantz Fanon, *Toward the African Revolution (Pour la Révolution Africaine* [1964], Paris: Maspero), trans. Haakon Chevalier, London: Penguin, pp. 7-10.

Mazrui, A. A. (1990), *Cultural Forces in World Politics*, London: James Currey.

Mekidèche, M. (2000), *L'Algérie entre économie de rente et économie émergente*, Algiers: Editions Dahlab.

Merton, R. K. (1957), *Social Theory and Social Structure*, Glencoe, III/ London: Free Press/Macmillan.

Mignon, P. (1994), 'New Supporter Cultures and Identity in France: The Case of Paris Saint-Germain', in R. Giulianotti & J. Williams (eds.), *Game without frontiers: football, identity and modernity*, Aldershot: Arena, pp. 273-297

Miliani, M. (1997), 'National language vs. foreign languages: between political alibis and cultural blindness', *Confluences Algérie*, Oran/Paris: Editions CMM/ l'Harmattan, pp. 57-66.

Modigliani, F. & Miller, M. (1958), 'The Cost of Capital, Corporation Finance and the Theory of Investment', *American Economic Review*, 48: 3, pp. 261-97.

M'Rabet, F. (1966), *Les Algériennes*, Paris: Maspero.

Ndzinge, S. & Briston, J. (1999), 'Accounting and Economic Development: A Case for Africa' in Wallace R. S., Samuels J. M., Briston R. J. and Saudagaran S. (eds.), *Research in Accounting in Emerging Countries*. Supplement 1, Stamford, Connecticut: JAI Press, pp. 29-42.

Needles, B. E. (1976), 'Implementing a Framework for the International Transfer of Accounting Technology', *International Journal of Accounting Education and Research*, 12, pp. 45-62.

Nonaka, I. (1996), 'The Knowledge Creating Company', in Starkey K. (ed.), *How Organisations Learn*, London: Thomson Business Press.

Oufreha, F.-Z. (1998), 'Femmes algériennes: la révolution silencieuse?', *Monde Arabe. Maghreb Machrek*, 162, pp. 57-68.

Ouibrahim, N. & Scapens, R. (1989), 'Accounting and Financial Control in a Socialist Enterprise: A Case Study from Algeria', *Accounting, Auditing & Accountability Journal*, 2: 2, pp. 7-28.

PCN (1975), *Ordonnance*, No.75/35, 29 April, Algiers

Perroux, F. (1963), *Problèmes de l'Algérie indépendante*, Paris: Presses Universitaires de France.

Perroux, F. (1991), *L'Economie du XXième siècle* [1961], in *Œuvres Complètes. V Théorie Générale: Les Concepts*, Grenoble: Presses Universitaires de Grenoble.

Plant, R. (1987), *Managing Change and Making it Stick*, London: Fontana.

Pollard, S. (1989), *Britain's Prime and Britain's Decline - the British Economy, 1870-1914*, London: Edward Arnold.

Quandt, W. B. (1998), *Between Ballots and Bullets, Algeria's Transition from Authoritarianism*, Washington DC: Brookings Institution Press.

Radebaugh, S. J. & Gray, S. J. (1997), *International Accounting and Multinational Enterprises*, 4th edition, New York: John Wiley and Sons.

Raffinot, M. & Jacquemot, P. (1977), *Le Capitalisme d'état algérien*, Paris: François Maspero

Reich, W. (1932), *Der Einbruch der Sexualmoral,* Berlin: Verlag für Sexualpolitik.

Roberts, H. (1993), 'Historical and Unhistorical Approaches to the Question of Identity in Algeria', *Bulletin of Francophone Africa*, 2: 4, pp. 79-92.

Roberts, H. (2003), *The Battlefield. Algeria 1988-2002. Studies in a Broken Polity*, London/New York: Verso.

Rouadjia, A. (1991), *Les Frères et la Mosquée: enquête sur le mouvement islamiste en Algérie*, Algiers: Bouchene.

Rybczynski, T. M. (1991), 'The Sequencing of Reform', *Oxford Review of Economic Policy*, 7: 4, pp. 26-34.

Saad, M. (2000), *Development Through Technology Transfer - Creating New Organisational and Cultural Understanding*, Exeter: Intellect.

Saadi, N. (1991), *La Femme et la loi en Algérie*, Algiers: UNU/Wider, Bouchène.

Sadler, P. (1991), *Designing Organisations - The Foundation of Excellence*, London: Mercury Books.

Said, E. W. (1993), *Culture and Imperialism*, London: Chatto & Windus.

Samuels, J. M., Groves, R. E. V. & Goddard, C. S. (1975), *Company Finance in Europe*, London: The Institute of Chartered Accountants of England and Wales.

Sartre, J. P. (1961), Preface to F. Fanon, *Les Damnés de la terre*, Paris: Maspero, pp. 5-22

Sartre, J. P. & Lévy, B. (1991), *L'Espoir maintenant. Les entretiens de 1980*, Paris: Verdier.

Schuler, C. (1968), *Zur Politischen Ekonomik der Armen Welt*, Munich: Beck.

Sebaa, R. (1996), *L'Arabisation dans les sciences sociales*, Paris: l'Harmattan

Sebaa, R. (1997), 'La démocratie introuvable ou la quête des fondements', in *Confluences Algérie*, Oran/Paris: Editions CMM/ l'Harmattan, pp. 23-31

Smith, A. (1977), *The Wealth of Nations* [1776], London: J M Dent & Sons Ltd.

Soliman, N. H. (1991), *Perspectives in the Privatisation of the Public Sector*, Egypte Comptiere.

Solomons, D. (1980), Foreword to AAA Report, *Accounting Education and the Third World*, Sarasota, Florida: American Accounting Association.

Stora, B. (1992), *La Gangrène et l'oubli. La mémoire de la guerre d'Algérie*, Paris: La Découverte.

Tahi, M. S. (1992), 'The arduous democratisation process in Algeria', *Journal of Modern African Studies*, 39: 3, pp. 397-419.

Taleb Ibrahimi, A. (1976), *De la décolonisation à la révolution culturelle*, Algiers: SNED.

Taleb Ibrahimi, A. (1981), 'Réflexions sur la décolonisation culturelle en Algérie' [1973], in *De la décolonisation à la révolution culturelle, 1962-1972* [1973], Algiers: SNED.

Taleb Ibrahimi, K. (1995), *Les Algériens et leur(s) langue(s)*, Algiers: Editions El Hikma.

Temmar, H. (1973), *Approche structurelle du phenomène du sous-développement. La structure de l'économie sous-dévelopée*, Algiers: SNED.

Textes fondamentaux du Front de libération nationale 1954-68 (1976), Documentary dossier 24, Algiers: Ministry of Information and Culture.

Touati, A. (1996), 'Femmes en Algérie: Etat des lieux et des luttes', *Bulletin of Francophone Africa*, 5: 9, pp. 1-9.

UNDP (1998), *Human Development Report*, New York: United Nations.

Vince, R. (1996), 'Experiential Management Education as the Practice of Change', in R. French & C. Grey (eds.), *Rethinking Management Education*, London: Sage.

Walch, J. (1975), *Michel Chevalier. Economiste Saint-Simonian 1806-1879*, Paris: Librairie Philosophique J Vrin.

Wallace, R. S. O., (1999), 'Accounting and Development: A special Case for Africa', in 'Accounting and Economic Development: A Case for Africa' in Wallace R. S., Samuels J. M., Briston R. J. and Saudagaran S. (eds.), *Research in Accounting in Emerging Countries*. Supplement 1, Stamford, Connecticut: JAI Press, pp. 1-25.

Walton, R. E. (1985), 'From Control to Commitment in the Workplace', *Harvard Business Review*, 63: 2, March-April, pp. 76-84.

Xenikon, A. & Furnham, A. (1996), 'A Correlation and Factor Analytic Study of Four Questionnaire Measures of Organisational Culture', *Human Relations*, 49: 3.

Yuval-Davis, N. (1997), *Gender and Nation*, London: Sage.

Zahar, R. (1970), *L'Oeuvre de Frantz Fanon: colonialisme et aliénation dans l'œuvre de Frantz Fanon*, Paris: Maspero.